ESSAYS ON RACE AND EMPIRE

ESSAYS

ON RACE AND EMPIRE

Nancy Cunard

edited by Maureen Moynagh

broadview literary texts

National Library of Canada Cataloguing in Publication Data

Cunard, Nancy, 1896-1965
  Essays on race and empire / Nancy Cunard ; edited by Maureen Moynagh.

(Broadview literary texts)
Includes bibliographical references.
ISBN 1-55111-230-2

1. Race relations. 2. Blacks. 3. Imperialism.
I. Moynagh, Maureen Anne, 1963-   II. Title.   III. Series.

JV305.C85 2002   305.8   C2002-902940-6

Broadview Press Ltd., is an independent, international publishing house, incorporat-
ed in 1985.
North America:
P.O. Box 1243, Peterborough, Ontario, Canada K9J 7H5
3576 California Road, Orchard Park, NY 14127
TEL: (705) 743-8990; FAX: (705) 743-8353;
E-MAIL: customerservice@broadviewpress.com

United Kingdom and Europe
Plymbridge North (Thomas Lyster, Ltd.)
Unit 3 & 4a, Ormskirk Industrial Park
Old Boundary Way, Burscough Road
Ormskirk, Lancashire L39 2YW
TEL: (01695) 575112; FAX: (01695) 570120; E-MAIL: books@tlyster.co.uk

Australia:
UNIREPS University of New South Wales, Sydney, NSW 2052.
E-MAIL: infopress@unsw.edu.au   TEL: 61 2 9664099   FAX: 61 2 9664520

www.broadviewpress.com

Broadview Press gratefully acknowledges the financial support of the Book
Publishing Industry Development Program, Ministry of Canadian Heritage,
Government of Canada.

Series editor: Professor L.W. Conolly
Advisory editor for this volume: Michel W. Pharand

Text design and composition by George Kirkpatrick

PRINTED IN CANADA

Contents

Acknowledgements

A number of people and institutions have provided assistance during the preparation of this edition. The University Council for Research at St. Francis Xavier University provided travel grants which enabled me to consult the Cunard papers at the Harry Ransom Humanities Research Center of the University of Texas at Austin. At the HRHRC, Barbara Smith-Laborde, David Coleman, and Pat Fox were particularly helpful. I wish to thank my colleague Richard Nemesvari for patiently enduring all my questions about editing and for providing sound advice. I wish to thank my research assistants, Jonathan Cormier, Alanna Jamieson and Kathleen Reddy. Thank you also to Victor Ramraj for suggesting this project in the first place.

The Editor of this book and the Publisher have made every attempt to locate the authors of the copyrighted material or their heirs and assigns, and would be grateful for any information that would allow them to correct any errors or omissions in a subsequent edition of the work.

For permission to reprint material under copyright, I thank the following publishers and individuals:

"Harlem Reviewed," "Jamaica — The Negro Island," *The White Man's Duty: An Analysis of the Colonial Question in Light of the Atlantic Charter, Black Man and White Ladyship*, "The American Moron and the American of Sense — Letters on the Negro," "Scottsboro — and Other Scottsboros," and "A Reactionary Negro Organisation" are reprinted by permission of the Heirs of Nancy Cunard.

Excerpt from *West African Passage* by Margery Perham reprinted by permission of Peter Owen Ltd., London.

Excerpt from *The Case for West Indian Self-Government* by C.L.R. James reproduced with permission of Curtis Brown Ltd., London, on behalf of The Estate of C.L.R. James 1992, Copyright © 1992.

Reprinted with the permission of Scribner, a Division of Simon & Schuster, excerpt from *The Fruit of the Family Tree* by

Finally, for his support and companionship, his intellectual engagement with all I do, and for being there when it mattered most, I thank my partner, Rod Bantjes.

Introduction

Alternative Modernisms

As a modernist expatriate living in France, as poet, editor, publisher, journalist and political passionaria, Nancy Cunard (1896-1965) embodies much of what one typically associates with the Parisian avant-garde and with left political commitments of the 1930s. But she represents much of what is atypical as well. The great-granddaughter of the founder of the Cunard shipping lines, Nancy Cunard spent much of her life resisting that imperial legacy. Notes for a projected autobiography invoke what was to become the mantra of cultural politics in the 1990s: "When of SELF writing: Re the three main things. 1. Equality of races 2. of sexes 3. of classes."[1] A collector of African art like so many European modernists with a voguish fascination for things primitive, Cunard also devoted much of her considerable energy to the cause of racial justice. The essays assembled in this volume offer a window onto this dimension not only of Nancy Cunard's life, but of the modernist, imperial world in which she moved in the early part of the twentieth century. A study of Cunard offers an opportunity to reconsider the connections between modernism, race, gender and empire, for as Susan Stanford Friedman has suggested, hers is a name that "crisscrosses the map of modernism—not so much as a poet but more as a tireless advocate, a progressive spirit, a charismatic dynamo, a woman who fascinated and frightened people with her passions."[2]

Central to Cunard's cultural and political work as well as to this collection is the publishing project she undertook from 1930 to 1934: *Negro, An Anthology.* "Harlem Reviewed," "Jamaica—The Negro Island," "The American Moron and the American of Sense," "Scottsboro—and Other Scottsboros," and "A Reactionary Negro Organisation" were all originally published in *Negro.*

---

1   From a notebook dated 1956, MS Nancy Cunard, Harry Ransom Humanities Research Center, The University of Texas at Austin.
2   Susan Stanford Friedman, "Nancy Cunard," *The Gender of Modernism*, ed. Bonnie Kime Scott (Bloomington: Indiana UP, 1990) 63.

Black Man and White Ladyship was privately published as a pamphlet during the first year of Cunard's work on the anthology, and *The White Man's Duty: An Analysis of the Colonial Question in Light of the Atlantic Charter*, although published nearly a decade later, was co-authored by one of Cunard's key collaborators on the anthology, George Padmore. *Negro*, a massive, 850-page tome, remains a fascinating document. A "panorama" of the black diaspora, to borrow Cunard's own description, the volume contains a bewildering array of articles on racial injustice, music, ethnology, black history, imperialism, and folklore, together with glossy photographs of black singers, dancers, boxers, and film stars, plates of African art, snapshots Cunard took in her travels, poetry, maps, tables, and manifestos. Among the contributors are the key African-American intellectuals of the day: W. E. B. DuBois, Walter White, Alain Locke, E. Franklin Frazier and many figures associated with the Harlem Renaissance, including Langston Hughes, Sterling Brown, Countee Cullen, and Arna Bontemps. Several of Zora Neale Hurston's early essays on folklore were first published in *Negro*. There is a good deal of serious scholarship and some solid journalism. Melville Herskovits was a contributor. George Padmore, an important intellectual and Pan-Africanist originally from Trinidad, contributed several articles. Jomo Kenyatta, then a student in London, and later independence leader and first president of Kenya, contributed to the collection. There are also contributions from the international coterie of modernists Cunard knew in Paris and London: the Surrealists contributed a manifesto, Ezra Pound and William Carlos Williams contributed some of the more frivolous and troubling pieces in the anthology, Theodore Dreiser gave permission for the reprinting of his speech on the Scottsboro Boys, Benjamin Péret wrote about Brazil, Georges Sadoul analysed racist and colonial stereotypes in French children's publications, Samuel Beckett did several translations from French to English, and Brazilian modernist Mario de Andrade contributed a piece on Afro-Brazilian culture.

Cunard represents the anthology as a record of "the struggles and achievements, the persecutions and the revolts against them, of the Negro peoples";[1] it is this and more. In speaking of Rich-

---

1   Nancy Cunard, *Negro, An Anthology* (London: Wishart, 1934) iii.

ard Wright's experience of blackness and modernity, Paul Gilroy writes: "The image of the Negro and the idea of 'race' which it helps to found are living components of a western sensibility that extends beyond national boundaries, linking America to Europe and its empires."[1] This transatlantic or, in Gilroy's terms, *black Atlantic* linkage and this western sensibility are exemplified and anatomized in Cunard's anthology. One of the values of the anthology, for a contemporary reader, is the way it lays a modernist transatlantic matrix alongside a black transatlantic matrix, for it exposes the extent to which modernism is dependent on not only the "*image* of the Negro and the *idea* of 'race'" but on the labour of blacks and of black cultural producers. In the essays that Cunard contributed to the anthology, and in her role as editor more generally, the reader will find several of the tensions important for understanding modernism. The same may be said of the pamphlets, *Black Man and White Ladyship* and *The White Man's Duty*. Both gender and left politics emerge as key issues in Cunard's representations of race and empire. Most importantly perhaps, Cunard's project compels recognition of the interdependence of empire, gender, race politics, and the left.

While Cunard's work on race and empire may not, at first blush, seem to have much to do with gender, I will argue that *Negro* and related projects, including her political activism, were inexorably crosscut by gender. This is not to suggest that Cunard wrote about gender very extensively — in fact, even where she did, she tended either to brush it aside or address it indirectly through other questions. Rather, it is to suggest, first of all, that a woman who undertook the kind of work she did in the 1920s, '30s and '40s could not avoid gender issues; and secondly, it is to argue that the particular kinds of issues she took on in her work were in fact a means of grappling head-on with contemporary constructions of gender, even though she did not often speak of them.

At the time Cunard embarked on the *Negro* project, very few women were interested in anti-imperialism in Britain, nor were feminism and anti-imperialism closely linked. As Inderpal Grewal

---

1   Paul Gilroy, *The Black Atlantic: Modernity and Double Consciousness* (Cambridge, MA: Harvard UP, 1994) 159.

puts it, "feminism … did not create an automatic antipathy toward imperialism in late nineteenth- and early twentieth-century England."[1] In fact, feminists and imperialists were more generally in sympathy. Not only did organized feminism emerge "in the context of Victorian and Edwardian imperialism,"[2] feminists employed imperialist and nationalist rhetoric in the service of the women's movement. The circulation of the trope of the harem in nineteenth-century feminist writing is one instance of this rhetorical invocation of imperial culture and its axiomatic superiority. In Malek Alloula's account,[3] the harem is an eroticized symbol of male imperial penetration of unknown lands; for many nineteenth-century English women, on the other hand, the harem was synonymous with the barbarous treatment of Asian women and their lack of freedom, in contrast with their English sisters. Antoinette Burton points out that British feminists striving for inclusion in the public sphere as citizens drew on these stereotypes to advance their cause: "Arguments for recognition as imperial citizens were predicated on the imagery of Indian women, whom British feminist writers depicted as helpless victims awaiting the representation of their plight and the redress of their condition at the hands of their sisters in the metropole."[4] Two well-known works of fiction may serve as examples of this rhetoric at work. In Mary Shelley's *Frankenstein*, the Creature tells us that Safie, the "Christian Arab" whose mother was enslaved by Turks, was instructed by her mother "to aspire to higher powers of intellect, and an independence of spirit, forbidden to the female followers of Mahomet,"[5] and therefore Safie has escaped from her father to join her beloved in Switzerland, a republic representative of those Enlightenment ideals. An exchange between Jane and Rochester in Charlotte Brontë's *Jane Eyre* similarly invokes the trope of the "enslaved" woman in the harem. Rochester declares

1   Inderpal Grewal, *The Home and the Harem. Nation, Gender, Empire, and the Cultures of Travel* (Durham: Duke UP, 1996) 58.

2   Antoinette Burton, *The Burdens of History: British Feminists, Indian Women, and Imperial Culture, 1865-1915* (Chapel Hill: U of North Carolina P, 1994) 1.

3   Malek Alloula, *The Colonial Harem*, (Minneapolis: U of Minnesota P, 1986).

4   Burton, 7.

5   Mary Shelley, *Frankenstein*, ed. D.L. MacDonald and Kathleen Sherf (Peterborough: Broadview, 1994) 151.

that he "would not exchange this one little English girl for the grand Turk's whole seraglio,"[1] to which Jane retorts, "if you have a fancy for anything in that line, away with you sir, to the bazaars of Stamboul without delay," adding, "I'll be preparing myself to go out as a missionary to preach liberty to them that are enslaved — your harem inmates among the rest."[2] So ingrained were assumptions about the superiority of British culture, that even those most critical of the status of women in Britain did not scruple to assume that their sisters in empire were worse off. This understanding frequently entailed for feminists the moral imperative to undertake the liberation of their "sisters," an obligation that, as Burton puts it, "British women were required to discharge — for the benefit of colonial peoples and, ultimately, for the good of the imperial nation itself."[3]

This trope is not infrequently played out even in the work of feminists who were anti-imperialist, like Annie Besant and Margaret Cousins. Both Besant and Cousins were very involved with socialist and feminist movements in England and Ireland, and Cousins with Irish nationalism, before each moved to India where they became involved in India's independence movement and in the beginnings of Indian feminism. On the home front, and more contemporaneously with Cunard, Virginia Woolf and Sylvia Pankhurst are among the very few high-profile English feminists who came to take up an anti-imperialist stance. Woolf's famous rejection of patriotism in *Three Guineas*, "As a woman I have no country,"[4] links feminism with a rejection of nation, and by extension in the British imagination at the time, with a rejection of empire. Her denunciation of the connections between adolescent pursuits and the "glories" of empire in Kipling,[5] and the deep ambivalence about empire and war in her own writing, distinguish Woolf from many other feminists in Britain in the peri-

---

1   Charlotte Brontë, *Jane Eyre*, ed. Richard Nemesvari (Peterborough: Broadview, 1999) 355.

2   Brontë, 355.

3   Burton, 7.

4   Virginia Woolf, *Three Guineas* (1938; London, New York: Harcourt, Brace, Jovanovich, 1966) 109.

5   Virginia Woolf, "Mr. Kipling's Notebooks," *Books and Portraits*, ed. Mary Lyon (London: The Hogarth Press, 1977) 65.

od. Suffragette Sylvia Pankhurst's leftist and anti-imperialist sympathies separated her from the mainstream women's suffrage movement in Britain led by her mother and sister, Emmeline and Christabel Pankhurst. Sylvia founded the East London Federation of Suffragettes in order to work for the political interests of working-class women. Eventually she joined the Communist Party, and in the 1930s, when Italy invaded Ethiopia, she supported Haile Selassie in the struggle against fascism and colonialism. To this end she founded a newspaper, the *New Times and Ethiopia News* (to which Nancy Cunard contributed articles on the Ethiopian crisis), and published books critical of British colonial policies in Africa. Sylvia also came to oppose apartheid in South Africa and British rule in India.

Inderpal Grewal points out that the political commitments of someone like Sylvia Pankhurst "reveal a trajectory that connects the struggle for women's rights and freedom with other struggles for freedom," and that some Western feminists were able to work across imperial divides "by showing connections between patriarchal power in England and colonial practices."[1] The trajectory that Cunard followed in her political commitments makes this connection in a different way. In taking on anti-imperialist and anti-racist causes, in embracing left politics and anti-fascism, Cunard travelled across imperial divides both literally and figuratively, and in so doing transgressed established gender boundaries. Her journeys to Harlem and the Caribbean to collect materials for her anthology might today be viewed as a kind of political tourism to the extent that her work exhibits both the privileged gaze of the (imperial) tourist and the commitment of a partisan in the cause for social justice.[2] This tension marks all of the essays assembled here in different ways, as it does the anthology as a whole, but it cannot be reduced to the conventional binaries—black/white, male/female, colonizer/colonized. The particular expeditions of a privileged, white woman undertaking political solidarity with causes construed as not her own

---

1 Grewal, 78.
2 See my article, "Cunard's Lines: Political Tourism and its Texts," *New Formations* 34 (Summer 1998): 70–90.

ultimately chart a more complicated course through and across these divides.

If gender is a central, but submerged aspect of Cunard's work on race and empire, left politics emerge as an overt concern. Many commentators on Cunard's anthology have been either dismissive or critical of her explicit endorsement of the Communist Party line on questions of race. Cunard's assertion (reiterated several times in the anthology) that "the more vital of the Negro race have realized that it is Communism alone which throws down the barriers of race as finally as it wipes out class distinctions"[1] certainly bears the traces of privileged arrogance, and a limited understanding of the workings of race and racism, along with its evident passion for social justice. Yet what seems to some like an idiosyncratic and troubling emphasis on the intersection of communism with the struggle for racial justice, both in the US and internationally, ought rather to be seen as one of the valuable features of the anthology as a document of the period and of black Marxism. Not only does Cunard reiterate this connection in her own contributions, she devotes two sections of the anthology to the topic, and several of her contributors, black and white, were Communist Party members or fellow travellers.

Until recently, both the international and the left-wing dimensions of black cultural production tended to be occluded in literary-historical work. As Hazel Carby points out, "historians of the Harlem renaissance have little to say about the relation between left-wing literary circles and the Harlem intellectuals, even though people like Langston Hughes and Claude McKay were important figures in both movements."[2] In fact, several artists associated with the Harlem Renaissance and many of the black writers and intellectuals from the Caribbean were, at one time or another, associated with Marxism and/or with the Communist Party. Alfred Mendes, in speaking of a group of intellectuals and artists associated with Trinidadian journals *Trinidad* and the *Beacon*, explains the attraction of the left in these terms: "We had

---

1 Cunard, *Negro*, iii.
2 Hazel Carby, "Proletarian or Revolutionary Literature: C.L.R. James and the Politics of the Trinidadian Renaissance," *The South Atlantic Quarterly* 87:1 (1988) 45.

come to be known as the Communist group, and indeed in those years we were very sympathetic towards what was occurring in the Soviet Union."[1] C.L.R. James, in "Discovering Literature in Trinidad: The 1930s," recognizes how Marxism influenced his formation as a writer: "We were educated not only in the literature and material life of Western civilisation, but we also became marxists and were educated by marxism."[2]

In the same essay James makes quite clear that the international dimension of black cultural production in this time period was not, in the way it most often was for white writers and artists, a matter of choice. James names several men (and it is worth noting that he only names men), including Alfred Mendes, in his generation who were similarly intellectually and artistically gifted, and he remarks: "We went one way; these white boys all went the other way. We were black and the only way we could do anything along the lines we were interested in was by going abroad."[3] James's comment confirms and extends Raymond Williams's observation that "the key cultural factor of the modernist shift" was the general phenomenon of early twentieth-century migration to the metropolis.[4] Williams points out that the "new cultural dimension" of the metropolis in the early part of the twentieth-century "had much to do with imperialism: with the magnetic concentration of wealth and power in imperial capitals and the simultaneous cosmopolitan access to a wide variety of subordinate cultures."[5] James, George Padmore, Aimé Césaire, Claude McKay, Langston Hughes, and Paul Robeson were also part of an emerging international Pan-Africanism, and this international dimension to black intellectual, political and artistic work is an important feature underscored by Cunard's work on race and empire. The trajectories of Caribbean and African-American writers offer testimony to the parts they played in what Hazel Carby describes

---

1 Quoted in Carby, 46.
2 C.L.R. James, "Discovering Literature in Trinidad: The 1930s," *Spheres of Existence. Selected Writings* (Westport, CT: Lawrence Hill, 1980) 238.
3 James, 238.
4 Raymond Williams, "Metropolitan Perceptions and the Emergence of Modernism," *The Politics of Modernism*, ed. Tony Pinkey (London: Verso, 1989) 45.
5 Williams, 44.

as the "international development of negritude":[1] Langston Hughes travelled to West Africa, Europe, and the Caribbean, and translated works by Haitian poet Jacques Roumain and Cuban poet Nicolás Guillén; George Padmore moved from his native Trinidad to the US where he joined the Communist Party, which sent him to the USSR; from there he went to Germany, Austria, then England, and he eventually made his home in independent Ghana; C.L.R. James went from Trinidad to England to the US and back to Trinidad. This criss-crossing of the Atlantic between Africa, Europe and the Americas constituted an eccentric modernism, one not bound to a central metropole, and one whose trajectories reversed those of imperial travel. Cunard's writing on race and empire, her work as editor and journalist, can be seen as charting some of the routes linking empire and metropole, in both directions.

The essays gathered together here, while they comprise only a portion of Cunard's life's work, are important for what they can tell us about such intersections. My aim in assembling these essays is less to add Cunard to the canon of neglected modern women writers than it is to situate her writing on race and empire in a way that sheds light on relations between radical politics, gender, race and modernism. In this way I hope to contribute to revisions of modernism begun by scholars like Houston Baker in *Modernism and the Harlem Renaissance* (1987), Edward Said in *Culture and Imperialism* (1994) and Rita Felski in *The Gender of Modernity* (1995). It should follow from these examples that I understand modernism to be a rather more diverse phenomenon than the traditional Anglo-American and European canon might suggest. Raymond Williams offers an important reminder of the "internal diversity" of modernism:

> Even the basic range of cultural positions within Modernism stretches from an eager embrace of modernity, either in its new technical and mechanical forms or in the equally significant attachments to ideas of social and political revolution, to conscious options for past or exotic cultures as

---

1   Carby, 46.

sources or at least as fragments *against* the modern world, from the Futurist affirmation of the city to Eliot's pessimistic recoil.[1]

The perspective Williams is concerned with, nonetheless, remains that of the Europeans for whom the black diaspora represented in Cunard's essays on race and empire numbered among those "past or exotic cultures" that were to serve as alternatives to the modern world. As will become clear in the essays gathered together here, this perspective is also Cunard's much of the time, despite her clear efforts to present herself as an insider in the struggle. It is important, then, to keep in view the sharp differences in social, economic and political power among the diverse actors engaged in modernist cultural production. To this end, I read Cunard's life and her work against the horizon of relevant material and discursive histories. The appendices I have assembled are intended both to extend the historicizing work I do in this introduction, and to inspire new, perhaps contestatory readings.

Cunard's critical reception in the latter part of the twentieth century has been neither extensive nor unambivalent. Apart from Hugh Ford's collection of texts and reminiscences, *Nancy Cunard: Brave Poet, Indomitable Rebel* (1968) and the 1979 biography by Anne Chisholm, little attention was given to Cunard's work until she was included in Bonnie Kime Scott's anthology, *The Gender of Modernism* (1990). Since then, critical revisions of modernism have produced two sorts of responses to Cunard. One group of scholars, engaged in the process of recovering the work of neglected women artists from the modernist period, has been instrumental in bringing her work to light and in arguing that her neglect has been unjust. Jane Marcus, for instance, asks "why Nancy Cunard (1896–1965) has been eliminated or discredited as a producer of knowledge in all fields to which she contributed, why her voice has been silenced in the histories of the several modern(ist) discourses to which she contributed."[2] Marcus, who

---

1 Williams, 43, his emphasis.
2 Jane Marcus, "Bonding and Bondage: Nancy Cunard and the Making of the Negro Anthology," *Borders, Boundaries and Traces*, ed. Mae Gwendolyn Henderson (New York: Routledge, 1995) 34.

is working on a critical biography of Cunard, argues that Cunard has been discredited as "an intellectual historian of black culture" because of her race, class and gender, even though it is arguably the responsibility of the oppressors to undertake the cultural history of oppression.[1] For critics like Michael North and Ann Douglas who are principally concerned with the inter-relationship of modernism and race, on the other hand, Cunard remains in the problematic position of white patron to black artists and intellectuals, unable to free herself from a privileged discourse. According to Douglas, "Despite her good intentions and very real achievements, Cunard played out a variant of the White Ladyship-Black Man pairing."[2] For North, Cunard's anthology reproduced a common modernist dichotomy between art and political action that all too often operated either to exclude or to contain the work of African-American artists and intellectuals.[3] In presenting Cunard's essays on race and empire, I am also necessarily engaged in revising modernism, but rather than choose sides (or claim to resolve the differences), I argue that a more complex and more interesting picture emerges when, in taking account of Cunard's work, we attempt to think race, gender and empire together.

Daughter of Empire, Woman of the Left Bank, Political Tourist

Diana Fuss makes a useful distinction between identity and identification.[4] Identity is "an identification come to light," a public persona organized and enabled by identification, the private processes of taking on, trying out, performing available social roles. One may inhabit several identities simultaneously or consecutively, but the flexibility, even instability of identification as an activity enables the performance of identities one might seem excluded from inhabiting and the disavowal of others one might

---

1   Marcus, 33.
2   Ann Douglas, *Terrible Honesty: Mongrel Manhattan in the 1920s* (New York: Farrar, Strauss & Giroux, 1995) 281.
3   Michael North, *The Dialect of Modernism: Race, Language and Twentieth-Century Literature* (New York, London: Oxford UP, 1994) 193.
4   Diana Fuss, *Identification Papers* (New York: Routledge, 1995) 1-3.

seem to own. "Identification," Fuss tells us, "is a process that keeps identity at a distance" so that identity can never be taken for granted, never understood as immutable, as a given. With the descriptors "daughter of empire," "woman of the left bank," and "political tourist" I mean to offer synopses of some of Cunard's identities; more importantly, I mean to suggest a trajectory of some of the processes of identification that moved her from daughter of empire to political tourist and that disrupted, unsettled each identity in turn. The concept of identification as I have sketched it out here will be key not only for getting a handle on Cunard's life, but for situating her cultural production historically and for evaluating its significance.

It is as vital to begin by acknowledging Cunard's imperial background as it is to signal her efforts to reject it in the work she undertook from about 1930 on. The world into which Nancy Cunard was born in 1896 was imperial by virtue of the historical milieu and by virtue of her family's situation in that milieu. Particularly emblematic are the manor house where she grew up and the routes leading to it. The manor house, according to Ian Baucom, is a sign of "both Englishness and empire, the manifestation in England's built space of colonial capital and colonial discipline."[1] Many English country houses were built with imperial capital[2] and while this is not literally true of Nevill Holt, the Cunard family home, which dates from 1476, the estate was nonetheless purchased with revenue from a colonial enterprise. Cunard's was not an old English family of aristocratic lineage, but one fashioned of commercial success in the Americas: Nancy's father, Sir Bache Cunard, was the grandson of Samuel Cunard who founded the Cunard steamship line in Halifax in 1840, and who acquired a baronetcy for imperial service from Queen Victoria when he retired to England in 1859. Sir Bache's younger brother Edward purchased Nevill Holt in 1876, and when he inherited it after his brother's accidental death a year later, Sir Bache undertook the life of the English country gentleman as though confirming the exchange of colonial wealth for English-

---

1   Ian Baucom, *Out of Place. Englishness, Empire, and Locations of Identity* (Princeton: Princeton UP, 1999) 166.
2   Baucom, 168.

ness. Nancy's mother, Maud Burke, similarly used her wealth to exchange an American for an English identity. She was a Californian heiress who, like many of her generation, sought a titled husband to enhance her social standing, and who indeed used her position to become a society hostess and patron of the arts in London. Even the different rural-urban inclinations of Sir Bache and Maud (or Emerald, as she called herself) seem to replicate on a familial scale a similar split in imperial culture. The countryside has long been represented as a repository of Englishness, but London at the end of nineteenth and the beginning of the twentieth century was the imperial metropolis, "the place where new social and economic and cultural relations, beyond both city and nation in their older senses, were beginning to be formed."[1] If the metropolis in its modernity and cosmopolitan diversity was the product of imperialism, the idea of England as an imperial "homeland" that was so integral to British imperial discourse remained conceptually linked with the countryside.[2]

To grow up at Nevill Holt as Nancy Cunard did was to grow up at the heart of this articulation between nation and empire, but in circumstances that must have made explicit what might otherwise have been rendered seamless. The trajectories of her parents' lives de-naturalized such associations, even if such irregularities did little to dislodge the hold of these powerful myths of identity.

In 1920 Nancy joined the ranks of expatriate artists and intellectuals living in Paris, and through her friendships with Solita Solano, Janet Flanner, and Tristan Tzara, among many others, gained exposure to modernist and avant-garde writing, art, and performance. A woman of the left bank, to borrow Shari Benstock's phrase, Cunard led a life made possible by Paris's reputed tolerance for bohemianism, by the relative detachment from social conventions afforded expatriates, by the freedoms associated with the New Woman, and, not least, by her financial independence. Cunard wrote poetry, explored her sexuality, began to collect African art, travelled extensively, and hosted parties in her Île St. Louis apartment, which she decorated with paintings

---

1   Williams, 44.
2   Judy Giles and Tim Middleton, eds., *Writing Englishness 1900-1950* (London: Routledge, 1995) 193-94.

by Tanguy, de Chirico, and Picabia. A modernist salon of sorts, albeit on a smaller scale than those hosted by Gertrude Stein and Natalie Barney, these gatherings brought together some of Nancy's English and Irish friends with a mixture of American expatriates and French artists. George Moore visited with Arthur Symons and, on one occasion, sexologist Havelock Ellis. Eugene MacCown and Robert McAlmon, Man Ray, Peggy Guggenheim, Berenice Abbott, and William Carlos Williams were among the Americans. Her guests also included an impressive list of members of the French avant-garde: in addition to Tzara, there were René Crevel, Philippe Soupault, André Breton, Louis Aragon, Jean Cocteau and Drieu La Rochelle.

In the late 1920s Cunard turned from writing poetry to publishing it. She founded the Hours Press in 1928 to publish experimental poetry in hand-printed, limited edition books with artist-designed covers. The list of titles, although short, is nonetheless impressive and includes Samuel Beckett's *Whoroscope*, Louis Aragon's translation of Lewis Carroll's *The Hunting of the Snark* (*La Chasse au Snark*), poems by Walter Lowenfels, Robert Graves, Laura Riding, one of Havelock Ellis's essays, and *A Draft of XXX Cantos* by Ezra Pound. As a modernist cultural producer, Cunard, like the other expatriate women artists and intellectuals around her, moved in masculine spheres of activity. While she and other New Women in this period were able to take advantage of the new position of women "as political agents, as subjects of, rather than simply subject to, history,"[1] these same women would have been lightning rods for contemporary anxiety about changing gender roles. As patron of the arts, as publisher and *salonière*, Cunard did not violate the gendered divisions of modernist artistic labour, but as poet she potentially did. Her 1925 long poem, *Parallax*, published by Virginia and Leonard Woolf's Hogarth Press, presents a masculine speaker and thereby both acknowledges the conventional gendering of the poet as male and adopts the role for Cunard's own ends. *Parallax*'s clear links to T. S. Eliot's *The Waste Land* (1922) were identified by contemporary reviewers as evidence of the derivative, inferior quality of Cunard's poem. It

---

1 Rita Felski, *The Gender of Modernity* (Cambridge, MA: Harvard UP, 1995) 147.

seems not to have occurred to anyone that the appropriations might have been deliberate, even though the title explicitly identifies as the subject of the poem the apparent transformations an object undergoes when viewed from different perspectives. Poetry was not, however, Cunard's most significant contribution to modernist culture. In many respects, her multiple identifications across social boundaries of various kinds as recorded in the poetry, the editions, the pamphlets, and the photographs — both those she took and especially those taken of her — are more important.

To the extent that Cunard might be said to have identified with the socio-cultural construct of the New Woman, one imagines her sympathy with the figure as "a resonant symbol of emancipation, whose modernity signalled ... a bold imagining of an alternative future"[1] and with the links between identity, freedom and sexuality increasingly made by New Women in the early twentieth century. Sexologists like Krafft-Ebing associated the new social demands women began making in the last decades of the nineteenth century with cross-dressing, hermaphroditism and lesbian desire. But as Carroll Smith-Rosenberg notes, "The New Women of the 1920s and 1930s, imbuing male imagery with feminist meaning, transformed the sexologists' symbolic system. Boldly, they asserted their right to participate in male discourse, to function in a public (male) arena, and to act as men did — both in and out of bed."[2] Cunard's sexuality, perhaps more than her role as cultural producer, both attracted and repelled the male modernists in her circle. That she slept with women as well as men was less threatening to some of her lovers than her refusal to conform to the traditional feminine principle of fidelity. The ambivalence of many male modernists toward the political, social and sexual liberation of second-generation New Women like Cunard emerges in characters created by novelists Michael Arlen and Aldous Huxley, both of whom had affairs with her and both of whom translated those experiences into their art in ways not especially flattering to Nancy.

---

1 Felski, 14.
2 Carroll Smith-Rosenberg, *Disorderly Conduct. Visions of Gender in Victorian America* (Oxford: Oxford UP, 1985) 295.

At the same time, the New Woman's association with androgyny and "intermediate" sexuality made her a fascinating object for modernist art, as Carroll Smith-Rosenberg affirms: "In surrealistic and expatriate worlds, New Women float between genders and violate divisions between appearance and reality."[1] Thus Nancy appears as androgyne in a 1924 Man Ray photograph where she poses in silver lamé trousers with matching coat and top hat, while Tristan Tzara kneels to kiss her hand. In Eugene Mac-Cown's 1923 painting she is also represented in trousers, vest, tie, and top hat. Her pencil-thin silhouette seems to have appealed to several artists in her circle: she appears with her hair bobbed and holding a cigarette (both signs of the New Woman) in front of a mirror in a 1927 photograph by Curtis Moffat, and in similar guise in a drawing by Wyndham Lewis (1922) and a painting by Alvaro "Chile" Guevara (1919). As part of this group of modernist cultural producers, Cunard is no mere object of the male artist's gaze in these works. She must, I think, be seen as a self-conscious participant in these constructions of a particular vision of womanhood, performing gender transgressions for her own as well as for the artist's purposes.

Another common way of experimenting with social boundaries in this period, as we have seen, has to do with crossing racial and class divides. Cunard ventured increasingly in this direction as the decade progressed. Among modernist and avant-garde artists, particularly the surrealists, there was considerable interest in the so-called primitive arts. Introduced to the artists who were to develop surrealism as an avant-garde movement by Tzara, and drawn into further proximity with them when she and Louis Aragon became lovers in 1926, Cunard undoubtedly felt a good deal of affinity for these *rodeurs des confins* (prowlers on the borders) as they were called by Jules Monnerot, one of the black collaborators with surrealism. As Brent Hayes Edwards explains, Monnerot "meant that surrealism roamed the outermost bounds of the modern sensibility, constantly looking for ways to push them further, undo the limits."[2] In this instance, the literal and the figurative boundaries were interchangeable. Edwards continues:

1   Smith-Rosenberg, 289–90.
2   Brent Hayes Edwards, "The Ethnics of Surrealism," *Transition* 78 (1999) 84.

"the surrealists were also gnawing at the edges of Europe through their fascination with its others, its outcasts, and in particular its 'primitives' in the colonies of Africa, Asia and Oceania."[1] Cunard collected African art, particularly ivory bangles which she wore up and down the length of her arms; she frequented jazz clubs, taking in performances by Josephine Baker; in 1928 she began her liaison with Henry Crowder, the African-American jazz musician— although he was by no means to be her only black lover. In photographs and paintings of the late twenties and early thirties, Cunard's interest in the exotic is apparent. In a series of photographs by Cecil Beaton, Cunard appears with arms encased in ivory bracelets up to her elbows, kohl-rimmed eyes, and wearing a heavy necklace of carved wooden beads, and a close-fitting modernist helmet, in front of a bold black and white polka dot backdrop. A painting by American surrealist John Banting depicts her in strikingly similar fashion, with turbaned head, heavily kohl-rimmed eyes, and ivory-bangled arms ending in hands that appear black as though in a solarized photograph. A photograph taken by Barbara Ker-Seymer and frequently misattributed to Cecil Beaton presents Cunard against a tiger-skin backdrop, turbaned, wearing a leopard-skin collar and staring icily at the viewer through a veil wrapped around the top half of her face. Embodying a kind of radical chic, Cunard performs a primitivism that fluctuates between identification and appropriation. The very availability of tiger skin and ivory bangles in London and Paris is tangible evidence of imperial adventure in Africa and India. Is it possible to dress this way and oppose imperialism?

Such questions are raised in an even more pointed way by some of the other collaborations between Cunard and Ker-Seymer. The most dramatic staging of Cunard's engagement with blackness and sexuality is a series of solarized photographs (that make white look black and black white) by Ker-Seymer that depict a bare-headed and bare-shouldered Cunard, with a thick choker made from beads wound round and round her neck, in an attitude that, as Jane Marcus points out, can be read either as sexual abandonment or physical distress.[2] Are we to read Cunard as

---

1 Hayes Edwards, 84.
2 Jane Marcus, 43.

the "black" victim of a lynching, or the "white" victim of a rape, or no victim at all? The implicit identification with blackness in these images is particularly disturbing given the relationship between lynching and the myth of black men raping white women. Marcus, however, argues that Cunard's intentions were directed toward political solidarity:

> Nancy Cunard's reenactment of black slave bondage in the self-staging of her white body as a site for political protest against racism has not been read inside *her* semiotics, but instead as a perverse pornography, both political and sexual. But she really meant the performance of bondage to signify her political bonding with black culture.[1]

To the extent one can be confident about imputing intentions, Marcus is probably right, but good intentions do not limit the semiotic volatility of these images. In her roaming at the "outer-most bounds of modern sensibility," in her efforts to "undo the limits," Cunard risks reinstating the literal divisions she may be striving to erase in her figurative performance. This sort of boundary confusion is at the heart of primitivism itself.

A discourse which pervaded not only the arts, but anthropology, psychoanalysis, and colonial policy in the early part of the twentieth century, primitivism also frequently served as a justification for imperialism. Primitivism remains difficult to delineate conceptually in part because it was contradictorily embraced by widely different constituencies—both by those who had little compunction in declaring subjugated peoples inherently inferior to those in power, and by those who advocated their emancipation. One can gain a sense of both the character and the contradictions of the primitive by considering the qualities associated with it—simplicity, vitality, authenticity, fertility—in conjunction with the peoples deemed "primitive": children, peasants, the mentally ill, and the "savage" (non-white) races of the world. Julian Stallabrass points out that even among those who admired the qualities attributed to primitive art, there was often contempt

---

1 Marcus, 42.

for the people who produced the art.[1] In light of the ambiguities of primitivism, it is important to remain critical of Cunard's flirtations with racial boundaries, but it would also be a mistake to dismiss her primitivist performances out of hand. The intertwining of sex, race, and class difference that emerges in primitivism remains fundamental to Cunard's work. However problematically, an embrace of primitivism was often directed toward a critique of European values and societies, and the Surrealists in particular combined their interest in the primitive with a denunciation of imperialism. In her work of the 1930s especially, Cunard goes the route of political commitment, having first embraced the other via avant-garde performance.

In 1928, Cunard spent the summer in Venice with some friends and there she met Henry Crowder, an African-American jazz pianist. Nancy spent a good deal of time with Henry for the remainder of her stay in Venice; on her departure she proposed that he accompany her to Paris to work with her on the Hours Press. During their relationship, Cunard's interest in the African diaspora became increasingly political and gradually evolved into the *Negro* project. If their relationship operated in part along established lines of racial patronage, with Nancy supporting Henry financially, purchasing a sports car for him, and controlling his coming and going by alternately providing and withholding funds for travel, it was also more complicated. In his strange, ghost-written account of his affair with Cunard, Crowder acknowledges that she "was to open up new avenues of thought for me and because of her I was to change my ideas of life."[2] For her part, Cunard said simply "Henry made me."[3] Signifying both her identification with Henry and with what he represented for her — "this Man-Continent-People"[4]— this acknowledgment itself resonates with the ambiguities of Cunard's work on race and

---

1 Julian Stallabrass, "The Idea of the Primitive: British Art and Anthropology 1918-1930," *New Left Review* 183 (1990): 99.

2 Henry Crowder, *As Wonderful as All That? Henry Crowder's Memoir of his Affair with Nancy Cunard*, ed. Robert Allen (Navarro, CA: Wild Trees P, 1987) 17.

3 Quoted in Anne Chisholm, *Nancy Cunard* (New York: Knopf, 1979) 299.

4 Quoted in Anthony Thorne, "A Share of Nancy," *Nancy Cunard: Brave Poet, Indomitable Rebel, 1896-1965*, ed. Hugh Ford (Philadelphia: Chilton, 1968) 295.

empire even as it signals in a profound way her building of an identity through her engagement with blackness. In her efforts to speak from a position outside of imperial constructions of whiteness in her political identifications with black struggles, Cunard repeatedly risked a rehearsal of the imperial script, for as Gayatri Spivak has argued, "[n]o perspective *critical* of imperialism can turn the Other into a self, because the project of imperialism has always already historically refracted what might have been the absolutely Other into a domesticated Other that consolidates the imperialist self."[1] So how might we come to terms with Cunard's investment in race politics?

Understanding Cunard's identification, not only with black struggles for social justice, but with the other causes she devoted her energies to over the course of her life, as a kind of political tourism—the work of an outsider travelling inside "foreign" territory—enables us to take account of these problems of identity and identification alongside our analysis of the work itself, and to take seriously what might otherwise be seen as either frivolous or too troubling to touch. As a "tourist" who crossed race, class and gender boundaries as well as international borders, Cunard opened herself to experiences that would challenge any simple notions of identity. In the spring of 1931, Nancy travelled to Harlem with Henry Crowder to begin work on her anthology. Crowder introduced her to W. E. B. DuBois, who had been one of his professors, and she met several other key African-American intellectuals and artists. She also encountered American race politics first-hand. "Harlem Reviewed," which was written two years later, records some of these experiences, and tells us quite as much about Cunard as it does about Harlem in the 1930s. Her second trip to Harlem was made almost exactly one year later, this time in the company of John Banting, and this time Cunard's arrival occasioned a sex scandal in the press. The tabloids circulated a rumour that Cunard had come to New York in pursuit of her lover, Paul Robeson. Cunard's efforts to deny the story and to reroute press attention to her anthology were largely unsuccessful, and she ultimately had to leave Harlem for a time until things set-

---

1 Gayatri Spivak, "Three Women's Texts and a Critique of Imperialism," *Critical Inquiry* 12.3 (1985) 253, her emphasis.

tled down. She writes about this episode, and the hate mail she received as a consequence of it, in "The American Moron and the American of Sense." In her travels, through her research, and in her correspondence with contributors (as well as "interested" members of the public), Cunard encountered the vicissitudes of racial identification, learning necessarily not only about blackness but about whiteness as well.

By the time of her second trip to the United States, Cunard had begun fund-raising for the Scottsboro Boys and had learned more about lynchings and the conditions of black labourers. She declared an interest in travelling to the southern states to see some of these conditions first-hand, but eventually was dissuaded from doing so; the potential repercussions for her black associates of undertaking such a journey must have been impressed upon her. She nonetheless hired a black secretary from Boston to accompany her to the Caribbean, and again prurient representations of their relationship surfaced in the press. Cunard's political touring, although ostensibly directed at dissolving racial and economic structures of privilege, inevitably reproduced many of those structures since freedom of movement was largely a matter of white and, to some degree, male privilege. Cunard's repeated efforts to dismantle these structures of privilege emerge in different ways in her essays. In "Jamaica—The Negro Island," for instance, she finds no place for whiteness on the island at all, declaring it obsolete. In "Scottsboro—and Other Scottsboros" and in "A Reactionary Negro Organisation" she is focused on class privilege, whether occupied by the white capitalists or the black middle classes, even as her sweeping dismissal of the NAACP reinstalls her own. The ambiguities of gender inflected by race and class privilege emerge in *Black Man and White Ladyship*.

If many of Cunard's other political activities seem more within the purview of European left activism in the first part of the twentieth century, set alongside her work on race and empire, they define concrete trajectories of allegiance between left politics, gender politics, anti-racism and anti-imperialism. In 1935 she travelled to the Soviet Union, making the almost obligatory pilgrimage, for communists and their fellow travellers, to the site of the revolution. In 1936 she went to Spain, as did so many others, to witness the Spanish Civil War and to write about and campaign on behalf of republican Spain. After the triumph of Franco's fascist rebels, she worked on behalf of Spanish refugees in France. When Mussolini invaded Ethiopia in 1935, she became a defender of Haile Selassie and a vocal opponent of fascism, once again contributing articles to Sylvia Pankhurst's *New Times and Ethiopia News* as well as to the American Negro Press. At the outset of the second world war, she set off for Chile to visit Pablo Neruda, whom she had befriended in Spain. From there, she went to Mexico, to Trinidad and to Cuba before returning to Europe, all the while contributing articles, chiefly about the war, to the American Negro Press as well as to newspapers in Trinidad during her sojourn there. Not only was she, as Jane Marcus puts it, "a full time political organizer"[1] in this period, she organized on the move and most often for causes deemed not her own.

She lived in London for the next several years, prevented from travelling by the war and exiled from Nazi-occupied France. England became her place of residence again, as opposed to a frequent stopping place, for the first time since 1920, and her writing registers a divided allegiance. On the one hand, her anti-fascism inclined her toward Britain for its role in the war; on the other hand, she remained critical of Britain's role as an imperial power, as the pamphlet she co-authored with George Padmore, *A White Man's Duty*, makes clear.

Cunard's work after the war seems to look back more than it forges ahead. In 1949 she printed a pamphlet containing poems about fascism and civil war in Spain. She published memoirs about Norman Douglas (1954) and George Moore (1956), and wrote a memoir about her own Hours Press that was published posthumously. She undertook an autobiography, but after the publisher rejected an initial draft, she abandoned the project. A projected book on African ivories was similarly never realized. In 1957, the physical and mental illnesses that were to dog her remaining years began. Nancy Cunard died in a Paris hospital in 1965.

---

1 Marcus, 35.

Imperial Eyes

Mary Louise Pratt's important study of travel writing in the context of colonialism, *Imperial Eyes: Travel Writing and Transculturation* (1992), provides a useful figure for considering Cunard's work, both because she at times seems to cast an imperial gaze on the subjects of her writing and because the anti-imperial, anti-racist work she carries out is itself conducted under imperial eyes. Cunard's activities, in other words, are shaped and constrained by the conditions of empire, even as she struggles to work against those same conditions. Travel is linked to seeing in the figure of imperial eyes, and travel is also an important dimension of Cunard's work in the 1930s. She travelled to Harlem and the Caribbean to collect materials for the anthology and to "see for herself" the conditions, the struggles, the cultural production she was in the process of writing about and collecting. She also planned to travel to Africa in the company of Norman Douglas and Henry Crowder, but Douglas was reluctant to take on the problems they would encounter travelling with a black man in colonized Africa. Travel in empire was not an innocent undertaking; it carried considerable cultural baggage, particularly for a woman, and so Cunard's journeys must be situated in relation to more common modes of imperial travel.

While the project of colonial exploration was largely at an end by the turn of the century and therefore transmuted into a nostalgic trope celebrated in popular narratives of adventure for adults and children alike, fascination with the exotic continued to entice travellers into empire and provided a ready audience for travel writing. Mary Louise Pratt has delineated the ways imperial travel literature not only represented "exotic" landscapes from and for a distinctly European perspective, but enacted a rhetorical claim to heroic discovery that had to do with translating a foreign scene into something of significance for European readers. The gaze of the European tourist in colonized lands is inevitably structured by imperial patterns of racial, gender and politico-economic dominance, and the traces of this imperial gaze mark the writing in discernible ways. Travel in empire by Victorian and Edwardian women was often perceived as a means of gaining freedom from the constraints of gender roles in England; thus empire meant the possibility of a career for women like Mary Kingsley and Margery Perham, as well as for many missionary women, or self-realization and adventure for women such as Freya Stark or Mary Gaunt, both of whom had careers as travel writers. While Cunard was not a travel writer, a number of the essays she wrote during her travels to Harlem and the Caribbean to collect material for her *Negro* anthology exhibit the ambivalent gaze of an imperial tourist who is nonetheless attempting to undertake anti-racist and anti-imperialist work.

"Harlem Reviewed" is simultaneously part travel narrative, part ethnography and part cultural criticism. While Cunard deploys many of the common tropes of travel writing, adopting the guise of tour guide to Harlem and presenting exotic spectacles for the consumption of her readers, her version of the urban travel text also works against the grain of the genre. In focusing on Harlem, she follows the pattern of well-known late nineteenth-century urban travel texts like Jacob Riis's *How the Other Half Lives* (1890), Horatio Alger's *Ragged Dick, or, Street Life in New York* (1868), and Stephen Crane's sketches of New York,[1] in attempting "to reclaim slums and poverty stricken areas for middle-class understanding."[2] Yet Harlem, as Cunard presents it, is never completely "other," nor completely within the grasp of the tour guide who is meant to "decode the signifiers of city life."[3] Harlem, for Cunard, is both vaguely familiar — "When I first saw it, at 7th Avenue, I thought of the Mile End Road" — and resistant to her efforts at representational mastery: "Is it possible to give any kind of visual idea of a place by description? I think not, least of all of Harlem." Part of the challenge Harlem represents for the (imperial woman) traveller is that of negotiating race relations and, for an anti-racist

---

1 Crane published numerous vignettes of New York in newspapers and magazines from approximately 1892 to 1902. These works, most previously published, but some unpublished in Crane's lifetime, have been collected in *The New York City Sketches of Stephen Crane*, ed. R.W. Stallman and E.R. Hagemann (New York: New York UP, 1966).

2 Justin D. Edwards, "Henry James's 'Alien' New York: Gender and Race in *The American Scene*" *American Studies International* 36:1 (1998) 69.

3 Edwards, 70.

traveller, of negotiating racism. Something of the dilemma Cunard faced can be discerned in the following passage:

> This capital [of the "Negro world"] now exists, with its ghetto-like slums around 5th, bourgeois streets, residential areas, a few aristocratic avenues or sections thereof, white-owned stores and cafeterias, small general shops, and the innumerable "skin-whitening" and "anti-kink" beauty parlours. There is one large modern hotel, the Dewey Square, where coloured people of course may stay; and another, far larger, a few paces from it, where certainly they *may not*! And this is in the centre of Harlem. Such race barriers are on all sides; it just depends on chance whether you meet them or no. Some Negro friend maybe will not go into a certain drugstore with you for an ice-cream soda at 108th (where Harlem is supposed to begin, but where it is still largely "white"); "might not get served in there" (and by a coloured server at that—the white boss's orders). Just across the Harlem River some white gentlemen flashing by in a car take it into their heads to bawl, "Can't you get yourself a white man?"—you are walking with a Negro, yet you walk down-town with the same and meet no such hysteria, or again, you do.

The signposts Cunard is meant to interpret for her readers are those of racial difference; that she presents them as contradictory and haphazard has the designed rhetorical effect of implying that racism is illogical. At the same time, this passage suggests Cunard's own confusion at having to navigate this terrain. The experiences she describes in an impersonal register were in fact her own during her first trip to Harlem in 1931 in the company of Henry Crowder. The logic of these racist practices clearly eluded Cunard, yet she is meant to be instructing her readers on the workings of race and racism through her essay.

If Cunard's failures in this regard make her a dubious guide in many respects, the moments in the text where her authority seems most fragile are paradoxically the richest for a late twentieth-century or early twenty-first century reader.

Certainly she strives for a kind of authority that would distinguish her from other colonial travellers and from other writers about Harlem to whom she might easily be compared. In particular, Cunard is anxious to disavow Carl Van Vechten's *Nigger Heaven* (1926), accusing him of painting a sleazy portrait of Harlem in this controversial novel that was denounced by many, though not all, African-American writers and intellectuals. She is similarly dismissive of Paul Morand's representation of Harlem in his urban travel book, *New York* (1930). Cunard cites with some approval, in contrast, Harlem Renaissance writer Claude McKay's representations of Harlem in *Gingertown* (1932), oddly failing to mention his *Home to Harlem* (1928) perhaps because, not unlike *Nigger Heaven*, it takes the reader on a tour through the seamier side of life in Harlem. Here we see a strategy Cunard deploys throughout the essay: distancing herself from whites, particularly those with a prurient interest in Harlem, she aligns her efforts implicitly with those of the black writers she cites, not only McKay, but James Weldon Johnson and Edwin Embree.

Perhaps the most striking technique Cunard uses in an effort to distinguish her essay from other urban travel texts is to describe the typical tour in one section of her essay, embedding it in her own narrative in such a way as to suggest she is not the tour guide here, and this is not necessarily the Harlem she would want to show us. "If you are 'shown' Harlem by day ..." she begins; "At night you will be taken ..." she continues. By day one sees the inequities in housing, the charitable institutions, the library. By night one visits the jazz clubs and is entertained by black dancers, musicians, comedians. Cunard has clearly taken this tour, and she is anxious to represent it as the standard tour for a visitor to Harlem — note the impersonal structure of address. But she is also keen to establish that she has gone beyond the standard tour, and that she wants her readers to see more than the nightlife, so a critique of whites that seek out Harlem for these purposes follows immediately on her description of the "tour."

Notice how many of the whites are unreal in America; they are *dim*. But the Negro is very real; he is *there*. And the ofays know it. That's why they come to Harlem—out of curiosity and jealousy and don't-know-why. This desire to get close to the other race has often nothing honest about it; for where the ofays flock, to night-clubs, for instance, such as Connie's Inn and the Cotton Club and Small's, expensive cabarets, to these two former the coloured clientele is no longer admitted! To the latter, only just, grudgingly. No, you can't go to Connie's Inn with your coloured friends. The place is *for whites*. "Niggers" to serve, and "coons" to play—and later the same ofay will slip into what he calls "a coloured dive," and there it'll be "Evening, Mr. Brown," polite and cordial, because this will be a real coloured place and the ofay is not sure of himself there a-tall....

Cunard's desire to "get close to the other race" is, in contrast, meant to be honest; she is not merely a tourist, but a *political* tourist whose aim is solidarity and partisanship. The authority she strives for is ultimately not that of the imperial traveller, commenting on the "other" from above (although she slips in and out of this position in the text), but that of the insider, who can pronounce that Claude McKay had "that wrong kind of race-consciousness," who can deride class pretensions among African-Americans in Washington, who can declare communism the only solution to the race problem in the United States. That these claims are among the most discomfiting to readers today suggests her failure, but it is the failure of a woman passionately committed to the cause of racial justice, striving to find a place outside of imperialism from which to speak.

In "Jamaica—The Negro Island," Cunard's efforts to evade an imperialist subject position also tend toward a disavowal of whiteness. In this case her position is not to assume a careful distance from particular kinds of whiteness; it is rather to claim that whiteness has no place in Jamaica at all. Much of this essay is taken up with the (recorded) history of the island, and with descriptions of current conditions, particularly for the black peasant labourers. In this respect, "Jamaica—The Negro Island" appears to follow the "scientific" neutrality of colonial travel accounts written by men, with none of the "feminine" interest in personal relations, in the autobiographical that, according to Sara Mills, characterizes colonial travel narratives by women.[1] On the other hand, the naturalizing of a European presence around the globe that is typical of imperial travel narratives by both men and women is here not only absent, it is countered by the narrative Cunard constructs.

Cunard opens her essay with reference to that first European traveller to Jamaica whose tale is so well known: Columbus. She continues with the English colonization and the history of slavery. The history of Jamaica from the time of Columbus, she implies, is a history of interlopers who have no rightful place there. That she concludes that Jamaica is "the place of black peasantry" and that it "must be unconditionally theirs" is clearly intended not only as a critique of imperialism, but an implicit call for decolonization. The injustice of slavery, of the treatment of former slaves subsequent to emancipation, as exemplified in the infamous Morant Bay Rebellion, and the inequities suffered by labourers on the banana plantations at the time of Cunard's tours, fuel this call for a radical change. Yet even as she argues that Jamaica is a Negro island, Cunard finds a place in the history of British imperial relations with Jamaica that she can occupy, an ethical stance she can identify with.

Alongside the history of slavery, Cunard narrates the history of abolition, and in that latter narrative she finds an Englishness that is bound up with the role of liberator. Catherine Hall points out that in English representations of Jamaica between 1830 and 1860, plantation society came to be the antithesis of Englishness, and Englishness was both what "the freed slaves might be" and what "the freed slaves were not."[2] In other words, while the position on slavery was quite clear—among respectable middle-class English folk in the period, "only the paid lackeys of the planters would publicly defend slavery"[3]—the attitudes toward the former slaves were a good deal more ambivalent. An imperial inequality remained at the heart of this abolitionist orthodoxy: "slaves were

---

1   Sara Mills, *Discourses of Difference: An Analysis of Women's Travel Writing and Colonialism* (London: Routledge, 1993) 51.

2   Catherine Hall, *White, Male, and Middle Class: Explorations in Feminism and History* (New York: Routledge, 1988) 208.

3   Hall, 208.

brothers and sisters ... but younger brothers and sisters who must be educated and led by their older white siblings."[1] Hall points out, too, that the close conceptual tie between the English and their colonized brothers and sisters was relatively short-lived; by 1865, the date of the Morant Bay Rebellion, English discourses had shifted once again to a more open racism.

Cunard, for her part, shifts back, at this point in her narrative, to a critique of the role the English continued to play in Jamaica, from Eyre's treatment of the alleged perpetrators of the rebellion to the social stratification based on race that she witnesses during her travels. If she was able to identify with the Englishness of the abolitionists, however problematic a position that was, she is constrained to reject the British role in the Jamaica she travels through:

> And the Jamaica of today? Evidently and most essentially a land of black people. It is ridiculous and bound to strike any traveller there overpoweringly that this island should be anything but a black man's territory. Africa is peopled by Negroes. So is Jamaica. As clearly and categorically as that. Of Kingston, the capital, I cannot say otherwise than that I found it a very ugly town, contrived by that singular British spirit which is quite desperately without any concept of even the existence of plan, architecture or form. Yes, totally in keeping with the administrative and official atmosphere, which in other words signifies no geographic or human atmosphere of any kind.

With this passage Cunard emerges from historical narrative into travel narrative, from an accounting of the racial demographic in Jamaica from 1844 onward to an assertion of Jamaica's essential blackness—from a rhetorical deployment of the "objective" historical voice to an abrupt declaration of partisanship. That her condemnation of the British presence in Jamaica takes the form of an aesthetic critique seems peculiar unless one considers that part of the function of a conventional travel narrative is to com-

---

1   Hall, 208.

ment on the sights, and in this context, for Cunard, the ethical-political and the aesthetic are intertwined. Thus the built evidence of the British presence is both ugly to look at and produces, through its administrative structures, ugly results: "no ... human atmosphere of any kind." In contrast, the Jamaican countryside, the market day with its "sea of black people," the "old washerwoman" caught in a cloudburst, the "low knotted hills of the old Maroon country," are beautiful. It is not difficult to recognize the primitivist impulse in the contrast Cunard sets out here between the ugly trappings of European modernity and the "natural" beauty of the land and "its" people. And the political direction of Cunard's descriptions of Jamaica and its black population are easy enough to discern from the interpolated comments about the inequitable workings of the imperialist economy.

Cunard attempts to persuade her readers that Jamaica's status as a "Negro Island" is self-evident ("bound to strike any traveller there"), but such a conclusion is neither obvious nor historically necessary. It is rather, I would argue, strategic in two ways. It is politically strategic in relation to a bid for decolonization, and it is rhetorically strategic in relation to Cunard's construction of her partisanship. With respect to politics, first of all, Stuart Hall, writing in 1987, has this to say about the racial identity of Jamaica:

> People now speak of the society I come from in totally unrecognisable ways. Of course Jamaica is a black society, they say. In reality it is a society of black and brown people who lived for three or four hundred years without ever being able to speak of themselves as 'black.' Black is an identity which had to be learned and could only be learned in a certain moment. In Jamaica that moment is the 1970s.[1]

There are important differences in the semantic registers of the terms "Negro" and "black," not the least of which is the historical specificity of each term, so I do not mean to conflate Hall's remarks with Cunard's declaration about Jamaica. What I think is

---

1 Stuart Hall, "Minimal Selves," *Black British Cultural Studies: A Reader*, ed. Houston Baker, Jr., Manthia Diawara, and Ruth Lindeborg (Chicago: U of Chicago P, 1996) 116.

instructive about this passage is its denaturalizing of identity and its recognition that identities have their moment and their structures of possibility. One of the structures of possibility for the learning of blackness as an identity in Jamaica was independence. One of the structures of possibility for Cunard's declaration that Jamaica is a Negro island is Pan-Africanism, with its consciousness of race as a potentially unifying force and its collective approach to anti-imperialist action. Yet Pan-Africanism, at least as represented by Marcus Garvey, comes in for some criticism here.

As a rhetorical strategy, Cunard's assertion that Jamaica is a Negro island dissociates her from imperialism by aligning her with those who are calling for decolonization and independence, and as such gives her a place in the text from which to speak. She also locates her authority in an international discourse which she represents as superior to Garvey's Pan-Africanism. After commending Garvey as a member of the black peasantry "that British rule has not been able to keep out of sight," and praising his role in raising race-consciousness and in advocating in behalf of African and African-descended populations in international venues such as the League of Nations, Cunard nonetheless finds fault with his program:

> He has protested very outspokenly against the maintenance in various forms of slavery of the black races. Yet this conclusion is inevitable: his conception of the breaking down of this slavery is in no way linked up with the struggle to abolish the exploitation of the toiling masses of other races. The one will never be accomplished without the other, and this Garvey does not see. He does not see that the white imperialists will never *give*, but that they must be *forced*, and for this that the actual condition, the system itself, must be revolutionarily changed.

One need not disagree with Cunard's argument here to recognize that in setting Garvey up as a representative black political thinker and then countering his program with the Communist Party line, Cunard seems to garner for herself the role of liberator, once again. That is, in seeming to know better what the effective solution to racial oppression really is, Cunard ironically slips back into the imperial subject-position she has been trying to evade.

If "Jamaica—The Negro Island" may be read, in part, as an early engagement with Pan-Africanism, in *The White Man's Duty: An Analysis of the Colonial Question in Light of the Atlantic Charter* Cunard returns to the discourse, this time in the company of George Padmore, an important Pan-Africanist in his own right. Published in January 1943, *The White Man's Duty* can be read as anti-colonial critique, beginning with its title. A clear allusion to Rudyard Kipling's infamous contribution to debates over the New Imperialism, "The White Man's Burden," the pamphlet co-authored by Cunard and Padmore counters Kipling's position, neatly reversing the nature of the burdensome duty he describes. Kipling's poem, which was written in 1899, urges the sons of empire on to the thankless task of bringing enlightenment to the backward races through imperialism:

> Take up the White Man's burden—
>> Send forth the best ye breed—
> Go, bind your sons to exile
>> To serve your captives need;
> To wait, in heavy harness,
>> On fluttered folk and wild—
> Your new-caught sullen peoples,
>> Half devil and half child.

In representing imperialists as bound in servitude to devilish and child-like peoples, Kipling inverts the moral order of imperialism and encapsulates a central trope of colonial discourse: the notion that imperialism is a benevolent undertaking. For Cunard and Padmore, in sharp contrast, "the white man's duty" is to accord the colonized their right to sovereignty and equality; in other words, the white man's duty is to *de*colonize.

The occasion for this published conversation between Cunard and Padmore is the Atlantic Charter, a signed agreement between the US President, Franklin Roosevelt, and the British Prime Minister, Winston Churchill, who met in secret aboard the USS Augusta in Placentia Bay, Newfoundland in August of 1941. The aim of the charter was to set out a series of principles that might serve as a basis for international relations after the war; the eight principles outlined in the Atlantic Charter came to serve as the basis for the United Nations Charter. Cunard and Padmore are chiefly concerned with the third principle, which initially excited a good deal of hope and expectation among colonized leaders. The third principle of the Charter reads: "they [Roosevelt and Churchill] respect the right of all peoples to choose the form of government under which they will live; and they wish to see sovereign rights and self-government restored to those who have been forcibly deprived of them." As Cunard and Padmore make clear, however, Roosevelt and Churchill understood themselves to be talking about European nations and independent settler colonies like the US, Canada, and Australia, and not the colonized nations of the South. The forcible deprivation of sovereign rights to which they refer was apparently meant to apply exclusively to Nazi-occupied European nations, and not to the peoples deprived of those rights by European imperialism and colonialism. *The White Man's Duty* exposes the hypocritical double standard scripted into the Atlantic Charter, and makes a case for extending the third principle beyond Europe to its colonies.

George Padmore was, as Cunard suggests when she introduces him to the reader, particularly well-suited to commenting on the Charter and on the conditions in Britain's colonies. Padmore was born Malcolm Nurse in Trinidad in 1902. He attended university in the US, enrolling in law first at Fisk, then at Columbia. He joined the Communist Party shortly after his arrival in New York, and party activities prevented him from completing the degree. George Padmore was the cover name he adopted when conducting Party business, and he kept the name even after he had broken with the Communist Party. Padmore was soon posted to the Soviet Union and made head of the Negro Bureau of the Red International of Labour Unions. In that capacity, Padmore helped to organize an international conference of Negro workers in Hamburg in 1930. Representatives from the US, the Caribbean, and Africa were in attendance. Padmore was beginning to articulate a connection between anti-colonial struggles in Asia and the condition of blacks in Africa and the diaspora, although he ironically argued against Pan-Africanism at this point.[1] In the wake of this conference, Padmore became involved with a monthly publication that was in effect the first international review directed at Negro workers around the world. During this period Padmore published a number of pamphlets as well as one of his best-known books, *Life and Struggles of Negro Toilers* (1931), which was quickly banned by colonial governments.

In 1932 in Paris, Padmore met Nancy Cunard for the first time; they had already corresponded fairly extensively as she gathered materials for *Negro*, and according to her testimony, Padmore was to become, along with Raymond Michelet, one of her most important collaborators in work on the anthology.[2] It was Padmore who put her in touch with the International Labour Defence and William Patterson, even before they met in Paris, and as Padmore's biographer notes, the views Cunard expresses throughout the anthology are heavily influenced by those represented in *The Negro Worker*, the journal Padmore was involved with.[3]

In 1933, with the triumph of Hitler in Germany, the Hamburg office of *The Negro Worker* was closed and many of those connected with it, including Padmore, were imprisoned. Some months later Padmore was deported to England (he held a British passport), and he began to edit the journal from London. The rise of Nazism also had an impact on Padmore in another way. In order to begin to smooth relations with the West, the Soviet Union decided to disband the International Trade Union Committee of Negro Workers and, in Padmore's words, "to put a brake upon the anti-imperialist work of its affiliate sections and thereby sacrifice the young national liberation movements in Asia and Africa."[4] In anger at what he regarded as a betrayal of anti-racist, anti-imperialist principles, Padmore resigned. As a consequence, he was eventually formally expelled by the Communist Party,

---

1 James Hooker, *Black Revolutionary: George Padmore's Path from Communism to Pan-Africanism* (New York, London: Frederick Praeger, 1967) 17-18.
2 Hooker, 27. Cunard's testimony is in a letter to Hooker written in 1964.
3 Hooker, 28.
4 Quoted in Hooker, 31.

accused of "petty bourgeois nationalist deviation."[1] Padmore continued his anti-colonial work, and pursued a socialist analysis independent of the Communist Party; his London apartment gradually came to be an important centre of anti-colonial activism through the 1940s and 1950s.

In London in the 1930s, Padmore met up with his childhood friend, C. L. R. James, with whom he established the International African Service Bureau, and through activities such as this he expanded his contacts throughout the colonies and increased his knowledge of colonial affairs, about which he published regularly. This activity continued during the Second World War — the publication of the pamphlet on the Atlantic Charter with Cunard was only one of his undertakings. In 1944 Padmore was among the founders of the Pan-African Federation, and in 1948 he was involved in planning for the Fifth Pan-African Congress alongside Francis N. Kwame Nkrumah, who arrived in London with a letter of introduction to Padmore from C. L. R. James. The fifth Congress saw higher participation of African delegates, and for the first time demanded independence for Africa and the right of all colonized peoples to self-determination. Soon afterward, Kwame Nkrumah returned to Gold Coast (later Ghana) to begin working toward independence. When Nkrumah became prime minister of an independent Ghana in 1957, he appointed Padmore his secretary on African affairs, but Padmore did not hold the position long before succumbing to a liver ailment in 1959.

Cunard's collaboration with Padmore, first in the context of her *Negro* anthology, and then on this co-authored pamphlet, helps to frame some of the positions she took up. Her criticisms of DuBois and Garvey, for instance, echo Padmore's own at the time *Negro* was published, although Padmore later came to work with and proclaim admiration for DuBois. More importantly, her collaboration with Padmore helps to credential her anti-imperialist work. Certainly, the arguments and analysis in *The White Man's Duty* are largely Padmore's, and Cunard's role more that of partisan interviewer than co-author, strictly speaking. The text itself is usefully placed in the context of both anti-colonial agitation and

---

1   Padmore quoted in Hooker, 32.

anti-imperial writing in the period, bearing in mind that it was destined for a broad-based readership as a Hurricane "political"[1] and not for an intellectual readership. Thus, while it is not on a par with C.L.R. James's *Black Jacobins* (1938), in its call for decolonization and its analysis of the contradictions in Britain's national and imperial policies, it can be compared with James's *A Case for West Indian Self-Government* (1933). It is appropriate to place this pamphlet in the tradition of anti-colonial literature that developed further after the Second World War as decolonization unfolded, a body of writing that would include the works of more famous analysts of colonialism such as James, but also Aimé Césaire, Albert Memmi, Frantz Fanon, Amilcar Cabral.

It is also appropriate, as Edward Said has argued, to situate this body of anti-colonial writing in relation to the modernist cultural production with which Cunard is more typically associated. The influx of non-Europeans into the "heart" of empire in the early part of the twentieth century had a broader impact on modernism than is apparent from the discourse of primitivism alone. Said has been pivotal in initiating the "remarkable adjustment in perspective and understanding [that] is required to take account of the contribution to modernism of decolonization, resistance culture, and the literature of opposition to imperialism," arguing that

> The cross-fertilization between African nationalism as represented by George Padmore, Nkrumah, C.L.R. James on the one hand, and, on the other the emergence of a new literary style in the works of Césaire, Senghor, poets of the Harlem Renaissance like Claude McKay and Langston Hughes, is a central part of the global history of modernism.[2]

This "adjustment" in critical conceptions of modernism entails taking account of literatures produced in Africa, the Caribbean,

---

1 W.H. Allen published a series titled "Hurricane" books, which sold for nine pence and were intended for a broad readership (a minimum of 50,000 copies). At the time Cunard and Padmore produced *The White Man's Duty*, the publisher began a new series, called Hurricane "politicals," that consisted of shorter works, directed at a more serious (and presumably more modest) readership.

2 Edward Said, *Culture and Imperialism* (New York: Vintage, 1994) 243.

and Harlem not typically part of the modernist literary canon as it was established in the years following the Second World War, and it entails examining the ways European and Euro-American literature is marked by the "crisis" in imperialism as well. Both a malaise about empire and a "new imperialist" fervour are manifest in European literary culture around the turn of the century and both are transmuted, in different ways, in modernist literary culture. That Euro-American malaise is usefully illuminated by being set against the literary works of the African diaspora, but also against anti-imperialist writing like *The White Man's Duty*, as inter-locking parts of the "global history of modernism." Cunard, with projects like *Negro* and *The White Man's Duty*, allies herself with those travellers to the heart of empire, like Hughes and Padmore, helping to enlarge and rewrite the modernist project and chart the imperial connections.

Miscegenation Blues[1]

Feminist scholars have long recognized how deeply the sexual is implicated in the politics of race and nation. In "Making Empire Respectable" Ann Laura Stoler argues that "the very categories of 'colonizer' and 'colonized' were secured through forms of sexual control that defined the domestic arrangements of Europeans and the cultural investments by which they identified themselves."[2] In the early part of the twentieth century, changes in colonial relations coincided with a new discourse of sexual control as the guarantor of imperial power. In both the United States and Europe, eugenics constructed European women as the foundation of racial purity, and in the colonies the newly perceived vulnerability of white rule was to be shored up by new regulations of sex and gender. Two of Cunard's essays are testimony to the ways she ran afoul of imperial gender relations in her work and in her trav-

---

1 I owe my heading to the title of a collection of fiction by writers of mixed racial heritage, *Miscegenation Blues: Voices of Mixed Race Women*, ed. Carol Camper (Toronto: Sister Vision, 1994).

2 Ann Laura Stoler, "Making Empire Respectable: The Politics of Race and Sexual Morality in Twentieth-Century Colonial Cultures," *Dangerous Liaisons: Gender, Nation and Postcolonial Perspectives*, ed. Anne McClintock, Aamir Mufti, and Ella Shohat (Minneapolis: U of Minnesota P, 1997) 345.

els. Cunard's political work offers an opportunity to consider the ways national and imperial inscriptions of race and gender underwrote and perhaps undermined the political commitments of a woman who tried to intervene in those narratives.

The early decades of the twentieth century are now commonly associated with a "crisis" in imperialism. Apart from those who were increasingly opposed to imperial exploits and looked forward to the end of empire, many proponents of empire developed a sense of malaise about its viability. Indicators of this dis-ease were varied. In Britain, one marker had to do with increasing doubts about Britain's capacity to contend with its European competitors and, while it could hardly be admitted, with growing resistance movements such as Indian and Irish nationalism. Bernard Porter has argued that the social questions that dominated debates on the national level, questions about the health of Britons, about labour, education and, not least, the "woman" question, can also be understood as questions central to imperialism.[1] The development of the discourse of eugenics was one approach to these concerns: if the poor, unhealthy working classes could be induced to have fewer children, working-class mothers educated to raise healthier children, and middle-class women persuaded to have more children, the result would be a fitter, better-educated populace—one better equipped to deal with the challenges of empire. As Stoler puts it, the "management of European sexual activity" by administrative and medical discourses was fundamentally "related to the racial politics of colonial rule,"[2] both in empire and at home.

Concern about increasing flaws in Britain's moral fabric was also part of this picture and can be seen as an extension of the various efforts to police sexuality, gender roles and racial purity. Porter cites expressions of alarm about indecencies of dress, the degradation of the British way of life by "foreign riff-raff," homosexuality, the circulation of pornography, and growth in the use of birth control.[3] Women's suffrage and pacifism, both read as threat-

---

1   Bernard Porter, "The Edwardians and their Empire," *Edwardian England* (New Brunswick, NJ: Rutgers UP, 1982) 130.

2   Stoler, 345.

3   Porter, 132.

ening to traditional gender roles, were perceived as endangering the integrity and strength of the nation and its empire. The "new woman" with her short hair, her cigarettes, and her interest in public life and politics, was deemed inappropriately masculine, aggressively sexual and therefore immoral. That she was also typically middle class fed fears about the declining birth rate among bourgeois families. Similar sorts of anxieties were prevalent in the US, where black migration from the South to northern industrial centres and increases in immigration were perceived political threats that shaped eugenics discourse. Madison Grant, a leading American eugenicist and historical anthropologist, called for an end to non-white immigration to the US and condemned miscegenation in his 1916 bestseller, *The Passing of the Great Race*. Here also, political anxieties were articulated in sexual terms, as Cunard would discover.

Nancy Cunard's life and work could scarcely have been better suited to trigger these sorts of anxieties, both at home and in empire. That Cunard carried her public preoccupations with matters of race and class into her private life and vice versa, rendering these boundaries all the more fluid, heightened responses to her work both on the domestic front (*Black Man and White Ladyship*) and the international one ("The American Moron and the American of Sense—Letters on the Negro").

Black Man and White Ladyship was published privately as a pamphlet in December of 1931, the first year of Cunard's work on the *Negro* anthology. In it, Cunard explicitly challenges the intersection of class and racism, but does so through an attack on a particular construction of white womanhood, revealing perhaps unwittingly the extent to which gender is implicated in imperialist notions of respectability. The pamphlet arose out of a dispute between Cunard and her mother over Nancy's relationship with Henry Crowder. *Black Man and White Ladyship* takes the incident with Lady Cunard as a pretext for a critique of racism, and while some of Cunard's contemporaries clearly viewed her analysis of racism in the pamphlet as an excuse for a personal attack on her mother, it is more interesting to read the text as Cunard's break with a particular gendering.

The title is evocative of the divisions and inequality Cunard was preoccupied with, since it expresses not only differences in race and sex, but class. In her choice of the term "ladyship," Cunard betrays her concern with a particular construction of white womanhood. "Her Ladyship" was Cunard's nickname for her mother, but in the essay "ladyship" is also exemplary of a particular social identity. In the half of the essay subtitled "Her Ladyship," Cunard sketches a sardonic portrait of an upper-class society hostess who takes seriously her role as guardian of class position, respectability and, implicitly, Englishness. The race incident at the core of the text is a scandal, Cunard intimates, largely because of the significance it takes on in British society circles. Cunard's rendering of English society women and the values they uphold predominates in her recounting of the mother-daughter split:

> At a large lunch party in Her Ladyship's house things are set rocking by one of those bombs that throughout her "career" Margot Asquith, Lady Oxford, has been wont to hurl. No-one could fail to wish he had been at that lunch to see the effect of Lady Oxford's entry: "Hello, Maud, what is it now — drink, drugs or niggers?" ... The house is one in Grosvenor Square and what takes place in it is far from "drink, drugs, or niggers." There is confusion. A dreadful confusion between Her Ladyship and myself! ... Half of social London is immediately telephoned to: "Is it *true* that my daughter knows a Negro?"

As much as it is a critique of the values of a particular class and race, Cunard's portrait is a critique of a particular gender role, one she may well have been expected to take up. Her assessment of the source of the racism — "with you it is the other old trouble — class" — is accompanied by an indictment of the kind of femininity her mother represents. Her Ladyship is described as "petite and desirable as per all attributes of the nattier court lady," whose extravagance in matters of dress is unrivalled, and who is governed completely by the social fashions of the London upper crust: "Negroes, besides being black ... have not yet penetrated into London Society's consciousness. You exclaim, 'They are not received!' … They are not found in the Royal Red Book. Some big hostess gives a lead and the trick is done!" Such a "career" as this Cunard is determined to escape.

If, as I am suggesting, we read Cunard's break with her mother as a break with a particular gendering, it becomes possible to read her efforts to shed the mantle of race privilege in her work and in her travels as a means of effecting an alternative position for herself as a white English woman. In this respect she replicates the patterns of Victorian women travellers in the Empire, for whom travel was often a means of gaining freedom from gender constraints at "home." Her reluctance to see herself in a position of dominance in matters of race and class has to do with the ways whiteness and class privilege articulate with gender to produce "ladyship." Her relative silence on the subject of gender—apart from this pamphlet, Cunard rarely touches on gender in her writing—can be understood as a displacement of gender onto her preoccupation with race and class. I do not mean to suggest that Cunard's political identifications with black and working-class struggles were merely an excuse for reinventing herself as a woman. The pattern of her allegiances and identifications must be understood and evaluated in the context of available social categories and their historical resonance. Cunard explicitly presents herself as a class and race traitor in this pamphlet, but there can be little doubt she would have been perceived as betraying her sex as well. If she does not sufficiently acknowledge the way she too is implicated in raced and gendered discourses (in critiquing her mother, she might seem to place herself outside of whiteness as well as outside of a particular kind of womanhood), she "colours" herself through her associations, and is ultimately unable to evade gender inscriptions, as we will see.

In addition to the domestic scandal documented in *Black Man and White Ladyship*, another sort of sex scandal erupted during Cunard's work on the *Negro* anthology, confirming the extent to which her political work transgressed not only racial but gender boundaries. Shortly after Cunard arrived in Harlem for the second time in the spring of 1932, the New York *Daily Mirror* printed a story linking her to Paul Robeson and intimating she had come to New York in pursuit of him. Both denied the allega-

tions, and Cunard called a press conference at which she attempted to set the story straight regarding Robeson, and to redirect
publicity to her anthology and the cause of the Scottsboro boys.
While she did not succeed in deferring scandal, she did publicize
her interest in blacks, and the publicity generated hundreds of letters, among which were two or three dozen filled with threats
and obscenities. Cunard provides her own account of this incident in "The American Moron and the American of Sense,"
reprinting excerpts from some of the letters and offering an
analysis of the interracial sex scandal as a feature of American race
politics.

Almost without exception, the letters she received impugning
her interest in African-Americans as a betrayal of her race charged
her with betraying her gender as well. Her intellectual and political interests were refashioned as the most prurient of sexual
obsessions. This pattern is graphically clear in some of the letters
that Cunard, in the more conservative climate in which she was
writing and publishing, abstained from reprinting:

> I don't know what they call your kind in England but here
> in America they call them plain nigger fuckers or prostitutes
> of the lowest kind ...

> You dirty lowdown cocksucker, you are trying to convince
> the white race of NYC that you came here to write a book
> about the Negro race, we know that you came here to suck
> the black pricks ...

> I feel certain that in the eyes of this world of white humani-
> ty, you Miss Nancy Cunard, are lower than the lowest of
> prostitutes, in your phoney outbursts, and belley-hoo[sic]
> you are making since your arrival to this country. If you for
> one moment think that you are fooling the US people with
> your book writing pretext, you are mistaken ...[1]

If these letters are extreme, they are but a more explicit and less

---

1 MS Nancy Cunard, (Recip.), Harry Ransom Humanities Research Center, The
   University of Texas at Austin.

sanctioned version of what the press was publishing. Several papers ran a photograph of Cunard with Harlem novelist Taylor Gordon. The painter John Banting, who had accompanied her to Harlem, had been cut out of the original photograph in an effort to support claims about the sexual character of Cunard's interest in Harlem. That the image of a white woman on a street corner with a black man is sufficient "evidence" of sexual exploits tells us that the logic articulated in the obscene letters was more general than one might initially credit. Cunard was besieged with tele-phone calls and visitors at the Grampion Hotel in Harlem; reporters attempted to track down Henry Crowder; Cunard was pursued even at the home of the restaurant manager she had befriended at the Grampion and who had offered her accommo-dation when it became necessary to leave the hotel. Finally she retreated to a farm in upstate New York for a month, hoping the scandal which was interfering with the making of the anthology would die down.

In Cunard's account of these letters and the "sex scandal" in the press, she presents an analysis of what she sees as an effort to detract from her anti-racist work. "Any interest manifested by a white person," she explains, "even a foreigner to America (such as myself), is immediately turned into a sex 'scandal.'" Sex is used to delegitimize the work, to discourage challenges to racist institu-tions; sex is the stick anti-racists are beaten with: "No chance is ever missed by the American press ... to stir up as much fury as possible against Negroes and their white friends. To do this the sex motive is always used. As in the South it is always the lie of the 'rape' of white women by black men, so in the North it is always the so-called 'scandal' of inter-racial relations." In alluding to the practice of lynching black men on the pretext of their hav-ing raped white women, Cunard grasps both the fundamental violence of efforts to contain political action on the part of blacks and whites in the battle against racism, and the sexual subtext.

For her understanding of lynching—touched on here and developed in "Scottsboro—and Other Scottsboros"—Cunard is undoubtedly indebted, indirectly, to Ida B. Wells-Barnett, whose sophisticated analyses of lynching gained currency through her journalism and public speaking. As Hazel Carby attests, although she was writing at the turn of the last century, Wells-Barnett's "analysis of the relationship among political terrorism, economic oppression, and conventional codes of sexuality and morality … has still to be surpassed in its incisive condemnation of the patriarchal manipulation of race and gender."[1] Wells published her positions on lynching both in newspaper articles and in the form of pamphlets, such as *Southern Horrors* (1892) and *A Red Record* (1895). She also travelled extensively throughout the US and to Britain, presenting her arguments in the form of public lectures. Key points in her analysis concern the historical emergence of lynching as a practice during the period of Reconstruction, when the institution of slavery had been abolished and black men were legally able to compete economically with white men for the first time, and the injustice of miscegenation laws which defined rape in racial terms, making it illegal for a black man to have sexual relations with a white woman, but normalizing the rape of black women by white men. These laws effectively carried the practices of slavery, when white plantation owners regularly raped their women slaves and literally controlled black men economically and politically, beyond the official end of that institution, when "protecting" white women became an excuse for continuing to control black men through the terror of lynching.

That Cunard's political interest is recoded as sexual by the press and in the letters she received is not surprising in this context and was indeed a way of attempting to contain the threat posed by the kind of work she was doing. The violence of some of the more extreme letters registers the symbolic power of Cunard's challenge to the institutions of racism and gender discrimination. For a white woman publicly to declare intellectual and political interest in the lives of blacks in America was to engage in a kind of prostitution according to the cultural codes governing the behaviour of black and white, male and female. Stepping outside of middle-class white womanhood, coded as private and chaste, Cunard "coloured" herself with the public sexuality widely ascribed to black womanhood, necessarily coded as the opposite of white femininity. It is important to remember that when

---

1   Hazel Carby, *Reconstructing Womanhood: The Emergence of the Afro-American Woman Novelist* (Oxford: Oxford UP, 1987) 108.

Cunard was editing the *Negro* anthology anti-miscegenation laws were still on the books in most US states. Indeed, as late as 1967 fifteen states still had statutes proscribing inter-racial marriage. That Cunard deals only with the ways the "sex scandal" is used to discredit her work, and does not tackle inter-racial relationships head-on in this instance the way she does in *Black Man, White Ladyship* is perhaps not surprising. Her strategy, instead, is to characterize as "moronic" those who would either sanction her behaviour or dismiss her political work, and to represent as "sensible" those who support her anti-racist endeavours.

Apart from their mutual preoccupation with issues of sex and race, both of these essays are quasi-autobiographical—more than any of the others in this collection. The one narrates an intensely personal family break, albeit in a manner that strives to depersonalize the incident and to underplay its intensity; the other reflects upon a dimension of the process of preparing the anthology. Yet Cunard remains curiously elusive in each piece, as both anecdotes are presented as pretexts for addressing larger concerns. That is, while each essay centres on a key moment in Cunard's life, neither is *about* her. Yet it is in these two essays that she emerges most evidently as a gendered, classed, and raced social agent, running up against the material and discursive conditions in which she lived and worked. If Cunard's efforts at evading the social roles assigned her were only partly successful, it can at least be said that she managed to contest the limits and constraints of the raced and gendered boundaries she encountered in her travels.

The Red and the Black

Although Cunard's invocation of Communist Party rhetoric throughout her writings on race and empire has been taken as evidence of her imperialism and eurocentrism, the historical links between Marxist movements and African diasporan struggles provide another way of looking at this dimension of her racial justice work. This is not to suggest that Cunard's writing does not bear traces of her class and race privilege, but it is to argue that her work ought nonetheless to be positioned at the intersection of these international struggles for racial and economic justice—an intersection that has been underplayed in most accounts of modern American cultural production.

Cunard herself never took out membership in the Communist Party; indeed two of the African-American communists she came to know while working on the anthology, William Patterson and Louise Thompson, later characterized her commitment to social and racial justice as a passion rather than a politics.[1] Yet Cunard was a consistent "fellow traveller," to use the Party coinage for its allies, from her association with the Surrealists and especially Louis Aragon in the mid to late 1920s, through to her work on the anthology, and her involvement in the Spanish Civil War. Beyond this ideological affinity, the communist position on race politics at the time Cunard was working on the anthology created a place for her in what might otherwise have seemed someone else's struggle. The race policy of the Comintern in the 1930s was assimilationist, oriented to uniting black and white workers around a common cause, in contrast to many of "the most powerful and progressive impulses in Afro-American life"[2] which were nationalist. Yet as Robin Kelley points out, "by the late 1920s and early 1930s, Black nationalism(s)—especially as it was expressed in culture—had much more in common with American Communism than most scholars have admitted."[3] Cunard's embrace of black communists, the prominent place accorded to them in her anthology, and her critique of Garveyism as "the wrong kind of race politics" need to be situated in relation to the complex articulation between African-American politics, Pan-Africanism, and communism at the time she was working on the *Negro* anthology.

The rapprochement between the left and black intellectuals and artists in the twenties, thirties and forties, and, perhaps especially, the disenchantment with Communist Party politics experienced subsequently by some black American Marxists are well known. This latter narrative is to be found both in fiction and

---

1   Chisholm, 202-03.

2   Mark Naison, *Communists in Harlem During the Depression* (Urbana: U of Illinois P, 1983) 45.

3   Robin D.G. Kelley, "'Afric's Sons with Banner Red': African-American Communists and the Politics of Culture, 1919-1934," *Imagining Home: Class, Culture and Nationalism in the African Diaspora*, ed. Sidney J. Lemelle and Robin D.G. Kelley (London: Verso, 1994) 37.

non-fiction by Richard Wright, Ralph Ellison, and Chester Himes. Yet even a selected list of other African-American writers, artists, and intellectuals who were at one point or another either affiliated with the Communist Party or were fellow travellers suggests the breadth of red and black interaction in this period: Claude McKay, Langston Hughes, Louise Thompson, Paul Robeson, Margaret Walker, Sterling Brown, Countee Cullen, Jessie Fausett and, eventually, W. E. B. DuBois, in addition to Wright, Ellison, and Himes. Wright offers one way of understanding the appeal, for African-Americans, of Marxist discourse. In the manifesto *Blueprint for Negro Writing* (1937), Wright argued that black writers should look to Marxism as it provided "the maximum degree of freedom in thought and feeling ... for the Negro writer" and "restore[d] to the writer his lost heritage, that is, his role as a creator of the world in which he lives, and as a creator of himself."[1] Marxism, in other words, was a source of agency for those who had historically been deprived of the power to order their own lives.

American communists were, for their part, beginning to recognize the importance of making common cause with African-Americans in the struggle for racial justice. Mark Solomon explains the logic this way: "The pivotal issues then [1917-1936] ... involved the basic character of American society. Capitalism's cornerstone was seen to have been laid by slavery and fortified by racism. Therefore, the achievement of equality implied the ultimate transformation of the nation's economic and social foundation."[2] The influence of black communists and the need to engage with the legacy of slavery and the problems of racism were shaping forces in American communism in the early decades of the twentieth century. If the specific operations of race and racism made for important tensions between black Marxists, the US Communist Party, and the Comintern, the articulation of race and class struggles also made for tremendously creative

---

1 Richard Wright, *Blueprint for Negro Writing* in *The Norton Anthology of African-American Literature*, ed. Henry Louis Gates and Nellie McKay (New York: W.W. Norton, 1997) 1384.
2 Mark Solomon, *The Cry was Unity: Communists and African Americans, 1917-1936* (Jackson, MS: UP of Mississippi, 1998) xviii.

responses to the social conditions of the period, both in terms of activism and in terms of artistry.[1]

The two essays by Cunard that I want to consider under the rubric of the red and the black, although all of her work on race and empire can be viewed in these terms, are best understood as the products of her activism, specifically her activism in relation to the famous Scottsboro case. "Scottsboro—and Other Scottsboros" and "A Reactionary Negro Organisation" are products of Cunard's involvement with the mass action in behalf of the Scottsboro boys organized by the International Labour Defence, the legal defence organization of the US Communist Party. The ILD undertook a dual approach to fighting what came to be known as "race" cases, coupling legal defence with mass action to bring public pressure to bear against the racism in the judicial system. Thus while it may seem odd to a contemporary reader that her essay on the Scottsboro boys should be as much about International Labour Defence involvement in the case as it is about an analysis of lynching and the specifics of the Scottsboro case, the ILD was at the crux of efforts to forge an alliance between the left and black civil rights politics. As Mark Naison attests, "The campaign to free the Scottsboro boys, more than any single event, marked the Communist Party's emergence as a force in Harlem's life."[2] Cunard's championing of the ILD role in the Scottsboro campaign and her condemnation of the NAACP are, moreover, two sides of the same coin. Not only did the ILD make its struggle with the NAACP a key aspect of the Scottsboro campaign,[3] contempt for the black middle classes and black betterment organizations like the NAACP and the Urban League had been a standard Communist Party position since the 1920s,[4] and a standard feature of the work of black radicals like Cyril Briggs.

The style of "Scottsboro—and Other Scottsboros" is reminiscent of the Living Newspaper form of theatre developed in the wake of the Russian revolution of 1917 as a means for the new

---

1   See in particular the important recent study by James Edward Smethurst, *The New Red Negro: The Literary Left and African American Poetry, 1930-1946* (New York: Oxford UP, 1999).

2   Naison, 57.

3   Naison, 58.

4   Naison, 20.

communist government to disseminate news, education, and propaganda in a geographically vast and culturally diverse nation. The form soon spread beyond the Soviet Union, reaching Britain and the US in the 1930s. A dynamic and multi-faceted theatrical form, the Living Newspaper presented topical issues in an interpretive frame through a mix of media and theatrical styles: visual projections, puppets, dramatic sketches, satire, crowd scenes. Cunard's essay is a verbal collage of newspaper clippings, letters from ILD organizers, lists of racist "frame-ups," lists of lynchings and racially-motivated murders, quotations from legal briefs, and photographs, all used as evidence for her interpretation of the Scottsboro case. Framed by this cut-and-paste of the activist's archive is a detailed narrative of the Scottsboro case.

Read as an archive of mass action around a cause, "Scottsboro — and Other Scottsboros" works both as a petition in behalf of the Scottsboro boys, and as a record of political ephemera. The rhetorical power of the piece has to do with the sense it conveys of Cunard's immersion in what Laura Lyons has aptly dubbed "the dailiness of struggle."[1] The essay's value as a historical document has to do with the ways ephemera, to quote Lyons again, constitute "a uniquely resonant site for understanding the nexus" of specific political struggles and their larger social context. Cunard strives to place her reader at the scene as far as possible:

> Knight is shaking his fist at Haywood Patterson and calling him "that black thing over there." Leibowitz has made a four-hour summing up. Insults to Ruby Bates, Lester Carter, Leibowitz and Brodksy have been spat out by Knight and other prosecuting counsel. Leibowitz and Brodksy are "New York jews, but jew money can't buy Alabama justice;" all four have received many death threats. And another of the prosecuting attorneys has made a lynch-inciting speech which has increased the number of fiery crosses (Ku Klux manifestations) that have burned nightly for over a week in all the surrounding villages....

---

1   Laura Lyons, "Daily Espousals: Ephemera, Social Movements, and Irish Republicanism," paper delivered at Marxism 2000, Rethinking Marxism's 4th International Gala Conference, University of Massachusetts-Amherst, September 21-24, 2000.

This description of the proceedings at the Decatur retrial provides the context of race hatred and judicial corruption for the present-tense representation of the prosecuting attorney's violent gestures and racist epithets, giving the reader simultaneously a sense of immediacy and the background that allows for an interpretation of these gestures. Yet beyond such narrative techniques, the cut-and-paste approach Cunard takes to providing evidence for her claims offers another sort of immediacy. Part of the "dailiness of struggle" entails compiling information on lynchings, on the number of blacks murdered in a given six-month period—together with the putative circumstances of those killings which indicate how senseless they were. Part of it involves protests and demonstrations, and here the photographs that accompany the original article provide the evidence: a manifestation in Washington D.C. on the day the US Supreme Court reviewed the case and granted an appeal for a retrial; a protest meeting in Trafalgar Square, London—part of the international mobilization around the Scottsboro case; an anti-lynching march in Harlem; the mother of one of the boys walking down Fleet Street in London on her way to meet with newspaper editors as part of the campaign. Cunard also records a number of petitions, listing the well-known signatories. This is all the standard stuff of mass action, but Cunard's collection of Scottsboro ephemera dramatizes the history of this particular case and her involvement in it in a way that brings to life the larger "culture" against which the drama was played out.

Central, of course, is the lynch "culture" itself. Cunard's principal claim, that the Scottsboro case is not anomalous and that "every Negro worker is the potential victim of lynching, murder and legal lynching by the white ruling class, simply because he is a worker and black," is a clear rejection of what William Maxwell calls the "triangular lynch myth": the notion that white men need to protect white women from black male rapists.[1] Equally important, though, is the extent to which Cunard's representation of the Scottsboro case also goes some way toward redressing the "anti-lynch triangle" that the left produced in response to the lynch

---

1   William Maxwell, *New Negro, Old Left: African-American Writing and Communism Between the Wars* (New York: Columbia UP, 1999) 131, 140-41.

myth, uniting black and white male workers against the accusations made by white women. While the status of the two girls as prostitutes was used by the defence as a means of undermining the credibility of their testimony, Cunard at least makes it clear that this status made them vulnerable to police pressure to testify against the Scottsboro boys. She also stresses that neither of the young women had actually accused the nine black men and boys of rape, arguing instead that the two women were themselves victims: "The girls were not individuals with alleged wrongs, but had been transformed into part of the lynch machinery which 'keeps niggers in their place' by such frame-ups, so that other 'niggers' shall not dare to ask for their rights." If Cunard stops short of a fully developed gender analysis here, that is not surprising. According to Robin Kelley, the nature of the red and black symbiosis in the period "essentially precluded a serious theoretical framework that might combine the 'Negro' and 'Woman' questions."[1]

"A Reactionary Negro Organisation" exposes, perhaps more than any other piece, some of the problems with Cunard's approach to questions of race. That she should critique the NAACP in the context of the Scottsboro case is, in light of her own involvement with the mass action organized by the ILD, perhaps to be expected. That she should also attack W. E. B. DuBois and print this attack in an anthology that claimed to represent the breadth of the "struggles and achievements" of the African diaspora seems not to be particularly well thought out, to say the least. There is also some irony in the fact that DuBois resigned from the NAACP in 1934, the year *Negro* was published, and took up a position at Atlanta University. He also, at this time, according to Arnold Rampersad, began "a slow but steady turn away from a primary interest in Afro-American affairs to a deepening concern with the fate of international socialism and the rise of the colonial peoples."[2] He became a champion of the USSR, and continued to move increasingly to the left over the years until, in 1961, he joined the Communist Party and left for Africa where he died a

---

1   Kelley, 44.
2   Arnold Rampersad, *The Art and Imagination of W.E.B. DuBois* (New York: Schocken, 1990) 223.

few years later. It is important to understand that the problems with Cunard's essay are signs of more than a lapse of judgment on her part, or flaws in her character. They are better read as the traces of her social signature; that is, of her particular trajectory through radical race and class politics as a privileged white woman with partisan political desires. In berating DuBois and the NAACP for bourgeois complacency, she seeks to place herself, rhetorically, outside of class privilege; in taking up the anti-lynching cause, she seeks to step outside of whiteness and, implicitly, outside of the role it assigns the white woman in the lynch-myth triangle. Yet such an escape is ultimately impossible; the desire for a position beyond race, class and gender is itself marked by the very positions she seeks to evade.

The limits to Cunard's understanding of the nuances of race and racism, as they emerge in essays like "A Reactionary Negro Organisation," can also be understood in terms of her means of access to racial justice activism, and that is, once again, the ILD. If the Communist Party stood to gain from its association with black communists and with black struggles more broadly, and in fact did transform accordingly in particular cases, the experiences of a number of black Marxists are ample testimony to the frequent failure of the Comintern and nationally-based Communist Party locals to incorporate a thorough enough understanding of and commitment to racial justice. On the occasion of his resignation from the Communist Party in 1956, Aimé Césaire declared:

> What I demand of Marxism and Communism is that they serve the black peoples, not that the black peoples serve Marxism and Communism. Philosophies and movements must serve the people, not the people the doctrine and the movement.... We consider it our duty to make common cause with all who cherish truth and justice, in order to form organizations able to support effectively the black peoples in their present and future struggle — their struggle for justice, for culture, for dignity, for liberty....[1]

---

1 Quoted in Cedric Robinson, *Black Marxism: The Making of the Black Radical Tradition* (London: Zed, 1983) 260.

For Césaire, as for George Padmore, Richard Wright, and others who broke with the Party at various junctures, communism no longer served the black peoples effectively. To be sure, many other black radicals then and since have continued to work within a Marxist framework, including membership in the Communist Party, developing ever-more sophisticated analyses of the inter-relationship of race, class, gender and imperialism. What emerges in Césaire's declaration, however, is a dissatisfaction with philoso-phies and movements that do not adequately grasp the full specificity of the struggles of the African diaspora, struggles for justice, for culture, for dignity, for liberty. Cunard's writing on race and empire, and her work as editor and political organizer track these struggles, even as she attempts to chart a particular course through them. Yet Cunard, too, in her dismissal of DuBois, in her championing of the ILD over the NAACP, in her passion-ate commitment to a particular vision of the path to racial justice, mistakes the breadth and range of the very black struggles she seeks to represent and celebrate.

The merging of black nationalism with revolutionary socialism during the period Cunard was editing *Negro* and writing about race and empire represents what in contemporary terms we might think of as a local–global symbiosis. The specificity of black oppression in the US, in the Caribbean, in African colonies, made for a reaching out across national divides and an embrace of the Marxist analysis of capitalism and imperialism as the international mechanisms of that racial oppression. At the same time, the specificity of black oppression came to be acknowledged, to vary-ing degrees, by the Comintern and nationally-based Communist Parties, in a way that reshaped the theorizing and the policies of the international organizations. The so-called "black nation the-sis" came to characterize the approach taken by the US Com-munist Party to the question of race at this time. Cunard's work was enabled, both conceptually and literally, by this local–global intersection. The dialogue is frequently one-sided in her own writing, as we have seen, and it is consequently important to fol-low the traces of the larger debate that emerge in her work beyond the boundaries of those individual essays.

Conclusion

As modernist expatriate, Cunard travels through and inhabits foreign territory as a means of reinventing herself and of carving out a space for the kind of work she wants to do. In making "exile" her home, she follows a path well worn by imperial explorers, traders, adventurers, missionaries, scientists, anthropologists, not to mention her fellow modernists. In writing about race and empire in solidarity with another set of travellers, those moving from the colonies into the heart of empire and back out again with the weapons of decolonization, Cunard opens herself and her readers to a "remarkable adjustment in perspective and understanding," to quote Edward Said again, that entails recognition of the discontinuities between these two groups of travellers quite as much as of the scope for collaboration. In other words, in the crossing of paths between a Cunard and a Padmore, there lie both a history of unequal political and economic relations, cross-cut by gender and race, and the common ground of a desire for a more just future. To assess Cunard's writing on race and empire, then, we must take account of its place in these intersecting histories of cultural production, and we must ask what we might learn from the particular course she charts across cultural, social and geopolitical divides.

Cunard's writing on race and empire resists easy categorization precisely because it retains traces of her privilege even as she strives to eschew privilege in the name of social justice. We find tropes of imperial travel alongside calls for decolonization; primitivist fascination with black performance alongside denunciations of white slumming in Harlem; collaboration with Pan-Africanists and black communists despite the limitations of her understanding of race and racism. What we gain by considering this work in all of its ambiguity is an enlarged understanding of the processes of identification and affiliation that subtend modernist culture. If, as Said contends, "many of the most prominent characteristics of modernist culture ... include a response to the external pressures on culture from the *imperium*,"[1] in Cunard's writing, that response

---

1 Said, 188.

entailed collaborating with those applying the pressure. Hers was an oppositional aesthetic. In lieu of the formal innovations of high modernism, the encyclopaedic form, the novelty derived from juxtaposing disparate fragments, the irony, that Said argues are responses to empire,[1] Cunard embraced journalism, the pamphlet, the political essay, cultural criticism, and political activism. No less modern and no less imbued with universalizing impulses than a James Joyce or Joseph Conrad, Nancy Cunard flamboyantly performed political commitment as her art form.

Not surprisingly, the reviews of that performance were mixed. Claude McKay charged Cunard with "taking a Negro stick to beat the Cunard mother," and certainly there is evidence that in her identification with black struggles, Cunard remade herself. Yet Cunard's writing on race and empire was more than a passing affair, and it is difficult to see how it translated into an advantage for Cunard. Unlike Margery Perham's African journeys, for instance, Cunard's travels in empire did not win her favour with the authorities, did not lead to a prestigious academic career, did not lead to a career at all—other than the one she already had as political tourist. As problematic as her identifications were, what we learn from Cunard's writing on race and empire—from her mistakes, if nothing else—are the ways national and imperial inscriptions of race and gender both informed and destabilized her political commitments. It is her desire to transform herself from imperial daughter to partisan in the cause for racial justice, a desire for filiation and engagement, that exposes the dynamics of race and gender. In fact, it is arguably Cunard's contradictory social location as a writer, the fact that she is both a privileged participant in the imperial economy and a conscious opponent of its exploitative operations, that makes considering her work a worthwhile endeavour. In tracing, through her texts, the processes of her political engagement across boundaries of social, cultural, and racial difference, we can learn about late imperial culture in ways that speak to our world as much as to hers.

---

1 Said, 189-90.

Nancy Cunard: A Brief Chronology

1896 Born at Nevill Holt, Leicestershire, England. Daughter
      of Sir Bache Cunard, grandson of Samuel Cunard,
      Loyalist founder of the Cunard shipping line, and Maud
      Burke, a Californian heiress.

1916 Marries Sydney Fairbairn.
      Selected poems published in *Wheels: An Anthology of
      Verse*, edited by Edith and Osbert Sitwell.

1918 Sydney Fairbairn returns to the front; Nancy shares a
      house in the country with Sybil Hart-Davis. Augustus
      John and Alvaro (Chile) Guevara are frequent guests.
      Nancy writes more poetry.

1919 Separates from Sydney Fairbairn and travels to south of
      France. Returns to England in June and lives society life
      in Grovesnor Square with her mother for a time. In
      September, leaves for a month in Paris.

1920 Moves permanently to France.

1921 *Outlaws* (London: Elkin Mathews and Marrot). First
      collection of poetry appears to reasonably good reviews.

1923 *Sublunary* (London: Hodder and Stoughton Ltd.).
      Poems.
      Increasingly settled in Paris; befriends Robert
      McAlmon, Walter Lowenfels, Eugene MacCown, Kay
      Boyle, Tristan Tzara, Man Ray, Constantin Brancusi,
      Nina Hamnett, Janet Flanner and Solita Solano.
      Meets Norman Douglas on a trip to Italy.

1924 Entertains expatriate Americans and French avant-
      gardists (including René Crevel, Jean Cocteau, Louis
      Aragon, André Breton, Phillipe Soupault) in new apart-
      ment on Île St. Louis.

1925 *Parallax* (London: Hogarth Press). Long poem. Covers
      designed by Eugene MacCown.
      Sir Bache Cunard dies, November 3, leaving the bulk of
      his estate (£14,418) to Nancy.
      Finally secures divorce from Sidney Fairbairn.

1926   Begins love affair with Louis Aragon.
Together collect primitivist art, including Nancy's famous African ivory bracelets.
Nancy moves increasingly in communist circles.

1927   Buys old peasant farmhouse in La Chapelle-Réanville. Purchases an old printing press and learns the art of printing by hand from a professional printer, M. Lévy. Establishes her experimental Hours Press, and begins by publishing George Moore's short story "Peronnik the Fool" in a small limited edition. Followed by Louis Aragon's translation of Lewis Carroll's *The Hunting of the Snark* (*La Chasse au Snark*).

1928   Meets Henry Crowder, African-American jazz musician, in Venice. Breaks off relations with Aragon and invites Crowder to help her with the Hours Press, and to live with her in La Chapelle-Réanville.

1930   *Poems* (Aquila Press). Two long poems published. Hours Press moves to Paris; publishes *Whoroscope*, Samuel Beckett's first poem; also *A Draft of XXX Cantos* by Ezra Pound, and poems by Laura Riding, Robert Graves, and Walter Lowenfels, among others.

1931   Hours Press closes after publishing a half dozen more books, including poems by Harold Acton, Richard Aldington, and a treatise, *The Revaluation of Obscenity*, by sexologist Havelock Ellis.
Conceives of *Negro* anthology and undertakes first trip to Harlem. Meets many of the leading African-American artists and intellectuals, including W.E.B. DuBois, Alain Locke, Arthur Schomberg, and Langston Hughes.
Learns of Scottsboro case and actively campaigns on behalf of the Scottsboro boys through 1933.
Publishes pamphlet, *Black Man and White Ladyship: An Anniversary*. (Privately printed by N.C. in Toulon and distributed to friends and acquaintances; second printing, London: The Utopia Press.)

1932   Second trip to Harlem; press scandal breaks out. Also visits Cuba and Jamaica for purpose of collecting materials for *Negro*. She meets Nicolás Guillén and Marcus Garvey.

1934   *Negro, An Anthology*, ed. (London: Wishart and Company). Published at Cunard's own expense with funds she received from out of court settlement for libel suit launched against several British newspapers for articles published in the wake of second visit to Harlem. George Padmore visits at Réanville, completing *How Britain Rules Africa* over the summer.

1935   Travels to the U.S.S.R. for a month. Meets up with black American communist party contacts, William Patterson and Eugene Gordon.
Becomes correspondent for Associated Negro Press (ANP) on Mussolini's invasion of Abyssinia (Ethiopia).

1936   Outbreak of the Spanish Civil War; Nancy leaves for Barcelona. Spends next three years writing about and campaigning for republican Spain. Writes for Associated Negro Press (ANP), Sylvia Pankhurst's *New Times*, and three papers edited by Charles Duff: *Spanish Newsletter, Spain at War*, and *Voice of Spain*.
Meets and befriends Pablo Neruda.

1937   *Authors Take Sides on the Spanish Civil War*, ed. Pamphlet published by Left Review in London.

1938   Nancy helps republican Spaniards fleeing Franco and campaigns on behalf of Spanish refugees. Writes articles for the *Manchester Guardian* as well as ANP.

1940   Travels to Chile soon after outbreak of WWII. Visits Neruda and other Chilean friends; from there she goes to Mexico, Trinidad, and Cuba on her way back to Europe.
Continues to write for ANP.

1941   Lives in London for next three years, working for Ministry of Information, and reviewing for *Our Time*. Reconnects with George Padmore.

1942   *The White Man's Duty* (W.H. Allen). Nancy's pamphlet with George Padmore on imperialism and the Atlantic Charter is published and sells very well.

1944   *Poems for France*, ed. (La France Libre). Collection of poems by English writers in celebration of occupied France.

Visits Sylvia Townsend Warner and Valentine Ackland in Dorset.

Learns from Morris Gilbert that her house in Réanville has been destroyed.

1945   Returns to France to salvage what is left from her house.

Pursues journalism.

1948   Lady Cunard dies of cancer of the throat. Nancy absents herself, but is not disinherited. Uses proceeds from estate to purchase old house near La Mothe Fénélon in the Dordogne.

1949   *Poems for Spain*. Pamphlet privately published in Perpignan.

1954   *Grand Man: Memories of Norman Douglas* (Secker and Warburg, 1954).

1955   Writes book about George Moore.

Has plans for a book on African ivories, *The Ivory Road*, and travels through Switzerland and Germany visiting museums to research the volume. Project never realized.

1956   *G.M.: Memories of George Moore* (Rupert Hart-Davis, 1956).

At Rupert Hart-Davis's prompting, begins drafting autobiography.

1957   Beginnings of depression and physical illness that persisted intermittently through remaining years. Visits Spain under Franco several times and runs into trouble with authorities; is jailed and expelled from the country in 1960.

1959   Draft of autobiography rejected by Hart-Davis; Cunard abandons project.

1960   Visits London; is psychologically unstable, apparently suffering from paranoia. Arrested for drunk and disorderly behaviour and for soliciting. Found in need of psychiatric treatment, is hospitalized for four months. Friends, including Aragon and Lowenfels, work to ensure she is not held prisoner in Holloway Sanatorium, as Cunard herself, having been certified insane, fears.

1960   Returns to La Mothe Fénélon. Writes poetry. Physical health precarious.

1963   Works on series of essays about the Hours Press with Hugh Ford.
Diagnosed with emphysema.

1965   After several days of physical collapse and mental derangement in Paris, dies in a public ward at l'Hôpital Cochin.

1969   *These Were the Hours*, ed. Hugh Ford (Southern Illinois University Press). Posthumously published memoir of the Hours Press.

A Note on the Text

Rupert Hart-Davis tells a story about Cunard's interview with Jonathan Cape when she was in search of a publisher for her *Negro* anthology. Cunard arrived with a bulging mock-up of the anthology, and Cape spent some time outlining options for streamlining the book and improving its format. Cunard was apparently unconvinced: "'But you don't understand, Mr. Cape,' she squeaked at him, 'this *is* the format'."[1] Cunard's insistence at retaining full editorial control over her idiosyncratic project has guided my treatment of her essays, particularly those taken from *Negro*. Beyond emending obvious typographical or spelling errors, and rectifying inconsistencies in capitalization, treatment of numbers, and punctuation, I have not altered Cunard's original texts. Cunard's style is nothing if not emphatic; the dash and the exclamation point appear to be her favourite punctuation marks, italics her favourite typeface. Untouched, too, are the redundancies, the stylistic and even grammatical infelicities, the neologisms. She liked lists, liked to cobble texts together out of quotations, newspaper articles, and letters. The result is often a kind of encyclopedic, omnibus text not unusual among modernist works, and in Cunard's case in particular, the style bears traces both of the personal scrapbook and the imperial traveller's diary. I have felt it important to preserve this stylistic signature as much as possible, for it is at once a marker of the way Cunard inhabited the position of author and editor, and an index of the historical and discursive conditions under which her texts were produced.

I have taken as my copy text for the essays from *Negro* ("Harlem Reviewed," "Jamaica—The Negro Island," "The American Moron and the American of Sense—Letters on the Negro," "Scottsboro—and Other Scottsboros," and "A Reactionary Negro Organisation") the original edition of that work inscribed on left inside cover in Cunard's handwriting: "Nancy Cunard-1934. Publication: Feb 15 (This copy for England. March, 1952)." At bottom in same hand, "My Own Copy. Nancy

---

1   Quoted in Rupert Hart-Davis, "The Girl at the Writing Table," *Nancy Cunard: Brave Poet, Indomitable Rebel* ed. Hugh Ford (New York: Macmillan, 1975) 30-31.

Cunard. Oct. 1941. London. What remained of the whole edition has been destroyed by bombs and fire last year (Sept), save 10 copies, saved by E.E. Wishart, as if in prevision." According to a leaf tipped into the anthology, the edition consisted of 1000 copies, and 150 extra copies were printed for the contributors. Not only was the preponderance of the unsold copies of the edition destroyed by the war, most of the manuscript materials appear to have perished in the looting and vandalism inflicted on Cunard's house in Réanville, France by German soldiers and by French villagers disgruntled with Cunard's way of life. In the absence of manuscript materials to consult, I have relied upon this first edition and the already cited evidence that she retained editorial control over the volume.

I have similarly relied upon copies of her published pamphlets in the collection of Cunard's papers at the Harry Ransom Humanities Research Center at the University of Texas at Austin. There were two printings of *Black Man and White Ladyship*, both paid for by Cunard. I have used the first, privately published by Imprimerie A. Bordato in Toulon, December, 1931, as my copy text. The second was printed in the same year by Utopia Press, London, and while it corrects a few typographical errors present in the first printing, it introduces a significant erratum: it omits the second subtitle dividing the text, "The Black Man." Cunard was understandably outraged at this omission, the two distinct halves of her essay being key to its argument. Thus, while I have followed the second printing in correcting the typographical errors, I have followed the first printing with respect to subtitles.

Judging from royalties statements from the publisher, W.H. Allen, Cunard and Padmore's pamphlet *The White Man's Duty* fared quite well. The first printing in January 1943 of 12,500 copies sold out by April of that year, and a second printing of 5,880 also sold out in subsequent months. Cunard's request for a third printing was turned down owing to "paper difficulties,"[1] as the publisher's representative described the shortages of paper during the second world war. I have taken as my copy text one of

---

1 Letter to Cunard from Mark Goulden of W.H. Allen, December 2, 1943. MS Nancy Cunard (recip.), Harry Ransom Humanities Research Center, The University of Texas at Austin.

the copies of the pamphlet in the possession of the HRHRC, choosing the one signed by both Cunard and Padmore. Dorothy Pizer, who was Padmore's common-law wife, transcribed conversations between Cunard and Padmore that she had recorded by shorthand; these transcriptions were subsequently "lightly edited," to quote Cunard. Perhaps these transcripts remained in Dorothy Pizer's possession, or with the publisher. They are not, at any rate, among Cunard's papers.

A Note on the Appendices

I have assembled a range of documents from roughly 1890 to 1940 in order to place Cunard's work in dialogue with other European and Euro-American writers on empire and race as well as with the work of African-American and Afro-Caribbean intellectuals. I have organized these documents under the same broad conceptual rubrics as her essays: Imperial Eyes — the question of imperialism and travel in empire, especially by women; Miscegenation Blues — the question of inter-racial sexual relations and the discourse of eugenics; and The Red and the Black — the question of a communist "solution" to racism and imperialism.

Imperial Eyes

Cunard's travels in empire are contradictorily marked both by her efforts to undertake anti-imperialist work and by the imperialist cultural baggage she inevitably carried along. To take the measure of Cunard's work, in all of its ambivalence, it is useful to set it alongside other texts produced through imperial travel. As I have suggested, "Harlem Reviewed" and "Jamaica — The Negro Island" are not instances of travel writing in the conventional sense, but they do cite and even cross over into that genre as Cunard constructs her sense of self in relation to her political work. Because gender is so key for understanding the ways that Cunard was herself constrained by imperialist discourse even as she borrowed its privileges, I have selected excerpts from two very different travel texts by women. Mary Eliza Bakewell Gaunt (1861-1942) was a popular novelist and travel writer who supported herself with her writing. Gaunt's emphasis on the independent, adventurous woman and her explicit endorsement of racist stereotypes about Africans and other colonized peoples place her work within the mainstream, not only of popular travel writing in the period, but, more problematically, of first-wave feminism. Dame Margery Freda Perham (1895-1982) forged an academic career in history through her travels in, and written accounts of, empire. The founder of the Institute of Colonial

Studies at Oxford University, Perham was also a close associate of important figures like Lord Lugard, and came to be widely consulted on matters of colonial administration. The work these women did in empire, and the ways they each constructed a voice and an identity through their travels, present a notable contrast with Cunard, even at her most discomfiting.

For this reason it is also useful to set Cunard's writing on empire alongside that of others engaged in anti-imperialist work. In reading Cunard and Padmore's pamphlet, *The White Man's Duty*, together with an excerpt from an essay by C.L.R. James (1901-1989), we can get a sense of the emergent opposition to empire that they were all a part of. James's work of the 1930s — especially *The Black Jacobins* (1938) and his play *Toussaint L'Ouverture* (1936)—was pivotal in contributing to a growing culture of resistance to imperialism; indeed, James came to be one of the most important anti-colonial thinkers, not only of this period, but of the century.

Miscegenation Blues

Cunard's work on race and empire was directly implicated in early twentieth-century anxieties about race and sexuality. The pervasiveness of eugenics in scientific research, in social policy, and in popular discourse made anti-racist and anti-imperialist activity particularly difficult. We have seen the ways Cunard's activities provoked outrage in explicitly gendered as well as racialized terms. I have chosen an excerpt from an essay on eugenics that explicitly addresses the role a (white, middle- or upper-class) woman is intended to play in "race improvement": Albert Wiggam's (1875-1957) *Fruit of the Family Tree* (1924).

For those engaged in the struggle for equality and civil rights in the United States in the early part of the century, combating the arguments of eugenicists was key. Anthropologist Franz Boas challenged the scientific basis for eugenicist claims; others, W.E.B. DuBois (1868-1963) among them, opted for a socio-political analysis of eugenicist anxieties. DuBois's "The Marrying of White Folks" (1910) offers calm, rational arguments for education and social justice as means of preventing "degradation," and incisive condemnation of the hypocrisy with which the daughters of white men are represented as endangered. If DuBois offers an important gender analysis in his arguments against anti-miscegenation laws, Ida B. Wells-Barnett (1862-1931) makes an analysis of the construction of white womanhood central to her essays on lynching. The excerpt from *Southern Horrors: Lynch Law in all its Phases* (1872) speaks to the ways gender and sexuality are implicated in race politics, and is consequently usefully set along-side Cunard's own efforts to grapple with these questions in *Black Man and White Ladyship* and "The American Moron and the American of Sense — Letters on the Negro." Wells's essay is also relevant for Cunard's essay on the Scottsboro boys, which expounds a theory of lynching developed and popularized by Wells.

The Red and the Black

Understanding the historical links between Marxist movements and African diasporan struggles can help contemporary readers to make sense of some of the idiosyncrasies of Cunard's writing on race and empire. Communism not only offered Cunard a way into struggles for racial justice, it offered a conceptual framework and an international organizational structure for many African-American, Caribbean, and African activists as well. There have, however, also been important tensions, historically, between Marxism and the Communist Party on the one hand, and African diasporan struggles for social justice on the other. These dif-ferences have been articulated both by those with a different political philosophy and by those working within a Marxist framework. The short essay by W. E. B. DuBois titled "The Class Struggle" (1921) and the excerpt from Richard Wright's (1908-1960) autobiography *American Hunger* ([1944] 1977) may be taken as representative. DuBois had not yet turned to Marxist theoriz-ing when he wrote this short essay, which defends the politics of the NAACP in addition to outlining what he regarded as the lim-itations of communism in the struggle for racial equality in the US. Wright, who had argued not long before (1937) that Marxism provided "the maximum degree of freedom in thought and feeling" for black writers, here records some of the contradictions and constraints he encountered while working within the Communist Party.

Finally, I have reprinted an excerpt from Claude McKay's (1889-1948) autobiography *A Long Way from Home* (1937), both for its pointedly critical assessment of Cunard's work and for its insights into the contradictions marking it.

ESSAYS

ON RACE AND EMPIRE

IMPERIAL EYES

"HARLEM REVIEWED"

Is it possible to give any kind of visual idea of a place by description? I think not, least of all of Harlem. When I first saw it, at 7th Avenue, I thought of the Mile End Road[1]—same long vista, same kind of little low houses with, at first sight, many indeterminate things out on the pavement in front of them, same amount of blowing dust, papers, litter. But no; the scale, to begin with, was different. It was only from one point that the resemblance came to one. Beginning at the north end of Central Park, edged in on one side by the rocky hill of Columbia University and on the other by the streets that go to the East River, widening out more and more north to that peculiarly sinister halt in the town, the curve of the Harlem River, where one walks about in the dead junk and the refuse-on-a-grand-scale left in the sudden waste lots that are typical of all parts of New York—this is the area of Harlem. Manhattan and 8th Avenues, 7th, Lenox, 5th and Madison Avenues, they all run up here from the zone of the sky-scrapers, the gleaming white and blond towers of down-town that are just visible like a mirage down the Harlem perspective. These avenues, so grand in New York proper, are in Harlem very different. They are old, rattled, some of them, by the El on its iron heights, rattled, some of them, underneath, by the Sub[2] in its thundering groove.

Why is it called Harlem, and why the so-called capital of the Negro world? The Dutch made it first, in the 17th century; it was "white" till as recently as 1900. And then, because it was old and they weren't rebuilding it, because it's a good way from the centre, it was more or less "left" to the coloured people. Before this they lived in different parts of New York; there was no Negro "capital." This capital now exists, with its ghetto-like slums around 5th, bourgeois streets, residential areas, a few aristocratic avenues or sections thereof, white-owned stores and cafeterias, small general shops, and the innumerable "skin-whitening" and "anti-kink" beauty parlours. There is one large modern hotel, the Dewey

---

1   A street in London.
2   Part of New York City's public transit system; the El is above ground, the Sub of course
    is the underground subway.

Square, where coloured people of course may stay; and another, far larger, the Teresa, a few paces from it, where certainly they *may not*! And this is in the centre of Harlem. Such race barriers are on all sides; it just depends on chance whether you meet them or no. Some Negro friend maybe will not go into a certain drug-store with you for an ice-cream soda at 108th (where Harlem is supposed to begin, but where it is still largely "white"); "might not get served in there" (and by a coloured server at that—the white boss's orders). Just across the Harlem River some white gentlemen flashing by in a car take it into their heads to bawl, "Can't you get yourself a white man?"—you are walking with a Negro, yet you walk down-town with the same and meet no such hysteria, or again, you do.

In his book, *Black Manhattan*, James Weldon Johnson[1] has made a map of Harlem showing the rapid increase of Negro occupation. This of course cannot be taken otherwise than as percentage, as there are some whites living in all parts of it. The Negro population is always increasing, but the houses do not expand; hence overcrowding in all but the expensive apartments and the middle-class lodgings. These last are pretty similar to our own Bloomsbury[2] kind. And why then do the Negroes continue to flock to Harlem? Because in most other parts of New York they simply "don't let to coloured," at least never *en masse*. More and more of the "white" streets on the fringes of Harlem "go black" and become part of it. It happens this way. A coloured family or two get houses in such or such a street. Prejudiced white neighbours remonstrate with the landlord, who may not care—the more so as he knows that other coloured families will be wanting to move in. The whites have complained of his houses, demanded

---

1 James Weldon Johnson (1871-1938), African-American poet and social activist best known for works such as *God's Trombones* (1927) and *The Autobiography of an Ex-Coloured Man* (1912). Important critic, editor and poetic contributor to Harlem Renaissance. In 1916 Johnson became national organizer for the National Association for the Advancement of Coloured People (NAACP); 1920 became first African-American elected head of NAACP. *Black Manhattan* (New York: Arno P, 1930) was Johnson's history of blacks in New York and Harlem.

2 A neighbourhood in London made famous by the group of writers and artists who lived there: Virginia and Leonard Woolf, Vanessa and Clive Bell, Roger Fry, Duncan Grant, Lytton Strachey are the principle figures in the Bloomsbury Group.

repairs. He won't make them, and for Negroes he can *double the rent* (this is invariably so), and no repairs need, or will, ever be made. The Negroes come, up go the rents, and the whites abandon that street. One of the reasons why Harlem is so concentrated is that this procedure takes some time; in housing themselves, as in every single other thing, they have to fight and fight; they are penalized for being black or coloured in every imaginable way, and, to the European, in many unthinkable ones.

Some 350,000 Negroes and coloured are living in Harlem and Brooklyn (the second, and quite distinct, area in greater New York where they have congregated). American Negroes, West Indians, Africans, Latin Americans. The latter, Spanish-speaking, have made a centre round 112th St. and Lenox Avenue. Walk round there and you will hear—it is nearly all Spanish. The tempo of the gestures and gait, the atmosphere, are foreign. It is the Porto-Ricans, the Central Americans and the Cubans. Nationalisms exist, more or less fiercely, between them and the American Negro—as indeed does a jealous national spirit between American Negro and black Jamaican. The latter say they are the better at business, that the coloured Americans have no enterprise. (Are we to see here the mantle of the British as a nation of shopkeepers on West Indian shoulders?) The American Negro regards the Jamaican or British West Indian as "less civilised" than himself; jokes about his accent and deportment are constantly made on the Harlem stage. And so they are always at it, falling out about empty "superiorities" and "inferiorities," forgetting the white enemy.

The Jamaican is "a foreigner"—and yet it was Marcus Garvey,[1] from Jamaica, who, more than any living Negro, roused the black people of America just after the war with his "Back to Africa" movement. This sort of Zionism, after a lightning accumulation of millions of dollars, collapsed entirely. "Back to Africa" was held out to all the Negroes in the American continent, a Utopian

---

[1]   Marcus Garvey (1887-1940) popular founder of UNIA (Universal Negro Improvement Association) whose aim was the "general uplift of the Negro peoples of the world." Born in Jamaica, Garvey traveled to the US, initially for the purpose of raising funds for UNIA projects; once he arrived in Harlem in 1916, he decided to remain, making Harlem his base for activism.

impossibility at both ends—for how can 12 million transport themselves *en masse*, as Garvey urged them to do, and in what part of Africa would the white imperialists allow such, or even a small part of such, a settlement? Apart from this, the Africans were, not surprisingly, angered by Garvey's self-given title of "Provisional Emperor of Africa." The African country chosen by Garvey was Liberia, which, as is known to everyone, is really an American (Firestone) colony.[1] There is an anomaly now in the position of the Garvey movement. Though he is himself discredited, his followers (and there are several inter-factions too) disavow him but continue to call themselves Garveyites and proclaim his doctrine. Those extraordinary half salvation army, half British military uniforms that you see in the streets occasionally are Garvey's men; you come across them speaking at street corners, holding a large crowd. But it is all hot air. It is not organized in any direction or built on anything solid. Individually they have not the drive of the black Communist orator, for they are not speaking of anything serious; Garvey's theory was "all-black;" he wanted his people to be independent of, to cut away from, the white race entirely. The wrong kind of pride; a race pride which stopped at that, and paid no heed to the very real and concrete misery, oppression and struggles of the Negro toiling millions throughout the States.

If you are "shown" Harlem by day you will inevitably have pointed out to you the new Rockefeller apartments, a huge block towering above a rather sparse and visibly very indigent part of 7th Avenue. These were built by the millionaire of that name, supposedly to better the conditions of Negro workers by providing clean and comfortable lodging for them, but inhabited, however, by those who can afford to pay their rents. The Y.M.C.A. and the newly built Y.W.C.A.—more institutes for "uplift." The Harlem Public Library, with its good collection of books on Negro matters, and just a few pieces of African art, so few that the idea strikes one vexingly: why, in this capital of the Negro world, is there no centre, however small, of Africanology?

---

1 Liberia was established on land purchased by the US for the purpose of creating a colony for freed American slaves. It became independent in 1847. Harvey Samuel Firestone (1868-1938), the American industrialist and president of Firestone Rubber Company, established a large (one million acre) rubber plantation in Harbel, Liberia in 1923.

The American Negroes—this is a generalization with hardly any exceptions—are utterly uninterested in, callous to what Africa is, and to what it was. Many of them are fiercely "racial," as and when it applies to the States, but concerning their forefathers they have not even curiosity.

At night you will be taken to the Lafayette Theatre, the "cradle of new stars" that will go out on the road all over America and thence come to Europe. It is a sympathetic old hall, where, as they don't bother ever to print any programmes, one supposes that all the audience know all the players; it has that feeling too. Some of the best wit I heard here, and they can get away with a lot of stiff hot stuff. Ralph Cooper's orchestra[1] was playing admirably that night they had "the street" in. This was to give a hearing to any-one who applied. They just went on the stage and did their stuff. And the audience was *merciless* to a whole lot of these new triers, who would have passed with honour anywhere out of America. The dancing of two or three of the street shoe-blacks, box on back, then set down and dancing round it, was so perfect that the crowd gave them a big hand. No-one who has not seen the actual dancing of Harlem in Harlem can have any idea of its superb quality. From year to year it gets richer, more complicated, more exact. And I don't mean the unique Snake-Hips and the marvel-lous Bo-Jangles,[2] I mean the boys and girls out of the street who later become "chorats" and "chorines" (in the chorus), or who do those exquisite short numbers, as in music the Three Ink Spots[3] (a new trio), adolescents of sixteen or seventeen perhaps, playing Duke Ellington's *Mood Indigo*[4] so that the tears ran down one's face. There was a new dance too, one of the sights of the world as

---

1 Ralph Cooper was at one time a compère (or master of ceremonies) at Harlem's Apol-lo Theatre. His orchestra played at clubs in Harlem in the 1930s.

2 Earl "Snake-Hips" Tucker was a well-known dancer in the 1920s and 1930s who popu-larized a variation of an old plantation dance, the Snake Hips. Tucker appeared regular-ly in Harlem Clubs like Connie's Inn and the Cotton Club, and in the film *Symphony in Black* featuring Duke Ellington and Billie Holiday. Bill "Bo-Jangles" Robinson (1878-1949) was a dancer famous for tap dance and soft shoe routines; Robinson appeared in Vaudeville, in Broadway reviews in the 1920s and 1930s; after 1930 he also began per-forming in film.

3 J. Sterling Russell, Hamilton Stewart, Jr., and P. Clifton Armstrong formed a musical trio known as the Three Ink Spots.

4 Duke Ellington (1899-1974), a composer, arranger and musician, began playing piano professionally in Washington D.C. in 1917. In 1923 he moved to New York with a

done at the Savoy Ballroom, the Lindy-Hop. The fitting third to its predecessors, the Charleston and the Black Bottom. These were in the days of short skirts, but the Lindy is the more astounding as it is as violent (and as beautiful), with skirts sweeping the floor. Short minuet steps to begin, then suddenly fall back into an air-pocket, recover sideways, and proceed with all the variations of leaves on the wind. For the Lindy is Lindbergh,[1] of course, created by them in honour of his first triumph. These Tuesday nights at the Savoy are very famous, as is the Harlem "Drag Ball"[2] that happens only once a year. To this come the boys dressed as girls—some in magnificent and elaborate costumes made by themselves—and of course many whites from down-town. A word on the celebrated "rent-party" that the American press writes up with such lurid and false suggestions. This is no more nor less than an ordinary evening dance in someone's house. The "rent" part is its reason for being, for the guests give about fifty cents to come in, thereby helping pay the rent, and they buy liquor there which, as everywhere in dry America (and doubtless it will go on even if prohibition is entirely abolished), is made on the premises or by a friend. The music, as like as not, comes from a special kind of electric piano, a nickel a tune, all the best, the latest ones.

But it is the zest that the Negroes put in, and the enjoyment they get out of, things that causes one more envy in the ofay.[3] Notice how many of the whites are unreal in America; they are *dim*. But the Negro is very real; he is *there*. And the ofays know it. That's why they come to Harlem—out of curiosity and jealousy and don't-know-why. This desire to get close to the other race

---

band called the Washingtonians; from 1927-1930 Ellington's orchestra became the house band at the Cotton Club and became known as the Cotton Club Orchestra. Weekly radio broadcasts from the Cotton Club established Ellington's national reputation. Ellington left the Cotton Club in 1931 and began touring the US and Europe. In 1928 clarinetist Barney Bigard joined Ellington's orchestra; in 1930 he and Ellington co-wrote *Mood Indigo* which became a signature piece for the band.

1 Charles Lindbergh (1902-1974) was the American aviator who made the first solo, nonstop transatlantic flight from New York to Paris on May 21, 1927.

2 The Harlem Renaissance saw the development of an important gay subculture, and drag balls were a frequent occurrence. Both men and women cross-dressed, and thousands attended, many as spectators.

3 [Author's note: Ofay: white.]

has often nothing honest about it; for where the ofays flock, to night-clubs, for instance, such as Connie's Inn and the Cotton Club and Small's, expensive cabarets, to these two former the coloured clientele is no longer admitted! To the latter, only just, grudgingly. No, you can't go to Connie's Inn with your coloured friends. The place is *for whites*. "Niggers" to serve, and "coons" to play — and later the same ofay will slip into what he calls "a coloured dive," and there it'll be "Evening, Mr. Brown," polite and cordial, because this will be a real coloured place and the ofay is not sure of himself there a-tall....

This applies of course to the mass of whites who treat Harlem in the same way that English toffs[1] used to talk about "going slumming." The class I'm thinking of is "the club-man." They want entertainment. Go to Harlem, it's sharper there. And it doesn't upset their conception of the Negro's social status. From all time the Negro has entertained the whites, but never been thought of by this type as possibly a social equal. There are, however, thousands of artists, writers, musicians, intellectuals, etc., who have good friends in the dark race, and a good knowledge of Harlem life, "the freedom of Harlem," so to speak.

"You must see a revival meeting," they said to me. "It's nothing like what it is in the South, but you shouldn't miss it." Beforehand I thought I wouldn't be able to stand more than ten minutes of it — ten minutes in any church.... When we got into the Rev. Cullen's on 7th Avenue (the Rev. is the father of the poet, Countee Cullen[2]) a very large audience was waiting for the "Dancing Evangelist" (that is Becton's title, because of his terrific physical activity). A group of "sisters" all in white spread itself fan-wise in the balcony. There was a concert stage with deacons and some of Becton's twelve disciples, and the seven or eight absolutely first-class musicians who compose the orchestra, of whom Lawrence Pierre, a fine organist and a disciple. Nothing like a church, an evening concert.

---

1   British slang for a smartly-dressed, usually upper-class, person.
2   Countee Cullen (1903-1946) was regarded as one of the most promising young poets of the Harlem Renaissance. Unlike Langston Hughes, Cullen did not experiment formally, but he published several volumes of poetry during the 1920s and won several important prizes.

The music starts, a deep-toned Bach piece, then a short allocution, and then the long spirituals, the robust soloist that a massed chorus, the audience, answers back. They begin to beat time with their feet too. The "spirit" is coming with the volume of sound. At this point Becton enters quietly, stands silent on the stage, will not say a word. They must sing some more first, much more; they must be ripe ground. How do they reconcile Becton's exquisite smartness (pearl-grey suit, top hat, cane, ivory gloves, his youthful look and lovely figure), the whole sparkle about him, with the customary ponderousness of the other drab men of God? A sophisticated audience? No, for they appear to be mainly domestic workers, small shop workers, old and young, an evidently religious public, and one or two whites.

A new spiritual has begun; the singing gets intenser, foot-beating all around now, bodies swaying, and clapping of hands in unison. Now and again a voice, several voices, rise above the rest in a single phrase, the foot-beat becomes a stamp. A forest shoots up—black, brown, ivory, amber hands-spread, stiffened-out fingers, gestures of *mea culpa*, beating of breasts, gestures of stiff arms out, vibrating ecstasy. Far away in the audience a woman gets "seized," leaps up and down on the same spot belabouring her bosom. It comes here, there—who will be the next? At one moment I counted ten women in this same violent trance, not two with the same gestures, yet *all* in rhythm, halftime or double time. A few men too, less spectacular. Then just behind me, so that I see her well, a young girl. She leaps up and down after the first scream, eyes revulsed, arms upstretched—she is no longer "there." After about a minute those next to her seize her and hold her down.

The apex of the singing has come; it is impossible to convey the scale of these immense sound-waves and rhythmical under-surges. One is transported, completely. It has nothing to do with God, but with life—a collective life for which I know no name. The people are entirely out of themselves—and then, suddenly, the music stops, calm comes immediately.

In this prepared atmosphere Becton now strides about the stage, flaying the people for their sins, leading their ready attention to this or that point of his argument by some adroit word, a wise-crack maybe. He is a poet in speech and very graceful in all his movements. His dramatisation is generous—and how they respond ... "yeah man" ... "tell it, tell it." Sin, he threatens, is "cat-foot," a "double dare devil." And the sinner? "A double-ankled rascal," thunders this "adagio dancer," as he called himself that night, breaking off sharp into another mood, an admonishment out of "that inexpressible something by which I raise my hand." There are whirlwind gestures when he turns round on himself, one great clap of the palms and a sort of characteristic half-whistle-half-hoot before some point which is going to be emphasised—and the eloquence pours out in richer and richer imagery. Becton is the personification of expressionism, a great dramatic actor. You remember Chaliapine's acting of Boris Godounov;[1] these two are comparable.

Then, "when the millenniums are quaking it's time to clap our hands." It is the moment for the "consecrated dime," and the singing begins again, but the trances are over; other preachers may speak later. This ritual goes on from eight till after midnight, about four nights a week, and sometimes both the faithful and the evangelist are so indefatigable that it goes on for twenty-four hours. These services, really concerts, are the gorgeous manifestation of *the emotion* of a race—that part of the Negro people that has been so trammelled with religion that it is still steeped therein. A manifestation of this kind by white people would have been utterly revolting. But with the Negro race it is on another plane, it seems positively another thing, not connected with Christ or bible, the pure outpouring of themselves, a nature-rite. In other words, it is the fervour, intensity, the stupendous rhythm and surge of singing that are so fine—the Christianity is only accidental, incidental to these. Not so for the assembly of course, for all of it is deeply, tenaciously religious.

Becton is the most famous evangelist of the coloured race in America. He has a following of more than two hundred thousand, from New York to Florida, from Baltimore to Kansas. Like

---

1   Fyodor Ivanovich Chaliapine (1873-1938) was a Russian/Soviet singer who famously performed the title role in the opera *Boris Godounov*, composed by Mussorgsky and based on works by Pushkin and Karamsin. Boris Godounov was Czar of Russia from 1590-1605.

Christ he has twelve disciples. "The reason I have my party comprised of all men is because Jesus' disciples were all men, and if it was right for him it is right for me." He is one of the most elegantly dressed men in the world. Another comparison: "If Jesus were alive he would dress like me," for "if I came out in a long black coat, a collar turned backwards and looked downcast and forlorn, people would say that if they have got to look like that to be Christians, they don't want to join the church." Some other sayings of Becton's which fetch the religious are: "I work for God on contract and he keeps his bargain." "I told you, Lord, before I started out that I was a high-priced man, but you wanted me." "God ain't broke!" The "consecrated dime" and its fellows of course supply all Becton's needs. His organisation is called "The World's Gospel Feast," which publishes a quarterly called *The Menu*, the motto of which is: "A Square Deal for God!"

I have given all this detail about the revivalist meeting because it is so fantastic, and, *aesthetically* speaking, so moving. But when one considers the appalling waste of this dynamic force of people, and this preying on the prayers and fervours of old-fashioned, misguided, religious Negroes, it is tragic. Some time during this last summer (1933); after a new point in horror had been reached in the Scottsboro case[1] at the Decatur "retrial," a young Negro minister frankly voiced his realisation of the truth; he said that the Communists were the only ones to defend his race, that they had proved it unquestionably throughout the whole history of Scottsboro; he said that for this reason although he was a man of God he was a Communist. Had Becton been honest, had he spoken thus, he would have swept the land. His followers would have had the same faith in these new words as in all his past "heavenly messages." But his was an individual racket.

I went to see Becton. A very handsome and courteous man. During our talk he leant forward earnestly: "In what manner do *you* think will come the freeing of my race?" "Only by organized and militant struggle for their *full* rights, side by side with Communism." He smiled. "And in what way do you think?"

---

1   See Cunard's essay on the subject in this volume.

I asked him. "I think it will be by prayer," he murmured. I wanted to shout at him "Be honest *now*. Use your great dramatic gift for the right thing; you could be a giant in the freeing of your people." He spoke of the new million-dollar temple he was going to build. "I have not the money, but I shall get it" — and no doubt he would have been able to collect it all by these consecrated dimes.... But now, one year after I saw him, Becton is dead. "Bumped off" suddenly and brutally by some gangsters, shot in a car.

Another spectacular man of God is the Rev. Father Devine, who that year was having a hard time with the authorities for what, in Jamaica, used to be called "night noises." The fervent assembled in too great numbers and their exaltation was too loud. Sensational vengeance followed Father Devine's arrest; the judge who condemned him died the next day.

It may seem odd that one's thoughts stay so long with these black priests and their terrific hold over their large following. But religion amongst the Negroes, those that have it (for the younger generation is shaking off its weight, and replacing this by a desire for, an acquisition of, racial and economic facts), their reaction to religion cannot be dissociated in my mind from their past collective reaction to tribal ceremony and custom in Africa. They are *honest* and at home in their belief; that is the whole difference as compared with whites. A white audience in church lifts one's heart in utter disgust; with the Negroes one longs for this collective force to be directed towards the right things, solidarity with those whites who are struggling for their rights too against the super-brutality of American "democracy."

The Negro ministers and churches vary in their attitude to the more and more violent struggle for Negro rights. Since the Scottsboro case and other equally vicious frame-ups, some have helped the International Labour Defence, the organisation which is fighting these cases; some have refused all aid. The same applies to the Negro newspapers. Scandals have occurred, such as misuse of funds collected by *The Amsterdam News*, an important Harlem paper, for the great march on Washington this spring by over

4,000 Harlem Negroes, protesting against the new legal lynch verdict on Haywood Patterson at Decatur.[1]

The Harlem Liberator[2] is the only honest Negro paper in the States, and there are some four or five hundred.... Controlled by jacks-in-office at the beck and call of American white money and black philanthropic support, this Negro bourgeoisie sits giving praise to each new president and each party that promises that "new deal to the Negro" that never comes (and will never come from Republican, Democrat or Labour), launching out frantic and crassly ignorant attacks on the Communists (see particularly the so-called "Symposium" of a dozen or so Negro editors in one of the spring 1932 numbers of *The Crisis*[3]). They are worse than the black imperialist lackeys in colonial countries, for they are not without money and some power, neither of which is ever applied to the crying needs of the race. There is not one paper (except *The Harlem Liberator*) that can be called a proper "Race" paper. Although they deal almost entirely with Negro doings, these doings are found to be mainly social events and functions. The coloured stage is much spoken of, which is very much to the good, for the white papers scarcely mention any Negro achievement; yet there is hardly a star who is not at some time or other of his or her career literally pulled to pieces by some scandal of press-invention. As to writing sanely about any inter-racial friendships or associations ... one might be reading a Southern white rag.

Confusion (and confusing the minds of its readers) is a strong newspaper characteristic. I say confusion, but it is by design.

---

1 Haywood Patterson was the first of the Scottsboro boys to be tried (see Cunard's essay in this collection), and when the jury returned a guilty verdict, *Amsterdam News* publisher William Davis called for a protest march on Washington and began circulating petitions throughout Harlem. Davis later spoke out against the idea of a march, and proposed instead a delegation. The ILD were extremely critical of Davis' shift in position, and of his presumption to collect funds for the Scottsboro boys' defence. This argument is perhaps the crux of Cunard's reference to a "misuse of funds." The march on Washington took place as scheduled on May 6, 1933; Davis and his delegation had arrived in Washington a day earlier and presented their petitions.

2 *The Harlem Liberator* was the official organ of the League of Struggle for Negro Rights, headed by James W. Ford (Communist Party vice-presidential candidate in 1932).

3 Magazine published by the NAACP (National Association for the Advancement of Coloured People).

Example: on several pages you will read vulgar, ignorant and abusive articles on Negro "reds;" misrepresentations, and every attempt at discredit. (For instance, the *Pittsburgh Courier* printed a baseless and indescribably vicious attack on Ruby Bates, one of the two white State witnesses in the Scottsboro case, because she admitted having lied in the first trial, thus being part responsible for nine innocent black boys being in jail under death-sentence for two and a half years, and because now she was speaking all over the country showing up the Southern lynch-terror and race-hate, on the same platform as Communist organizers.) And on another page will be found an honest account of some event in connection with these same Negro comrades. What is the explanation? The editor has been forced into this last by the remonstrances of militant Negroes who are bitterly aware of the sempiternal treacheries of the black bourgeoisie all along the line, but nowhere as vilely so as in their newspapers. The Negro race in America has no worse enemy than its own press.

If treachery and lying are its main attributes so is snobbery flourishing in certain parts of Harlem. "Strivers Row;" that is what 139th Street has been called. An excellent covering-name for "those Astorperious Ethiopians," as one of their own wits put it. There are near-white cliques, mulatto groups, dark-skinned sets who will not invite each other to their houses; some would not let a white cross their thresholds. The Negro "blue-bloods" of Washington are famous for their social exclusivity, there are some in Harlem too. I don't know if a foreign white would get in there, possibly not. The snobbery around skin-colour is terrifying. The light-skins and browns look down on the black; by some, friendships with *ofays* are not tolerated, from an understandable but totally unsatisfactory reaction to the general national attitude of white to coloured on the social equality basis. A number of the younger writers are race-conscious in the wrong way, they make of this a sort of forced, *self*-conscious thing, give the feeling that they are looking for obstacles. All this, indeed, is Society with a vengeance! A bourgeois ideology with no horizon, no philosophical link with life. And out of all this, need it be said, such writers as Van Vechten and Co. have made a revolting and cheap lithograph, so that Harlem, to a large idle-minded public, has come to mean nothing more whatsoever than a round of hooch[1]-filled night-clubs after a round of "snow"[2]-filled boudoirs. Van Vechten,[3] the spirit of vulgarity, has depicted Harlem as a grimace. He would have written the same way about Montparnasse or Limehouse and Soho.[4] Do places exist, or is life itself as described by Paul Morand[5] (another profiteer in coloured "stock")? Claude McKay[6] has done better. The studies in inter-colour relationships (in *Gingertown*) are honest. But his people, and himself, have also that wrong kind of race-consciousness; they ring themselves in, they are umbrageous. The "Negro Renaissance" (the literary movement of about 1925, now said to be at a halt, and one wonders on whose authority this is said) produced many books and poems filled with this bitter-sweet of Harlem's glitter and heartbreak.

This is not the Harlem one sees. You don't see the Harlem of the romancists; it is romantic in its own right. And it is *hard* and *strong*; its noise, heat, cold, cries and colours are so. And the nostalgia is violent too; the eternal radio seeping through everything day and night, indoors and out, becomes somehow the personification of restlessness, desire, brooding. And then the gorgeous roughness, the gargle of Louis Armstrong's[7] voice breaks

---

1   [Author's note: Drink.]

2   [Author's note: Cocaine.]

3   Carl Van Vechten (1880-1964) was an influential member of the New York literati in the 1920s and 1930s. A writer himself, he served as a kind of mentor to several African-American artists, including Zora Neale Hurston and Langston Hughes, finding them wealthy white patrons and promoting their work. He also wrote a novel about Harlem, *Nigger Heaven* (1928), which infamously depicts life there as seedy and exotic.

4   Located in Paris (Montparnasse) and London (Limehouse and Soho), these are areas associated with nightclubs, drugs and alcohol, and prostitution, as well as alternative bohemian lifeways.

5   Paul Morand (1888-1976) was a French writer who wrote a number of travel books, including *Paris, Tombouctou, documentaire* (1928) about French-speaking West Africa, and *New York* (1930), which offers a depiction of Harlem.

6   Claude McKay (1889-1948) was born in Jamaica but went to the US in 1912 to study at Tuskegee Institute. He quickly abandoned his studies to move to Harlem where he pursued his career as a writer, becoming an influential figure in the Harlem Renaissance with the publication of *Harlem Shadows* in 1922. In 1928 he published his first novel, *Home to Harlem*, which became a best seller. Critics of the novel claimed its success was largely due to its racy depiction of life in Harlem. *Gingertown*, a collection of short stories, was published in 1932.

7   Louis Armstrong (1900-1971) was an influential early jazz musician from New Orleans. He left New Orleans in 1919, moving first to St. Louis and then to Chicago in 1922

through. As everywhere, the real people are in the street. I mean those young men on the corner, and the people all sitting on the steps throughout the breathless, leaden summer. I mean the young men in Pelham Park; the sports groups (and one sees many in their bright sweaters), the strength of a race, its beauty. For in Harlem one can make an appreciation of a race. Walk down 7th Avenue — the different types are uncountable. Every diversity of bone-structure, of head-shape, of skin colour; mixes between Orientals and pure Negroes, Jews and Negroes, Red Indians and Negroes (a particularly beautiful blend, with the high cheek-bones always, and sometimes straight black hair), mulattoes of all shades, yellow, "high yaller" girls, and Havana-coloured girls, and, exquisitely fine, the Spanish and Negro blends; the Negro bone, and the Negro fat too, are a joy to the eye. And though there are more and more light-coloured people, there is great satisfaction in seeing that the white American features are absorbed in the mulatto, and that the mulatto is not, as so often in England, a coloured man with a white man's features and often expression as well. The white American and the Negro are a good mix physically. The pure black people — there are less of these (more than two-thirds of the race now being mixed with white). These are some of the new race that Embree has written of in his *Brown America*;[1] they are as distinct from the African as they are from the nordic.

The major part of Harlem's inhabitants are of course the Negro workers. Since the depression began the proportion of those that are unemployed is very much higher than that even of the white workers. They have been, they are being sacked, and their wretchedly underpaid jobs given to the whites. Unable to pay the rent, not a week goes by without numerous evictions, they are thrown out into the street. Bailiffs come and move out the few belongings they have. And it is here that the Communists have put up a strong and determined defence. Black and white comrades together go where the evictions are taking place and

---

where he joined the Creole Jazz Band and established his success as a cornet player and vocalist in the so-called New Orleans style.
1   Edwin R. Embree (1883-1950) published *Brown America: The Story of a New Race* (New York: Viking, 1931), a history of African-Americans and inter-racial relations.

move the things back. Police and riot squads come with bludgeons and tearbombs, fights and imprisonments, and deaths too, occur. In every form the oppression that the governing class carries out increasingly becomes more brutal as the need of the unemployed makes stronger and stronger demand for food, work and wages.

There is no finer realisation than that of knowing that the black and white proletariat is getting more and more together now on the only real basis that must be established and consolidated for ever: the equal rights of both under the Communist programme. And when this is in practice the full and final abolition of this artificially-bred race-hatred on the part of the whites, bred out of the enslaving of blacks, will be arrived at. In this and in no other way. There is no colour *problem*. The existence of the Negro race is not a problem, it is *a fact*. And in America, as in all other imperialist countries, this use of a wrong word is neither more nor less than a vicious lie on the part of the ruling class in urging the workers of each country into thinking that the Negro, the coloured race, was created by nature as a *menace*. The growing volume of the Communist consciousness among the black workers, and in some of the Negro intellectuals, dates chiefly from five years ago, and has in that time made, and is making, rapid increase. It is something new, *more and more tangible*, as here in England now, in the street as I go by I am immediately aware of a new expression in some of the faces, a look of purpose and responsibility.

One of the first things I was impressed by, the best thing that remains of Harlem, was the magnificent strength and lustiness of the Negro children. As I walked from end to end of it, down the length of 7th Avenue, the schools were just out. The children rushed by in rough leather jackets in the cold wind, some of them playing ball on roller skates, shouting and free. May these gorgeous children in their leathers be the living symbol of the finally liberated Negro people.

Up with an all-Communist Harlem in an all-Communist United States!

"JAMAICA—THE NEGRO ISLAND"

It was in 1494 that Columbus first saw the lofty outline of a new land and set foot on it in the name of Spain. The native fisherman with him said they called it "Xaymaca" in their language, a word signifying "a land of springs." "The well-wooded and well-watered," added Columbus, describing it on his return to the Spanish court as he crumpled up a sheet of paper in comparison of its mountainous, tumbled surface.

As in other countries of the Western Hemisphere the Spaniards were unable to force the natives, the Indians as they called them, to work; this new concept of life, enslaved suddenly to the brutal white interlopers, making the Indians prefer death. White colonists were insufficient; the tropical climate opposed and frustrated their efforts. But the land was obviously rich and full of promise. The importation of the "ebony cargo" began.

In the time of Cromwell[1] the English also discovered the wealth and advantages that would accrue from their possession of the island, and after numerous struggles with the Spaniards became virtually masters of it, although it was not until 1671 that by treaty Spain finally renounced all her claims. In 1656 the Spaniards, retreating before English attack, had liberated many of their Negro slaves. Sedgewicke,[2] the English governor of that time, is eloquent on the absolute need of destroying them all or of coming to terms with them at once if the colony were to continue. More especially in the wild northern parts were these freed slaves unvanquishable. The *Maroons* (named thus from *Cimarron* in Spanish, fierce, wild) were constantly reinforced by runaways from the plantations. They lived in the forests and rocky fastnesses as free as in Africa. The climate was their friend. When raids were sent against them no white man ever came back. The Maroons knew every detail of the impenetrable mountainous region where they had established themselves, from which they came forth to harry, plunder and defeat any invading whites. The whole history

---

1   Oliver Cromwell (1599-1658) was the Puritan who headed the Protectorate during the Puritan Commonwealth from 1642-1658.
2   Robert Sedgewick (?-1656), Governor of Jamaica and long-time colonial servant; also served in New England and against the French in Acadia in 1654.

of Jamaica is bound up with the heroic stand made by them against the colonisers' attempts to bring them into slavery; they have been conquered by treachery alone, by perfidy, and finally by the white man's breaking of his own treaties. In Dutch Guiana, the only place in the world where this is still so, the white man pays a yearly tribute in money to the black and observes his compact made with the *Djukas*,[1] who are the descendants of the fierce escaped slaves of the 16th and 17th centuries. The Djukas in the tropical forests of Guiana were of the same spirit and valour as the Maroons and have fared better than these.

Jamaica was in need of colonists. The mortality amongst English labourers was high, and small increases of souls, such as the sixteen hundred men, women, children and Negro slaves that arrived from the small island of Nevis in 1656, could not suffice. Permission to import Africans was granted by Cromwell. The Jamaican governor thought it useful to point out to Cromwell "that as their masters would have to pay for them they would feel a greater interest in the preservation of their lives than in that of mere labourers, and therefore be more careful only to work them with moderation" (Gardner's *History of Jamaica*[2]). This did not preclude the influx of white bond-servants. The colony now began to prosper. Tobacco, sugar-cane and flocks gladdened the hearts of the white masters; the fertile soil and its exploitation of Negroes and white bond-servants insured an augmentation of toil.

The Spaniards now attempted but failed to recapture the island. One of their slaves, St. Juan de Bolas,[3] whose name lives yet as a hero, and various Spanish and Negro guerrilla bands con-

---

1   The Djukas were escaped slaves who founded a Maroon society in Dutch Guyana. A band led by a slave named Arabi who launched a successful insurrection in 1757, the Djukas were granted independence by the Dutch on the condition that they take no new refugees.

2   Rev. William James Gardner (1825-1874) was a missionary who took charge of the Mission station at Chapelton in Jamaica in 1849. In 1856 he became pastor of the North Street Congregational Church in Kingston. In addition to his promotion of Christianity, Gardner founded the first building society in Jamaica and the "Society for Promotion of Pure Literature." His *History of Jamaica* was first published in 1873.

3   Juan Lubolo, alias Juan de Bolas, led a Maroon band of about 200 during Spanish rule over Jamaica. In 1660 Juan de Bolas negotiated a treaty with the English which guaranteed his group rights to land and freedom.

tinued to harry the north, and when Charles II became king[1] it was thought by many that Jamaica would be returned to Spain; but English domination had been well established; the king had no intention of giving back the island. From the sea buccaneers were bringing in rich prizes; it was seen that the land would flourish. Only, there were the Maroons. No new plantations could be started anywhere near them, it was considered folly. They were in most of the interior of the island and killed any white who tried to settle there. Conciliation was suggested; an offer was made to them of something which they had already in superabundance: land! Twenty acres and freedom was promised to each one who would *surrender*. Needless to say the Maroons refused this empty and treacherous offer.

It was during Modyford's[2] administration that the slave trade became one of the chief issues in Jamaican life. More and more slaves were now needed to tend the newly-planted cocoa groves, the increasing number of sugar-cane plantations. In 1673 there were 9,504 slaves. Cargoes coming from Africa had consisted heretofore mainly of young people, but now were added to these many warriors who had been taken in battle, whose spirit was harder to crush. An uprising of some three to four hundred slaves in 1690 terrified the white masters; they had set fire to the cane fields and killed some of the planters; after the soldiery had defeated them many of the survivors fled to the ever-welcoming Maroons.

The Declaration of Rights in William and Mary's reign[3] had sanctioned slave-trading by private companies, who, of course, vied with each other in hot competition. As sugar cultivation in-

---

1 Charles II was restored to the throne in 1660.
2 Sir Thomas Modyford (1620?-1679), a wealthy Barbadian planter and slave trading agent who became governor of Barbados in 1660 and subsequently governor of Jamaica in 1664. Although Jamaica fared well economically under his rule, he was tried for piracy in 1671 and sent home.
3 The English Bill of Rights (1689), the end to the concept of the divine right of kings, set significant limits on the Royal Family's legal prerogatives and decreed, among other things, that only parliament should have the right to taxation. William of Orange and his wife Mary were required to swear obedience to the laws of parliament at their coronation, and this royal consent to the new laws came to be known as the "glorious revolution." William and Mary governed jointly as king and queen from 1689-1694; thereafter, William ruled alone until 1702.

creased so did the number of Negroes imported. At one time a surfeit of these turned Jamaica into a depot from which slaves were sold out to other islands and to America. Rebellious ones were added to this number and shipped off mainly to Spanish colonies. And by no means at this time were Negroes the only slaves. This is how it operated for the white man. By all sorts of promises young men and boys from England were induced to come for a number of years as indentured labour; others arrived who had been deported for vagrancy, for political offences. Of the first, Esquimelling in his *History of the Buccaneers of America*,[1] 1695, and himself at one time bond-servant to a French master, wrote:

> Having once allured and conveyed them into the islands they were forced to work like horses, the toil they impose upon them being much harder than what they usually enjoin upon the Negroes, their slaves. For these they endeavour in some measure to preserve, as being their perpetual bondmen; but as for their white servants they care not whether they live or die, seeing they are to continue no longer than three years in their service.

If for the white it was an intensity of suffering, for the black it was an eternity of anguish lasting as long as life itself. Sloane, says Gardner, is the only writer who has fully described slave life on the estates. Sir Hans Sloane,[2] founder of the British Museum, published his big work on Jamaica in 1725. Of the punishments inflicted by overseers he says, "For negligence, whipping with

---

1   Alexander Olivier Exquemelin (transformed by the English into Esquimeling) (1645?-1707). Travelled to Tortuga in service of French West India Company in 1666. Left the service after three years to join buccaneers who made a living from piracy. Esquimeling returned to Europe in 1674 and published an account of his exploits in 1678, *De Americaensche Zeerovers*, which was translated into English in 1684 as *The Buccaneers of America*. Cunard is either mistaken about the publication date of this work, or is referring to a later edition.

2   Sir Hans Sloane (1660-1753) was a medical doctor with a passion for natural history. As a physician sought after by fashionable London society, Sloane was able to amass a considerable fortune that greatly facilitated his penchant for collecting a wide range of plants, skins, animal and human skeletons, and ancient artefacts of various kinds. In 1687 the Duke of Albemarle was made Governor of Jamaica and Sloane accompanied

lancewood switches till they be bloody and several of the switches broken." After the whippings "some put on their skins pepper and salt to make them smart; at other times their masters will drop melted wax on their skins." For running away "iron rings of great weight on their ankles, or pot-hooks about their necks ... or a spur in their mouth." Rebellion meant death by burning; half the foot might be cut off for attempting to escape. Branding and mutilating were tempered only by the fear that the Spaniards would refuse to buy the exported slaves marked in such manner indicative of their spirit. In the 1792 *Abstract of the Evidence presented to the British Parliament* by the abolitionists is the case of the pregnant woman who was made to lay her belly in a specially dug hole in the ground so that she might be whipped without danger of killing the child. Another witness speaks of the girl he saw hung by her wrists to a tree over a fire and set swinging so that the master had the added pleasure of cutting her flanks with a switch each time she came within his range....

As on the "Middle Passage," the name given to the agonising voyage from Africa to the New World, death had less terrors than slavery. There were many who killed themselves. Death was a return to their own land. More particularly the natives of Angola thought this. And the African belief that the *duppy*, or spirit, must be cared for until its departure for Africa was carried on in Jamaica. Food and rum were placed on the graves, amid lamentations, for several days.

"From Can to Can"

The routine on the plantations was to start work at daybreak and end only with darkness. "From Can to Can" this was called— "from can see light to can see dark." A blast on a conch shell or a bell woke the slaves. In the busiest seasons they would begin work an hour or two before dawn and sometimes labour on by the

---

him as his personal physician. Although the duke died a year later, Sloane took advantage of his short time in Jamaica to collect widely, returning to England with considerable materials for his collection and for a book, *The Natural History of Jamaica* (1725). On his death, Sloane's collection formed the basis for the British Museum and its Natural History Collection.

moon of the following night. They were worked in three gangs in the fields. The first or strongest lot cleared the land, dug and planted cane holes, cut cane, tended the mill house. The second lot, boys and pregnant women, weeded and did lighter jobs. The children weeded the gardens, collected food for the pigs, carried the smaller bundles and loads, and were always under the direction of an old woman with a switch. Infants were strapped on their mothers' backs as they bowed over the field. (Sloane even went so far as to attribute the flatness of the Negro's nose to this.) At midday one hour was given for eating. Those considered the more intelligent were trained as smiths, carpenters, masons. Parents were anxious for their children to get away from the rough field work where they might receive a slightly better treatment. The house-servants, often mulattoes, were better off. In all cases it was always on plantations from which the master was absent and the slaves under the sole control of the overseer that conditions were the worst. Considered purely as beasts of burden, worked as such and with more cruelty, all and any form of punishment was sanctioned. The slaves could also be seized for the master's debts; this was the outcome of a law made by George II[1] to facilitate the collecting of debts in the colonies. There were more male than female slaves and they lived in a state of polygamy; the women who were the hardest worked had the least children. Slaves that suffered from ulcers or sore legs were quickly put into stocks so that they might not delay healing by moving about. Yaws and smallpox were prevalent. Some of the Negroes, as occurs in certain parts of Africa, would eat earth; whether this was a disease or a cure for one is not quite clear, but they were punished when found so doing, for this practice had sometimes led to the death of large numbers. Gardner adds that "dissatisfaction or the fear of Obeah[2] seems to have induced it in many cases."

---

1   George II (1683-1760), king of Great Britain and Ireland. Ascended the throne in 1727 and reigned until his death.

2   Obeah is a form of Afro-Caribbean shamanism, related to Haitian voudon (voodoo), Cuban santeria and Brazilian candomblé. Practised predominantly in Jamaica and Trinidad, where it often interacts syncretically with other major religions (Christianity, Islam, Hinduism), obeah has historically served as a form of cultural resistance to imperialism.

The habitations were run up round a few posts in the ground, the space between filled in with wattle and mud and thatched above with palm or banana leaves. The floor was of beaten earth. A rough mat and some calabashes were the sole furniture and utensils. They cooked out of doors in a rude shed. And only on Sundays and half of Saturdays could they work for themselves. It was obligatory too, for they must raise all the food they required in the small grounds allotted them some way from the plantations. The only holidays in the year were Christmas and Easter, spent by them mainly in dancing. In speaking of these dances as "licentious" it is clear that Gardner is describing the African rhythms and gestures transplanted along with the traditional drums made anew in Jamaica. One of these drums caused the masters such uneasiness that it was long prohibited—a war drum.

Now given as explanation for the maintained power and independence of the Maroons was the increase, always welcomed by them, of slaves escaped from the plantations of absentee landlords. All the records agree that overseers were more brutal than most masters and many were killed in the slave-risings that added to the number of the Maroons. Mosquito Indians were now imported to hunt them, barracks erected in the mountains. The Journals of Assembly[1] of the early 18th century are filled with plans to capture and subdue for ever this relatively small number of five hundred or so free black men who kept the interior in perpetual alarm. At this time there were eighty thousand Negroes on the island. Of the eight thousand whites only some one thousand are described as "really reliable people," or masters. The greater part of the rest were indentured servants who had no desire to fight those who had escaped from slavery. "The black shot" was next devised against them—Negroes impressed into military service. The Maroon leaders were again promised their freedom if they would pledge themselves and their followers to recapture and deliver up escaped slaves; moreover their settlements were recog-

---

1   Records of the Jamaican Assembly, a body of Jamaican planters who gained control (1661-1689) over matters such as taxation and legislation regulating property and slavery, and who continued to struggle with colonial governors for constitutional power on into the eighteenth century.

nised as such by the whites. But had they not their freedom and as much land as they needed already?

Records of that time speak much of the "fierce and war-like Coromantyns,"[1] who were, however, appreciated for their superior strength. Some slaves were from Madagascar, less valuable because not so strong and "choice about their food." Best the colonists liked those born on the island; they were more tractable. Those with slight admixture of white blood were often employed as domestic servants or assistants to tradesmen. Hardly more than forty years after British conquest Sloane noted the great variety of colouring amongst the Negroes—mulattoes, quadroons and mustees (the last being the offspring of white and quadroon). The number of slaves imported varied from year to year; moreover many were exported to other colonies. An estimate for 1732 gives the figure as thirteen thousand; in 1767 only a quarter of that number. In 1775 the total of Negroes in the colony was two hundred thousand, and 12,737 whites. The colonists now began to protest against the influx, but from England Lord Dartmouth,[2] president of the Board of Trade, Bristol and Liverpool, slave-ports, declared they could not "allow the colonies to check or discourage in any degree a traffic so beneficial to the nation." A conflicting sentiment in that very year, from Kingston, Jamaica's capital, voiced by several slave-holders, declared that the trade was "neither consistent with sound policy, the laws of nature nor morality." That was a Jamaican opinion on the *trade*, lightly veiling to those easily taken in the economic fear of a surplus of the black beasts of burden. When it came to the abolition of slavery itself, to the freeing of all those already in captivity, the Jamaican masters were as frantically opposed as may be imagined.

The reason is clear. Sir John Costello of Kingston[3] was a veritable merchant prince in this traffic. Another planter sent home £50,000 in 1771 from the slaves he had sold. A good sugar estate was valued at some £30,000 to £40,000, rum and slaves counted in. One of the large properties, that of the father of William

---

1   A tribe from the Gold Coast with a reputation for being brave, proud and rebellious.
2   William Legge, second earl of Dartmouth (1731-1801), served as president of the board of trade and foreign plantations from 1765 to 1766.
3   Not specifically identified.

Beckford[1] the writer, comprised twenty-two plantations and a number of slaves varying between thirty-five hundred and four thousand. Apart from the value of each he estimated his yearly profits at about £10 per head on every one of them.

The Coromantyns were from the Gold Coast, composed of the Akim, the Ashantee and the Fanti peoples, and the whites seem to have been divided between the appreciation of their strength and activity and the apprehension of their fierceness, for in every rebellion would be found Coromantyns as leaders. An attempt to stop their importation failed. Other slaves were Eboes from the Bight of Benin, Mandingoes from the north coast of Sierra Leone; some of these latter being Mahommedans could read and write; the Papaws from Whiddah, "remarkable for their docility;" others from the Congo and Angola. In the course of time these tribes mingled and their different characteristics were lost. Always, encouraged to it by the old-established British policy of "divide to rule," the mulattoes considered themselves better than the pure blacks; likewise were they sustained in this by the better treatment they received; they would refer to the Africans as "Guinea birds" and "salt water Nagurs."

If the white masters could break their bodies and spirits they could not obliterate the only things the slaves had been able to bring with them from Africa—their customs, language and love of music. Certain African customs persisted for centuries, would in fact be kept alive by the constant new arrivals from Africa. It was thus that the powers of Obeah (*fetish*) were seen to be most active and widespread soon after the coming of new African slaves. Around Christmas the Negroes would be seen wearing masks, boars' tusks and cows' horns; a sort of carnival would take place at which John Connu,[2] a noted figure on the Guinea Coast,

1 William Beckford (1760-1844) was a Gothic novelist, a bibliophile, a traveller, a collector, and a builder of enormous, fanciful palaces: Fonthill Abbey and Lansdown Tower. His father was twice Lord Mayor of London as well as absentee owner of Jamaican plantations, and left his son a considerable fortune; indeed, Beckford was known as the wealthiest man in England. *The History of the Caliph Vathek* (1786) is Beckford's best-known work.
2 "John Canoe," according to Caribbean lore, is the name of an African tribal chief who demanded the right to celebrate with his people. Junkanoo is a festival of dance, costumes and masks celebrated at Christmas, the only time of year slaves were permitted to be with their families.

whose meaning is now a mystery, would be invoked by the brightly costumed crowds. The great being in the Coromantyn belief—and it was Coromantyn influence which came to dominate the Negroes of other origins—was Accompong, god and maker of humanity. Obboney was the symbol of evil, Ipboa, the sea-god, to Assaici were offered all first-fruits. Fetish, or Obeah, until the priests and missionaries were allowed to Christianise them, was their law, and the Obeah man was supreme.

A few kindly white figures emerge from the hideous record of slavery. William Beckford, who had inherited his father's vast plantations, was much concerned with the lot of his slaves on his visit to the island (for unluckily for them he was one of the absentee landlords), and tells somewhat naively of how when he had given them many small privileges and in general ameliorated their condition that they were always coming to him asking for more, that he could not understand what were their demands....

Through the activities of Jamaica's famous historian in the 18th century, Bryan Edwards,[1] the custom of not separating families who were on the same ship coming from Africa, and who would be sold on arrival, became law. At that time the slaves were allowed none of the white customs, marriage, religion, instruction. The testimony of any number of slaves was not accepted against a white man, though one slave alone could bring about the conviction of any number of blacks. The union of a couple was marked by some ceremony of their own making. As symbol of separation the *cotta*, or pad on which to this day Negroes carry immense loads on their heads, would be cut in two, each one keeping half.

In 1765 the Coromantyns took the fetish oath and met in council for rebellion. As with other revolts this was also put down with excessive brutality. If the Africans drank the blood of their vanquished enemies, as happened to the horror of the whites, this was done in exact following of African ritual which holds that the

---

1 Bryan Edwards (1743-1800) was a West Indian merchant and a member of the colonial assembly. An anti-abolitionist, his chief works were *The History of the British Colonies in the West Indies* (1793) and *Historical Survey of the French Colony in the Island of Sainte Domingo* (1797).

qualities of a dead warrior may thus be added to the valour of his conqueror, and not through any sort of cannibalistic or vague or empty ferocity. But, as in a previous rising when some sixty whites had been killed, the prisoners taken had been burned alive, hung up in iron frames for nine or ten days till they died from starvation. Often the heads of insurgents would be stuck on poles on the Kingston Parade. In that particular rebellion the colony had lost £100,000 in damaged property, and in the costs of its suppression. But instead of bettering the conditions of the slaves and thereby removing the main cause of revolt all laws were tightened up, and the black traitors who had informed against the insurgents were emancipated and pensioned. The history of so many of the risings is bitterly the same. The Negroes could not get together sufficiently, they were too quick to assume they had the victory after a first success, they were betrayed by other slaves who from fear or other causes remained faithful to the masters, and lastly the white man had at times been able to induce the Maroons to take sides against them.

By the middle of the 18th century there were a number of free persons of colour and of pure blacks who had been manumitted. Of these certain favoured ones were sent to England to be educated, generally the illegitimate children of planters. A pure Negro, Francis Williams,[1] protégé of the Duke of Montagu,[2] returned from Cambridge as a man of letters and opened a school in Spanish Town. His patron hoped for a seat in the council for him, where his talents might best be displayed, but the governor opposed this, saying that slaves would refuse to obey any longer if one of their race were thus exalted. Williams owned slaves himself, as might all free persons irrespective of race, and is described as being of the utmost severity with them, and as one more anxious to stand in well with the white ruling class than to take up the burdens of his own people. Other free people were the Maroons, by reason only of their unfailing and never relinquished

---

1   Not specifically identified.

2   John, second Duke of Montagu (1688?-1749) was granted the islands of St. Vincent and St. Lucia in 1722, but failed in his attempt to establish control.

resistance to all attempts at subjugation or useless treaties; they remained aloof and a menace, untouched by the white civilisation of succeeding decades.

Free-born and manumitted had different rights. The free-born were tried as white people, the ex-slaves were still judged as slaves, had neither civil nor political rights. When in 1763 an enquiry into the amount of property left to coloured beneficiaries showed this to be very considerable a law was quickly passed rendering void any amount exceeding £1,200 left by a white to a black or mulatto. Towards the end of the 18th century the missionaries, particularly the Moravian Brethren,[1] were allowed to approach the slaves, it now being judged that they were "advanced enough" to be christianised and in some sort educated. The missionaries found that some of the Mandingoes, being Mahommedan, already prayed in Arabic; the rest had no religion, nor had any time ever been given for it. In some cases it is true that the priests tried to better the slaves' lot but came up against either ferocious opposition or utter heedlessness from the overseers. Later, certain missionaries were even accused of urging slaves to revolt. Until abolition the owners' interests in getting as much work out of their slaves as possible, maintaining that neither religion nor instruction was necessary, proved strong barriers against the proselytising attempts of Christianity. Also when the clergy were given full rein it was a good number of years before the cult and belief of Obeah were set aside. Obeah remained firm in many baptised Negroes, certain characteristics being amalgamated or brought into the Christian faith. In present times there are still Obeah drums in the remoter hills. The Rev. Bedward[2] (dead not long ago) was quite obviously the direct descendant, at least spiritually, of the Obeah man and had an immense following much decried by the orthodox church. The great belief had been that buckra (white man) cannot kill Obeah man. But this too came to fail.

---

1 The Moravian Brethren preached to the slaves during the eighteenth century in St. Thomas, Antigua and Jamaica and converted many to Christianity. They were frequently blamed for slave rebellions and were consequently persecuted for their work.

2 Alexander Bedward was a colourful character known as the Mona prophet; he told followers they could fly if they had faith and he announced the end of the world. In 1895 he was tried for sedition and released on the grounds of insanity.

Anti-Slavery Struggle

The legality of the right to own slaves had first come up in England in William and Mary's reign, when Justice Holt[1] had decided that once a Negro arrived in England he was free, for "one may be a villeyn in England but not a slave." Yet this decision had been discounted entirely. Some forty years later the question was revived and other justices pronounced now for, now against it. The public showed no interest. The ports and London, due to constant new arrivals from Africa, often contained as many slaves as did the lesser West Indian islands. Advertisements such as this were frequent in English papers: "By sale, a chestnut gelding and a well-made, good tempered black boy."

In 1765 Granville Sharp[2] started his campaign against slavery. He had befriended an ill-treated slave called Strong who had escaped but who had been found after two years and reclaimed by his former master and sold to a Jamaican for £30. Granville Sharp took the matter to court. For preventing Strong from being carried onto the ship he was sued by the original owner, but the case was dropped. Other such incidents arose. In 1772 the matter of whether or no slavery was legal in England was settled. The words that record this are, "as soon as any slave sets foot on English ground he becomes free." Motions for abolition were now put forward in Parliament, America sent petitions, the public interest became aroused. One scandalous case of brutality brought out the full horrors of the slave trade. In 1781 the *Zong*[3] had left Africa with a cargo of 440 slaves for Jamaica. Sixty had died on

---

1   Sir John Holt (1642-1710) served as Lord Chief Justice of the King's Bench from 1689 to 1710. He was known for taking a dim view of treason and seditious libel.

2   Granville Sharp (1735-1813) was an abolitionist who engaged in the legal actions which, in 1775, resulted in the formulation of the principle that any slave would automatically be granted freedom upon setting foot on English territory. One of the founders of the Committee for the Abolition of the Slave Trade in 1787, and the author of many pamphlets and treatises.

3   The Zong was a slave ship made infamous when its captain in 1781 threw 132 slaves overboard—having first ascertained that the slaves were covered by insurance—when all on board were threatened by an epidemic. In 1783 Granville Sharp attempted to prosecute those responsible in the Court of Admiralty, but he was unsuccessful. The English artist John Turner later based a painting titled "Slavers Throwing Overboard the Dead and the Dying, Typhoon Coming On" (1840) on the history of the Zong.

the way, many more were so sick they might not recover. The captain argued that the losses incurred by these deaths on board would fall on the owners, but that the underwriters would have to pay if they were cast into the sea. He argued that lack of water and the extremes they were in would be reason enough for putting them out of their misery. Despite sufficient provision of water and the fact that Jamaica had already been sighted (the captain later affirming he had thought it was Hayti), fifty-four of the slaves were thrown overboard at first, then forty-two more, then twenty-six when Jamaica was but three or four miles off. From despair ten others leapt in of their own accord; thus 132 of the slave cargo were drowned. Probably the Jamaicans thought little enough of this, as some five percent of the Negroes usually died between landing and distribution in the island. After a trial to settle the dispute between owners and underwriters, the owners claiming £30 for each dead slave, the verdict was given to the latter. Granville Sharp was for bringing forward a prosecution for murder; he was told this was madness; "the blacks were property."

This event did much to create public indignation and was followed by a book full of revelations on the slave traffic and the treatment of slaves in the colonies by one Ramsay,[1] for some time a resident in the West Indian island of St. Kitts, who had observed his facts at close hand. Clarkson's *Essay on the Slavery of the Human Species*,[2] prior to his *History of the Slave Trade*, appeared; the Society for the Abolition of the Slave Trade was formed in 1787. Pitt,[3] himself expressing no definite opinion for or against, insti-

---

1 James Ramsay (1733-1789) naval surgeon and later Anglican minister in St. Kitts. He published *An Essay on the Treatment and Conversion of African Slaves in the British Sugar Colonies* (London: J. Phillips, 1784).

2 The exact title is *An Essay on the Slavery and Commerce of the Human Species, Particularly the African*. Thomas Clarkson (1760-1846) was one of the leaders, along with William Wilberforce and Granville Sharp, of the English anti-slave trade movement. Clarkson's interest in the cause of abolition began while he was a student at Cambridge in the 1780s, and he dedicated his life to anti-slavery work. He was one of the founding members of the Committee for the Abolition of the Slave Trade, organized in 1787, and his extensive research provided documentary materials for Wilberforce and the other abolitionists in parliament to present to the House of Commons.

3 William Pitt (1759-1806) became prime minister in 1783 at the age of 24. Pitt's Tory government did not support the abolitionist cause, although William Wilberforce was himself a Tory.

tuted a parliamentary enquiry into the traffic. Slight ameliorations, such as less overcrowding of the slave ships, the minute and hesitant moves that were to culminate finally in abolition, were now made.

But the opposition from the colonists and many of those who had Jamaican or other colonial interest was extreme; the slaves represented some £50 apiece; there were 450,000 in the West Indies. Wilberforce,[1] seconded by Fox[2] and Pitt, brought in a bill against further importations, but this was thrown out. William IV, then Duke of Clarence,[3] was a strong upholder of the trade; he had been in Jamaica and his opinion carried much weight. The French revolution and its effect on the Haytian self-liberation of the slaves greatly alarmed colonial slave-owners and at the same time found echo in the feeling of three hundred thousand people in England who refused to buy slave-grown sugar and sent in one year 517 petitions for abolition to Parliament.

The movement was successful in 1808 when the last act of Fox and Grenville's[4] ministry was to obtain the king's consent to the outlawing of the slave trade, no vessels being allowed henceforth to fetch slaves, or to land any in the English colonies.

During the agitation in England a few reforms had been passed in Jamaica. It was forbidden to flog, to mutilate; but as still a Negro's word could not be taken against a white man the flogging and mutilating could, and did, continue.

---

1 William Wilberforce (1759-1833) was a Tory parliamentarian and one of the leaders of the abolition movement. He became interested in social reform when he converted to evangelical Christianity in 1784, and was approached by Lady Middleton who asked him to use his political influence to end the slave trade. He was one of the founders of the Society for the Abolition of the Slave Trade (1787), and in May of 1789 he made his first speech against the slave trade in parliament. As most Tories were opposed to ending the slave trade, Wilberforce relied on Whig support from Charles Fox, Richard Brinsley Sheridan and William Grenville, among others.

2 Charles Fox (1749-1806) entered politics at the age of 19; after 1780 he became a parliamentary reformer. Supported the efforts of the abolition movement to bring about an end to the slave trade through parliament, and made passionate speeches in support of abolition.

3 William IV (1765-1837) succeeded George IV as King of Great Britain and Ireland in 1830.

4 Lord William Grenville formed a Whig government in 1806; Charles Fox acted as foreign secretary. As both were strong opponents of the slave trade, the Abolition of Slave Trade Bill was made law in March of 1807.

The Exiling Of The Maroons

In 1795 came the breaking up of the Maroons as a free and separate people. They had complained that a well-liked white overseer had been taken from them, that two of their number had been flogged amidst the jeering of the slaves, that their lands were worn out and that no notice had been taken of their demand for new ones. Balcarres,[1] then governor, took this as the occasion to pen them up in an unproductive district where they could live only by robbery and plunder. Wild tales were circulated that they intended to follow the example of Hayti, that they were about to rouse all the slaves. But the Maroons were tractable and had formulated their demands clearly. Balcarres however seized six of their leaders he had sent for and who were coming to him and put them in chains. Grandiloquent proclamations were issued and a large number of troops sent for; the Maroons were told they and their people were surrounded, that they must surrender unconditionally under pain of death and were given four days to do so. The older ones were for surrender; the younger protested that from all time they had been a free people by treaty made with the whites. The old chief, Montague, went down to the English with about forty men and the same number of women and children. Their reception was watched by the others from heights over the British camp. As soon as they arrived Balcarres had them put in chains and taken to prison. This decided the rest to resist to the utmost. And now some five thousand soldiers were sent against three hundred Maroons, who defied and harassed them for many months. The forests were even more impenetrable owing to the heavy rains; they roamed the wild lands, leading the soldiers into ambuscades in the desolate cockpits full of chasms and precipices that they alone knew. Chasseurs with bloodhounds trained to hunt fugitives in Cuba were imported; the alarm of the whites increased, for by now the cane fields were dry again and might be burnt wholesale; the French on the island were expelled from fear that they would encourage and aid the Maroons in their revolt to follow the example of the Haytian Negroes; the dread of the

---

1   Alexander Lindsay, fifth earl of Balcarres (1752-1825), was governor of Jamaica from 1794 to 1801.

rousing of all the slaves was increased. Fearing no man, news of the bloodhounds, however, was a consternation to them. Walpole,[1] the English general, had himself encountered their ferocity, they had nearly pulled him from his horse; he was ready to treat with the Maroons. The terms they themselves proposed were to kneel and ask pardon of his majesty, to agree to go to Old Town or such place as should be appointed them with new lands, and to deliver all runaways. In exchange Walpole gave them his oath that they should not be deported. But Balcarres intervening demanded immediate surrender, giving them no time to inform their people of the terms. As the liberated Maroons went back to the hills to convey their message they were fired on by white troops despite the pass which Walpole had given them and which was being held high in a cleft stick. The hostilities therefore started anew. The treachery of the English had once again proved itself, and they were more loath than ever to surrender their liberty. By persuasion, by diplomacy, by more promises but never by fighting were the Maroons finally vanquished, when Walpole at length succeeded in getting them once again into his camp. And now the governor Balcarres reversed Walpole's solemn promise and made it known to them that they would be deported from Jamaica. Walpole protested in vain. Later he went to England and in parliament showed how basely the Maroons had been treated. Yet there is here too an astounding revelation of the truth of this man's seeming partisanry. His concern was that his word had been set at nought by Balcarres, and, said he, he had "suggested that the Maroons should be settled near Spanish Town, or some other large town in the lowlands, where they would have access to spirits, the use of which would decrease their numbers, and destroy the hardy constitution gained in the mountains" (Gardner). This general likewise stated that had it not been for the "treaty" they could never have been conquered, their surrender alone had saved the island.

In this way a whole tribe was deported; known as the Trelawney Maroons they were sent to Nova Scotia in 1796. Balcarres was highly honoured and rewarded for his subjugation of this free

---

1   George Walpole (1758-1827) was a soldier in the British colonial service; as a local major-general he defeated the Jamaican insurgents (1795-96).

people by treachery in a war which had cost a mere £372,000!

By the efforts of Granville Sharp, and along with some slaves whom he had succeeded in getting freed and with some of the black soldiers who had fought in the American War of Independence and who at that time were in Nova Scotia, these unhappy people were not long after sent to the colony for the repatriated black slaves which had been founded in Sierra Leone.

Emancipation

In 1808 at the time of the cessation of the slave trade, there were 323,827 Negroes in Jamaica, bond and free, and over a million had been imported into the island since its colonisation by the English in 1656. In 1822 there was much excitement on account of many proposals to abolish slavery itself. This had already been suspected and opposed by planters and slave-holders. Wilberforce had maintained that emancipation must follow. Fowell Buxton[1] had moved certain resolutions in parliament. They were only gradual "reforms." Nor himself nor Canning[2] would ask for immediate and total abolition. They held that the slaves would not be "prepared" for this, civil rights and privileges should be granted slowly. They proposed that only children born after a certain date to be agreed on should be free, that women should be exempt of corporal punishment. The Jamaican House of Assembly and the entire master class were incensed: what pledges would be given them in compensation of the losses they would incur from the freeing of the slaves? An address was sent to the king stating that it was false that the slaves were ill-treated or discontented with their lot, protesting against this interference in their affairs and going so far as to say that if England would buy their land for the philan-

---

1   Thomas Fowell Buxton (1786-1845) formed the Society for the Mitigation and Gradual Abolition of Slavery in 1823. Elected to parliament in 1818, Fowell Buxton worked for changes in criminal law, for prison reform, an end to the slave trade and, eventually, slavery itself. In 1839 he published *The African Slave Trade and its Remedy*.

2   George Canning (1770-1827), an English statesman made chancellor of the exchequer by George IV in 1827. He endeavoured to reform the corn laws, introduced in 1815 to protect English landholders by limiting corn imports when domestic prices fell below an established price. The corn laws had detrimental effects on the poor and on manufacturing.

thropic experiment it proposed they would then themselves leave the island.

The slaves had heard these rumours of approaching freedom and in 1831 rose again in rebellion as their condition had not been improved. The immediate reply to this was that no date had been set for abolition; the slaves were likewise thought to have decided not to work any longer after January 1, 1832, without their freedom. Excitement in the island was extreme. The insurgents burned and destroyed much property, the whites fled before them. Death and merciless floggings came as retribution. And the planters proclaimed that it was not in the power of the king to make any slaves free. But the English held that the slaves were the king's property and must therefore be under his control. In 1833 further measures were proposed. That a £15,000,000 loan should be offered the planters in compensation; that children born after the Act became law and those then under six years old should be free; that older ones should work for their former masters as apprentices for twelve years in the fields, for seven if employed in the house. The outcome was a gift of £20,000,000 to the West Indian colonies, of which over 6 million went to Jamaica, and on August 1, 1834, emancipation was finally proclaimed. Yet as this was a gradual abolition that immediately concerned the children only, as seen, and a promise of four years to wait for the grown slaves, it was acclaimed without any outburst or demonstration; the black people had yet to wait these four years to become "full free."

Emancipation meant anything but security to the slaves. The masters could turn them off their estates if they considered them in any sense "unruly." This term of course covered all legitimate demands on their part, such as proper wages. No scale of wages whatever had been fixed. A shilling a day seemed to be the general idea; out of this house and ground rent had to be paid. And the small proprietors in particular had threatened to evict the black labourers in the hope of getting them to work for even less. Rent was now charged by the planters on each member of the ex-slaves' family. The extent to which this abuse was practised is seen by this one example on a certain property where the total asked of the black dependants, amounted to £1,300 a year! a sum that the property itself had scarcely ever been known to yield under slavery. Work could be exacted from each member of the family. The ex-slaves were not granted leases, rents could be raised by the proprietors on any pretext. To be really free the black people must go out and buy land on which to build their own villages. And what, in almost every case, were they to buy it with? So came freedom in Jamaica without any equality; economic and labour tyranny merely replaced corporal slavery.

In 1844 the census put the number of whites on the island at 15,776, coloured at 68,529, black at 293,128—a total of 377,433, or 361,657 black and coloured to 15,776 white. What is the comment on these and preceding figures? That the island was, and had been practically since importation of Africans began, increasingly a country of Negro and mulatto people. Black and coloured labour had built it up; but those of the white minority remained the same hard and grasping exploiters they had ever been. In one parish, in St. Thomas in the East, in 1861 we find 282 white and 23,230 black! Four years later in that same parish a rising took place under the leadership of the mulatto Gordon and the Negro Bogle,[1] who told the black people they must fight for their rights. The English, as before, crushed this revolt against over-taxation, underpayment, starvation and denial of political and judicial rights, with excessive cruelty. Of the 608 deaths which occurred it has now been shown by Lord Olivier[2] in his latest book, *The Myth of Governor Eyre*, that twenty-one white and coloured men

---

1   Paul Bogle and George William Gordon were participants in the famous Morant Bay Rebellion put down by Governor Eyre in 1865. Morant Bay occurred during a period of economic and racial tension throughout the Caribbean; what made the Jamaican case different was the reaction of governor Eyre to a relatively minor incident. Bogle was a local property owner and preacher in the Native Baptist church in Morant Bay, and the alleged leader of a riot against the police at a Saturday market. When the police arrived to arrest Bogle, they were overpowered by Bogle's supporters. Tensions escalated when local magistrates notified the governor and requested assistance. Eyre imposed martial law and dispatched troops who marched through the parish, killing all the blacks they encountered. Bogle was tracked down and executed. Gordon was a mulatto member of the Jamaican House of Assembly, a lay Baptist preacher and an active reformer who endeavoured to improve the conditions of Jamaica's poor blacks. A close associate of Bogle's, Gordon was also later arrested and executed as a leader of the rebellion.

2   Baron Sydney Haldane Olivier (1859-1943) wrote several histories of Jamaica and slavery.

and seven rioters were killed in the thirty-hour disturbances. The rest were black men and women put to death subsequently, as reprisals, Gordon, after an illegal trial, himself being hung. There were also some six hundred floggings, to say nothing of the thousand houses that were burnt. This attempt to obtain at least some of their rights was put down to the black peasantry as "the great rebellion." Lord Olivier has shown this to be, as known also at the time, a local revolt which was repressed with utmost brutality by the Negro-hating governor, Eyre.

The increase in population, and in proportion, of black and coloured to white after 1844 is shown in 1871 as: total population, 506,154—13,101 white, 493,053 black and coloured. *A proportion of thirty-eight Negro and mulatto to one white.* From then until now the same increase of black and coloured inhabitants to the extremely small number of whites has continued.

And the Jamaica of today? Evidently and most essentially a land of black people. It is ridiculous and bound to strike any traveller there overpoweringly that this island should be anything but a black man's territory. Africa is peopled by Negroes. So is Jamaica. As clearly and categorically as that. Of Kingston, the capital, I cannot say otherwise than that I found it a very ugly town, contrived by that singular British spirit which is quite desperately without any concept of even the existence of plan, architecture or form. Yes, totally in keeping with the administrative and official atmosphere, which in other words signifies no geographic or human atmosphere of any kind. Spanish Town is different; the Latins made it, and though frequent earthquakes have shaken half of it down the sort of warm yellow sunset colouring on the lovely 18th century buildings gives an idea of what the white man's past must have looked like.

Of the black man's past ... observe his present. Those wattled huts the slaves lived in, doing their cooking in still rougher shanties, or outside ... all this is swept away? Indeed no. In the north, at least in such parts as I saw, the description of the 17th and 18th century writers is exactly appropriate still. I went through the island in the hot July days. There are few inns for the tourist save along the sea-coast. In Mandeville, a large country town inland, there are one or two "white" hotels, and banks. The feeling of the rather tentative "luxuries" you visualise the white man in general, the British in particular, hazarding in lands wrested from the natives. But no white people visible. Not one. It was market day, a sea of black people, a most vivacious crowd. What are they selling? The fruits of the earth; akees, yams, plantains and various delicious exotic half-fruits, half-nuts. Twists of rough tobacco. And those superb "Jamaica cloths" at one shilling, six pence a square yard, which are made at Manchester in England. All the women wear them turbaned about their heads. You begin to wonder what these blue, red and yellow striped squares cost to produce in Manchester, begin to suspect the profit made out of these rough cottons, but of course you will never see one in England; they are reserved for export to the West Indian colonies. They are not just kerchiefs, they have the standing of a dress, one shilling, six pence being a sum to the black worker. I looked for the indigenous goods that black Jamaicans might, in their turn, make a profit on in white markets. Sugar? No, she would not sell me less than that keg for one shilling; you could hardly carry one shilling-worth of the rich brown melting cane sugar that has to be searched for as a delicacy in England. Five or six bananas cost one shilling; we know what we pay for them here. Who gets the profits on that? Never the Jamaican peasant grower! Fruits and plantations are largely in the name of the United Fruit Company. The posters of the United Fruit Company are enthroned throughout Jamaica; they sit on the eminent hills, and facing them on other feathery luxuriant heights are other inventions of white civilisation: tin or brick chapels. These and fine, not much travelled motor roads are the modernities of Jamaica inland. And in the valleys and gorges of Crooked River down comes the daily cloudburst in that season as the old washerwoman slams hurriedly together the dispersed items she has been trying to get clean "in all dese stones." Along the road there would suddenly be an expanse of English park land, not a palm or banana tree in sight. And then the rain made it all go black and dark green, as if one were looking up from under deep water at the low knotted hills of the old Maroon country. It is not possible to describe the rapid changes of this beautiful land; only a film will be able to give any

·sense of it. Black River, banana, plantain and palm fronds fiercely tossing in the rain, deserted roads on completely empty mountains, and then the region where the huts are so frail you wonder if people can live in these. They do. They live life out in them, things a man would run up in a day or two, with the smoke coming out through the old pressed-down palm thatch at one corner. Maroon Town, St. James — it was some trouble to find it, for several of the roads that seemed to go there ended after a time in a flank of forest. There were cows' horns on one or two of the houses in that place, perhaps as Obeah signs still, and the sense of the utter remoteness of a barely inhabited region, whose people though pay homage to Christian Sunday with tightly clasped bibles, very much "dressed up" and with black buttoned shoes. The "progress" lies in the shoes; the wistful longing for shoes you meet with is a class distinction, to possess them constitutes a "rise" in the black labouring class. After Maroon Town there were no more huts even; the forests closed in the steep roads with immense trailing and dripping lianas.

Montego Bay is a sharp contrast. You come down on to a flat sand-stretch. A white man's resort, a bathing beach and accessory hotels, at twenty-five shillings a day. But there were no white men. Again, that night, there was the dense, moving, vivacious black crowd, round a preacher in the open square. The whites have planted Christianity in Jamaica in such a way that it is as much *there* as the native vegetation. In Kingston the raucous crashing of the Salvation Army is as inescapable as it is insufferable. Imagine a landscape of gravel, of glaring white concrete posts, railings and flower-beds round an immense, exotic, though somewhat humanity-scarred tree, with a small arrogant statue of the good Queen in whitest marble like the apex of the Victorian wedding cake — that is the centre of Kingston under a flaming sun. A vast number of tropical plants, and again they would be impossible to portray otherwise than by the film, has been gathered into a special garden nearby. This too is a pineapple farm. For working on it the descendant of the slave told me he got about two shillings a day. And it comes to about the same for the man who carries those full banana bunches onto the boats. A full bunch must have between 150 and 200 bananas. If there are less "we bruise them" (destroy them), said the young black worker who was coming down barefoot from the hills to Banana Day in Frankfield.

The English want this colony to progress, they say. Yet it was years before the banana agent, an ex-Justice and schoolmaster, was able to get permission to have the railway brought some eleven miles from its previous terminus to the banana centre, to transport the bi-weekly consignments. He had applied again and again. One day an official came from England. Asked to see the leading citizen of the place. My friend the banana agent is a pure Negro. The Englishman, said he, seemed very surprised at finding a Negro with education and who could explain the situation with detail and authority — very soon after we were allowed to have our railway. Is the ignorance of the white man really as simple as all that? However, what is lacking in ignorance is fully made up in prejudice.

To one coming direct from a distorted America where all coloured people are, governmentally and socially, labelled "niggers," Jamaica may at first seem without any of this social dementia. The colour question is more "subtly" handled by the English. It has the atmosphere of an orderly place. British Authority respected — an old-fashioned tempo, excessively so. But soon enough you notice there is a positive minimum of really black people "in office." By "in office" I mean the shops, all kinds of trading establishments and all milieus of middle-class independent life. The pure black people are on the land, an agricultural peasantry. Or in menial employ. The maids of the inn at which I stayed are black — and shoeless. The harbour workers, the market sellers are so. But in the newspaper offices, the shipping companies, banks, etc., and nearly all upper or middle class strata they are mulatto. This is indeed the white man's doing. As there are so few whites they have established on the rock foundation of British empire custom the "mulatto superiority" to fill the place of the "white superiority" which, from their very lack of numbers, they cannot operate with the same prestige here. From all times this has been used to divide the peoples of African and semi-African descent. White at the top, mulatto in the centre and black at the bottom of the economic and social scale.

There is one figure that British rule has not been able to keep out of sight in the background of the black peasantry, Marcus Garvey.[1] As Eric Walrond, a well-known West Indian Negro novelist and journalist, who at one time worked on Garvey's paper, wrote:

Garvey is of unmixed Negro blood. On its surface this may not appear significant, but it is indispensable to any consideration of the man. Goaded on by the memory that the first slaves stolen from Africa were full-blooded Negroes, Garvey and the gospel he preaches appeal particularly and not unexpectedly to the very black Negro element. In the island of his birth, Jamaica, a land with as many colour distinctions as there are eggs in a shad's roe, and all through his life, the fact that he was black was unerringly borne in upon him. Wherever he went, whether to Wolmer's, the college patronised by the upper class mulattoes in Jamaica, or to Europe or Central America as a student and journalist, he was continuously reminded that he was black and that it was futile for him to rise above the "hewer of wood and drawer of water."

In Jamaica, as elsewhere in the United Kingdom, England differentiates between the full bloods and the half bloods. In Garvey's Jamaica the mulattoes are next in power to the whites. *The blacks, who outnumber them three to one, have actually no voice politically or economically.* (Italics mine. Ed.[2]) (From *The Independent*, January 3, 1925.)

Garvey founded *The Negro World*, a violently racial weekly. It was, at that time, published in English, French and Spanish, and often suppressed in African colonies because of its message of race-consciousness and race-determination to the black peoples. This paper is still alive in New York, although in the hands of Garvey's

---

1   Marcus Garvey (1887-1940) founded such enterprises as the Black Factories Corporation and the Black Star Line, a steamship line owned and operated by blacks (which collapsed in 1921 due to mismanagement). Garvey died in London.
2   The editor here is Cunard.

enemies, a split from the original association, who, however, still call themselves "Garveyites."

In 1916 New York saw the arrival of Marcus Garvey and the founding of the Universal Negro Improvement Association with a nucleus of thirteen only. The movement rapidly grew and attained immense proportions. The Negroes flocked to hear Garvey speak. "Africa for the Africans" was the slogan; a sort of Zionism. But while making the Negroes conscious of themselves as a racial and separate entity, while attacking and exposing the white nations for their centuries-old pillage and exploitation of Africa and black peoples, his solution of these evils was simply to be the repatriation to Africa of all such American Negroes as desired, and would pay, to go there, and the demand of a Negro Free State in Africa itself. These two projects were to have Garvey himself as leader and figure-head. He constituted around himself a court of nobles, royal surroundings with court titles and offices, ceremonies, uniforms. Himself, once the projected plan had been carried out, was to be "Provisional Emperor of Africa." A fleet was brought into being to transport American and West Indian Negroes; it consisted of some five or six steamers, the "Black Star Line."[1] The contributions of the American coloured people — and the idea had so caught on that between 2 and 3 million dollars poured in — paid for all of this. By which capitalist white power the land for this African Empire would be granted was not revealed. Liberia seemed his choice. But Liberia is virtually an American colony, by reason of the huge loans forced upon it by the U.S., and by the Firestone rubber interests that control the country.[2] Surrounded by charlatans and crooks of all sorts who dilapidated the monies that flowed into this fantastic scheme, his fleet actually unseaworthy and in the hands of adventurers, opposed by American officialdom and even by many American Negroes, the stupendous project, the dream of the black empire,

---

1   There is some irony in the fact that the shipping line founded by Cunard's great-grand-father was known as the White Star Line.

2   Liberia was established on land purchased by the US for the purpose of creating a colony for freed American slaves. It became independent in 1847. Harvey Samuel Firestone (1868-1938), the American industrialist and president of Firestone Rubber Company, established a large (one million acre) rubber plantation in Harbel, Liberia in 1923.

blew up. And Garvey, target by then of many personal as well as public enemies, was eventually brought to trial before the New York courts, and, on a charge of "using the mails to defraud," sentenced to four years in the Atlanta penitentiary. Never had such a racial dream been put forth. While Garvey has done great good in arousing the race consciousness of the Negro his scheme stopped short at the purely racial. It simply ignored the far deeper and only solid basis of any reform—revolution is the correct word—in the condition of the black races of the world, their economic, their class status. A people of between 13 and 14 million, almost one quarter of whom are literally tied to the soil or economically enslaved by industry, cannot and will not transport itself to the unknown. And the Negroes in the U.S. are such a people, and nothing had been said of the conditions in Africa they would be going to.

Garvey's "torrential eloquence," as it has been rightly called, and his theme of the necessary revolt of the black oppressed against the white oppressor, sufficed amply to rouse millions of partisans to his scheme. But Garvey's desire was to accomplish this alone. He failed, he fails now to see that only by the combined and organised struggle of the white as much as the black oppressed classes of the world will the coloured races of the world be, in that same day, free. Free of the diverse yet precisely similar rule of the white capitalist and imperialist powers. His "all-black" policy for the Negro race was to place them on an equal footing with the white races. This, Communists also desire and intend. But it is not by the empty parades of court figures and ceremonies, in short, by the totally impracticable approach to this major issue in world history, that such a vital revolution is accomplished. In this sense Garvey is a demagogue. In the sense of the awakening of race-consciousness in the Negroes of the western hemisphere Garvey stands as a fixed point in Negro history.

At the League of Nations in Geneva in 1928, Garvey exposed his demands of "Africa for the Africans," and repeated this later the same year at a meeting in the Albert Hall.[1] From the printed report of his speech he exposed ably and passionately enough the

---

1   Royal Albert Hall is a concert hall in London that was built between 1867 and 1871 in memory of Prince Albert, consort to Queen Victoria.

monstrous ills and wrongs to which the African populations are subjected, the whole scale of economic and social oppression, the penning up of natives on reserves where the land is of the worst quality, the infamous code of South African Pass Laws,[1] the equally infamous wage contracts, the disfranchisement of black voters. Garvey's wife is also a fine speaker, and one who attended the meeting at which she spoke tells of the visible shame apparent in the audience who heard her describe their arrival in London, the £4 spent in taxis in the hunt for rooms from place to place which refused accommodation "to coloured," the disgrace of the British colour bar which can never be sufficiently denounced.

The two chief points in Garvey's dynamic personality are his energy and his eloquence. He has protested very outspokenly against the maintenance in various forms of slavery of the black races. Yet this conclusion is inevitable: his conception of the breaking down of this slavery is in no way linked up with the struggle to abolish the exploitation of the toiling masses of other races. The one will never be accomplished without the other, and this Garvey does not see. He does not see that the white imperialists will never *give*, but that they must be *forced*, and for this that the actual condition, the system itself, must be revolutionarily changed.

We have noted already the tremendously dominant number of black and coloured over whites in Jamaica, and of pure Negro over coloured. There is hardly any middle class in the island. It is essentially, as are other West Indian islands, a place of black peasantry. One is apt to think of "slavery" as the name for the most frightful condition that can befall mankind. Yet the economic state of the mass of black Jamaicans is not far removed therefrom. One shilling a day for ten hours' work in a rope factory is one example of wages. The fruit packers of the United Fruit Company are almost as badly off. There is no

---

1 The infamous South African pass laws were a form of influx control based on the apartheid principle that Africans were only permitted in urban areas to serve the needs of whites. Dating back to the Natives (Urban Areas) Act of 1923, the pass laws required that all African men (and later women) carry a pass indicating their place of residence, of employment, and any temporary permits to seek employment in a given area.

other work to go to outside of the other equally ill-paid forms of labour in an island which, though ample in proportion to population, cannot employ all its natives as it is. So that large numbers have been emigrating to America to settle, have been going to Cuba for plantation work and have been repatriated therefrom soon after, the conditions in Cuba being even worse. Of natural resources Jamaica has plenty, but insufficient capital to develop these. And it is logical that enterprise and effort will decline when constantly thwarted. Yet the Jamaican Negro peasant is particularly energetic; this comes out most visibly in any chance conversation, for instance, along the roads. In no sense ever an *abruti* by the encompassment of the economic horizon. Jamaicans are as full of curiosity concerning the rest of the world as they are of talk, mother-wit and logic. A most lovable and interesting people. They give you a great sense of the *justice* in them. They are subtle, their minds work at such a slant angle (and how apparent this is in the very shortest exchange of words, and in their famous proverbs) that you have the impression no other people in the least like them exist in the world. Probably this is true. And they are a beautiful race, or rather, blend of black races. The women's hair is done in a wealth of twists and knobs and knots and curls — a perfect series in which no two seem alike in style but all suggest direct parentage to Africa. Their manners are exquisite; a lusty, strong and dignified people, without the least trace of any of the surface "inferiority" or exterior hesitancy that has been beaten and pumped into some of the American Negroes by the bestiality of the American whites.

I am walking along those blue winding macadam roads after rain, when the steam rises through the indescribably lovely trees, through the whole outpouring of these tender and dark green tropics that were so fluid after the dry and tawny Cuba. The black women come out of their houses laughing. "Take us to Eng-land with you" (in a rich sing-song), "we want to go a-way from here" (scanning it, unforgettably). To England, "mother country" of so many plundered black peoples, to the brutality of colour bar and all the talk about the "not wanting the damned niggers?" They know nothing about these things. "Oh we would like to see England so much." These are the loyalest subjects of Great Britain. I pass on wondering *how much longer* the roguery, insolence and domination of the whites must last.

In a street near the harbour in Kingston an old majestic black cripple hobbles over to me, peers into my face. "English missie going away again, we people here are very poor, very *very* poor — don't forget that." That was all he said. Have I not indeed seen it.... And the *busher* (property overseer), the only mulatto I met with in that inland region in ten days: "The poor people are the backbone of this country, and they have a shackle round their necks they cannot shake off." And the black boys in the harbour waters diving for money thrown from gaping passengers on shipboard, swimming miraculously right under the keel from side to side, cheeks bulging with coins, making a bit more maybe than the dockers and ship loaders on such days as passenger steamers do come in....

That is the Jamaica I saw. It culminates into a certainty that comes like a voice out of the soil itself. "This island is the place of black peasantry, it must be unconditionally theirs. It belongs undividedly and by right to the black Jamaican on the land."

THE WHITE MAN'S DUTY

AN ANALYSIS OF THE COLONIAL QUESTION
IN LIGHT OF THE ATLANTIC CHARTER

Preface

AUTUMN 1942—the third anniversary of the declaration of War has come and gone and at this time the thoughts of men and statesmen, particularly in Great Britain and the U.S.A., are focussed not only on the struggle, and on victory over Nazi-Fascism, but on after-the-war reconstruction and a new policy of life for humanity—for the whole of humanity.

Never before in history has so much been said and insisted on for a total remaking of existence in the different countries of the earth. At the cost of this, the Second World War, what transformation of the social and economic world situation is being envisaged? Are the white peoples to be the sole beneficiaries?

British and United States leaders in clear terms tell us: "No. This is to be for *all* peoples, for *all* races." Words pronounced by President Roosevelt[1] contain a hope: "A planet unvexed by wars, untroubled by hunger or fear, and undivided by senseless distinctions of race, colour or theory." Roosevelt has voiced the "Four Freedoms:" "Freedom of Speech, Freedom of Religion, Freedom from Want, Freedom from Fear." They are closely inter-related, inherent in democracy, non-existent in fascism, and an obvious necessity to all mankind. If these be won, and maintained, it is worth while being alive.

There are pledges, such as Cordell Hull's[2] on July 24th, when he broadcast to the world that the American people are fighting that all peoples, without distinction of race, colour or religion, should be free, on condition that these peoples accept to fight to

---

1   Franklin Delano Roosevelt (1882-1945) US president from 1933-1945. Famous for the "New Deal," an economic and social program aimed at countering the effects of the Depression, which greatly expanded the role of the federal government.
2   Cordell Hull (1871-1955) renowned US statesman, longest serving secretary of state and Nobel Prize winner. Known as "father of the United Nations."

safeguard their liberty. *There are also the findings of science to back up these sentiments on the material plane: the earth contains enough resources and man has attained knowledge sufficient to produce enough food and other matters of material welfare to bring every living being into a state of comfort, and even more, in one generation alone.*

For Great Britain this immense new vision of the future is bound up with the question of her Empire and the 500 million subjects in it. Our politicians and prominent leaders in various fields, and of different political opinion, have made public statements: "We have already condemned and rejected the old inequalities between ourselves and the so-called subject races" (Sir Stafford Cripps[1]). "We must make the Colonial peoples feel it is their Empire as well as ours ... we have got to make the Empire a people's Empire" (Captain Gammans,[2] Conservative M.P. for Hornsey). "It is obvious that the pre-war epoch of British Imperialism in the East is over for good and all ... The sooner we make up our minds to the realisation that the destiny of the East is no longer a part of the White Man's Burden the sooner we shall discover the foundations of an enduring peace there" (Professor Laski[3]).

A great case can be made out of the multiplicity of words, speeches, articles, sentiments voiced in Press and Parliament, of this kind—a case for hope.

Yet many of us, white as well as coloured, are in doubt as to whether or no these sentiments and promises will materialise. We do not want to be cynical; but we remember. And to-day (this has to be said) the coloured soldier of the U.S.A. over here in very large numbers, records, that although he may be the same as a white American soldier in democracy when democracy is a battlefield, he is not to be the same in daily relations with the

---

1   Sir Stafford Cripps (1889-1952) British statesman. Cripps was a lawyer who was knighted in 1930, and became the solicitor general in the Labour government (1930-1931). He later became minister of economic affairs and chancellor of the exchequer (1947-1950), positions through which he largely controlled Britain's economy.
2   Captain Leonard David Gammans (1895-?). Conservative member of parliament.
3   Harold Laski (1893-1950) was a professor of political science at University of London who had a large student following. He was a committed socialist and published several books, including *Liberty in the Modern State* (1930). He formed the Left Book Club, published a left-wing weekly called the *Tribune*, and in 1945, became chair of the Labour Party.

people of Great Britain, because some of his chiefs have requested that this not be so. What can he conclude, if he knows the pledges of Mr. Cordell Hull: "without distinction of race, of colour ... "?

Many of us feel that sincerity of purpose motivated the promises and pledges, as did perhaps in no less measure the realisation that such is the only policy which will maintain peace when it is won. Yet we know that between the promises and their realisation there is an immense No Man's Land.

What does it contain? Will the British "master" evolve terms that can be accepted by the coloured "subject?" Will grudging "reforms" be arrived at in some sort of "appeasement of native unrest"? Or will there be real, necessary, sterling one hundred percent democracy?

With the enemy at the gates of India no solution has been reached, and we are told that one of the reasons is that Indians cannot agree among themselves. To this Nehru[1] answers: "The people of England feel that this is their war and that they have a job to do. But this feeling is lacking in India." Is that the truth, or just the view of "an embittered man" as Nehru has sometimes been called by those who prefer anything to looking truth in the face?

Events moved very fast in the beginning and spring of 1942 in the Far East, and in the comments here which followed, British politicians and coloured leaders were of the same mind, for the facts were historically irrefutable. In a debate on Colonial Policy in the House of Lords (May 21st), Lord Listowel[2] asked if we had a policy which would rally the Colonial peoples in their own defence. In Burma, he said, local inhabitants had taken up arms against the British when the Japanese advanced; in Malaya there had been numerous fifth-columnists. Lord Wedgewood,[3] in the same debate, said that natives of the Colonies should be given

---

1 Jawaharlal Nehru (1889-1964) Indian nationalist leader who became the first prime minister of independent India (1947-1964). Between 1921 and 1945 he was imprisoned nine times for actions undertaken in the struggle for independence from Britain.
2 Lord Listowel (1906-1997) was undersecretary of state for India for a time, then secretary of state for India and Burma, then minister of state for the Colonies, and he became governor general of Ghana from 1957-1960.
3 Not specifically identified.

commissions in the army and become officials in the administration.

George Padmore, co-author with me of this pamphlet, pointed out in *The Crisis* (July, New York):

> The Singapore natives, like those on the mainland, had no voice in their own affairs. Surely it is not really surprising that when the crisis came, the Governor, Sir Shenton Thomas,[1] was unable to mobilize the common people— Malayan, Chinese, Indian—to withstand the Japanese onslaught. How could a people, whose existence has been entirely ignored, presumably because they were considered unfit to participate in the government of the country, suddenly resuscitate themselves, as it were, and assume responsibility in defence of the system which had until then failed to recognise their existence?

What do Africa and its descendants feel about the all-in fight against Nazism and fascism? Rudolph Dunbar,[2] the Negro journalist and composer from British Guiana, puts it very clearly: "You will not gain the full confidence and co-operation of coloured men and women by telling them they would be worse off under fascist rule. You will only do that by convincing them that they will be better off in free association with you."

The crux of it all is: In war—to defend what is one's own. In peace—equal rights.

★   ★   ★

The logical feeling exists among coloured peoples: "Now Britain is in trouble she needs us, but when it is all over we shall be as before." This could be removed—but to do so would call for a change of heart, and of policy, toward coloured peoples on the part of many of the authorities and officials *particularly in the Colonies*. In the United States the thirteen million Negroes see

---

1 Sir Shenton Thomas (1879-1962) Governor and Commander-in-Chief of the Straits Settlement and High Commisioner of the Malay States from 1934-1942.

2 Rudolph Dunbar (1907-?), a black journalist and composer from British Guyana. He is author of *Treatise on the Clarinet* (1939), and was a contributor to Cunard's *Negro* anthology.

the call to the Colours translated for their race into a matter of segregated regiments and army service groups. One of their four hundred newspapers, commenting on a proposal made here in London during the worst air-raids to create separate shelters for coloured people, wrote: "If this is all that Britain is fighting for, the status quo, then to ask American Negroes to fight and die for Britain is like asking them to fight and die for Mississippi" (land of lynchings). True, civilians and soldiers of Great Britain are against treating the American coloured soldiers differently to the white, as they are requested to do. Yet is it possible to say that colour prejudice and colour bar are on the decline?

We salute the forceful article by our Minister of Information, Mr. Bracken,[1] "Colour bar Must Go" (*Sunday Express* September 20th), but we firmly believe that an act of parliament making all colour bar manifestations an offence (as was the case, for instance, in France before Hitler) would be an efficacious and sensible basis for its eradication. Race prejudice (of Jew, Negro, or any people) belongs to Nazi-fascism and not to democracy. If the British government intends colour prejudice to end, as Mr. Bracken states it does, it will have gone a long way in initiating "the second freeing" of all coloured peoples in the world, over one hundred years, as this would be, after our abolition of slavery itself. The gratitude of those of colour and of those who understand the effects of race prejudice will be acquired in fullest measure.

What is said in this article of Brendan Bracken is to-day's parallel and continuation of the speeches of the great abolitionists during the twenty-year struggle in Parliament at the end of the 18th century. Let me quote some passages: "The barriers still standing in the way of the social equality of coloured people must be withdrawn." "This is a process which will take time, but responsible people in Britain are determined that it shall be carried through, and the sooner the better." "I should like to emphasise that the theory of equal rights is not a mere high-sounding phrase." "I wish to emphasise here only that we in Britain do not intend to stand fast upon theories of political equality and economic freedom without seeing to it that the victory for which we are striving will be as much theirs as ours."

---

1 Brendan Bracken, (1901-1958), member of parliament.

Colour bar, (*legally* non-existent in Great Britain, as says Mr. Bracken) all too often does exist in hotels, lodging-houses, restaurants, bars, public-houses and the minds of landlords. A new clause added to the legal regulations to which these places conform, punishing colour bar, as, say, disorderliness is punished, would be excellent. This outspoken article deals mainly with colour bar in our own country. It is Lord Samuel[1] who throws a revealing light on the colonial situation. In a letter to *The Times* (August 8th), Lord Samuel says that several recent articles on the Colonial Empire "all stress the need for a forward colonial policy," and quotes from one: "Until an end is put to public indifference there is no hope of a truly dynamic policy for the Empire ... The key is in the hands of the people at home." Lord Samuel then writes: "The fact is that, while Parliament and [the] public are becoming more and more uneasy about the Crown Colonies, they are still hardly alive to their own responsibilities." Further he states that the House of Commons "devotes *one day a year* (emphasis mine) to the colonial estimates ... There are useful discussions from time to time in the House of Lords. *But there is no normal agency, continuously at work* (emphasis mine), *which will link the democratic forces of the nation with the processes of colonial administration*, which will diffuse the spirit of British policy throughout the Colonial Empire."

What are the "democratic forces of the nation"?

Coloured people translate this, and logically enough, into those who understand and who will back up our plea for "equal rights." A year ago when I was in the British West Indies, black workers said to me constantly: "In England the government and the people talk a great deal now about 'democracy for all after the war'. Do they include *us* in this?" But back in England I was unable to find the slightest increase of interest, concern or knowledge of our coloured subjects' lamentable conditions, although there was, and continues to be an immense amount of talk and of writing and of hope about the future instauration of "the better life for all."

Democracy is not a difficult idea, or theory, or concept, or state of being to understand, and the colonized peoples have a very

---

1 Possibly Herbert Louis Samuel, Viscount (1870-1963), author of *The British Colonial System and its Future* (1943).

clear sense of what it means. *It is exactly what they are asking for*: equal opportunities as the white people in all fields of life. Full equal rights are of course freedom, and freedom has been set down last of all in the words of Clause Three of the Atlantic Charter: "The right of all peoples to choose the form of government under which they live." To-day constant efforts are being made in India to end the terrible deadlock there, and the two facts contained in one phrase of Mr. P.N. Sapru's speech in the Council of State at New Delhi (Sept. 22nd), are the heart-cry of the Indian millions: "The failure to include India in the scope of the Atlantic Charter; the totalitarian administration of India …"

★   ★   ★

What is to be concluded from the sentiments and promises I have quoted here as examples of a very great many more of the same progressive kind? Are they to be casually dismissed: "Oh, this is just talk; nothing is meant to come of it!" (frequently the feeling of "the man in the street")—or are we to believe that they spring from a true determination to put an end to all the worst abuses and conditions of to-day? If colonies are a national heartache to those who know them and who know also that coloured peoples are as human as ourselves and deserve the kind of life we ourselves desire, they could become the *real* British "Commonwealth" which, to-day, is a term on paper, and not more, as far as the native population of the colonies is concerned.

With all of this in mind I went to talk to George Padmore, the young leader of colour, who was born in Trinidad, British West Indies. Author of several books and innumerable articles on the Negro, Padmore has travelled much, absorbing political experience in many lands. Our premise was: "We will take the statesmen who have made these promises at their word." And so in several talks we examined the situation in the colonies, and I asked Padmore to give me his analysis and solution of the problem; it will be found in the following pages. My questions and Padmore's answers were taken down in shorthand and only very slightly edited for clarity and sequence later on.

Both Padmore and myself here render thanks to Miss Dorothy

Pizer,[1] who did the recording, for her valuable aid in this and for helpful and interesting criticism. And also to the American journalist, Morris Gilbert,[2] for his encouraging information concerning the importance of the fight waged against race prejudice in U.S. labour and war industries by the Congress of Industrial Organisations, and for his interest and constructive comment throughout.

DECEMBER, 1942.

A little time has passed since these lines were written and mention should be made here of an event which has taken its place since then in the history of colonial matters: the constitutional reform passed by the Netherlands government in London. The Dutch announced at the beginning of December that they would enact this reform immediately instead of only at the end of the war as had been their first intention. A few days later the queen of the Netherlands ratified it. *Holland becomes a Federal State*, and this means that in the Federal Cabinet at The Hague will sit representatives from Holland's far-distant colonies as well as those elected by Dutch citizens in the home country. Along with this, and comprised in it, goes the establishing of *the same status*; which means that a Javanese, for instance, can become a minister. That spells the end of any official stigma against colour. Moreover, the Dutch are a people who have always held the least race or colour prejudice.

"Being determined to repudiate the last particle of 'colonialism' (wrote the *Daily Telegraph* of December 3rd) the Dutch consider that there would be more risks in doing too little than in doing too much. They are anxious to conform with the Atlantic Charter." It is good that an allied government should go on record (and do so at this stage of the war) as interpreting the Atlantic Charter to mean, amongst other things, *racial equality in a constitutional form*. We salute the Dutch government and the

---

1 Dorothy Pizer was George Padmore's common-law wife.
2 Morris Gilbert was an American journalist attached to the US army and stationed in London during World War II. Cunard and Gilbert became lovers, but their relationship did not survive Gilbert's return to the US after the war ended.

queen of the Netherlands for this progressive, sensible and human measure.

At the time of the Royal Proclamation which ratified the new federation, the queen said that the Atlantic Charter represented exactly the Dutch conception of liberty and justice, that Dutch unity had been fortified by sufferings in common and that nothing would be undertaken before all the component parts of the Dutch territories had freely expressed themselves. After the war, said the queen, the Netherlands, along with the Dutch possessions could form four dominions indissolubly united as far as foreign questions were concerned, but that these four governments would be absolutely independent in what affected their interior or home administration. This division of the Netherlands, the Dutch East Indies, Dutch Guiana, and Curaçao into communities of independent character would allow for full equality between races and peoples. Dutch government policy will be based only on the merit of individual citizens and determined by the needs of the different sections of the population-groups.

"A partnership of peoples, each autonomous in internal affairs, linked to each other by an harmonious and voluntary co-operation," was the queen's definition of the effect of this legislation in her broadcast of December 6th, 1942. Let us also record what the governor-general of the Dutch East Indies said on New Year's Eve of 1941: "To get rid of the last vestiges of Colonial society and convert the East Indies into a society with individuality and character of its own."

The Dutch Federation will affect many million human beings. Whereas the Dutch number some nine million in Holland itself, their colonial territories are as follows: Dutch East Indies, 72 million; Dutch Guiana and Curaçao, 300,000. Though Curaçao is only a little island off the coast of Venezuela it is the most important petrol refinery in the world. And it is also one of the very few places in the Caribbean where I have seen black labourers with shoes on their feet, living in perhaps humble but certainly decent conditions — a striking contrast to the scandalous poverty and rags of our own West Indian possessions.

Chapter 1 Freedom for *All* Peoples

Nancy Cunard: Very much has been said and written about the new form of life that must come after victory over Nazi-Fascism, not only for the white peoples of the world but for *all* races. "Poverty must end. There must be work and good living for everyone," is the slogan. Now Padmore, you are not only a specialist in colonial matters, but a member and a leader of the national majority in the British West Indies, that is to say, of the people of colour, descendants of Africans. In your book, *Life and Struggles of Negro Toilers*, you have shown the miserable, the shocking conditions in which exist most of the Negroes of the world. *How Britain Rules Africa*, another book of yours, is a thorough study of the situation in the Dark Continent.[1] But to-day I am going to ask you a question about the future: a straightforward but also a very complex question: What should be done for the peoples of Africa, of the West Indies, of India, and all British colonial possessions, by the new type, the progressive type of administration that the pledges given by our public leaders, if they be carried out, entitle us to expect after peace has been declared?

George Padmore: Well, let us first consider the Atlantic Charter. That is a good basis on which to start.

N: Excellent. The convoy in which I came back to England from the West Indies was the one which crossed Winston Churchill[2] on his way to meet President Roosevelt.[3] No one knew at the time what the meeting was about.

1　Cunard uses the "Dark Continent"— a term coined by Henry Morton Stanley in his account of his search for the British explorer Dr. David Livingstone— interchangeably with Africa throughout the essay, apparently without any sense of irony. More perplexing perhaps, is that Padmore appears to do the same.

2　Sir Winston Churchill (1874-1965) distinguished British politician whose career spanned the first half of the twentieth century. He became prime minister in 1940, replacing Neville Chamberlain, and formed an all-party government to unite in the war effort. He was a key figure among allied leaders during World War II, establishing an important relationship with Franklin Roosevelt and forging a strategic alliance with Joseph Stalin.

3　The Atlantic Charter was a joint declaration by the United States and Britain, issued during World War II, which expressed a number of common principles to be pursued

P: You would suppose, from the way in which it is worded, that clause three of the Charter would have application to all the peoples of the world. It says: "They [the representatives of Great Britain and the United States] *respect the right of all peoples to choose the form of government under which they live*, and they wish to see sovereign rights and self-government restored to those who have been forcibly deprived of them." This, apparently, was the meaning given to it not only by colonial peoples, but even by prominent members of the British government. Now let me tell you the facts: When Mr. Attlee[1] made the announcement in August last about the Atlantic Charter, colonial peoples throughout the world became very excited. At last, they thought, freedom was to come their way. And when a few days afterwards Mr. Attlee spoke at a meeting of the West African Students' Union[2] in London, a member quite innocently asked whether it would in reality apply to the coloured peoples of the Empire. Mr. Churchill's deputy replied that there was not to be found "in the declarations which have been made on behalf of the government in this country on the war any suggestion that the freedom and social security for which we are fighting should be denied to any of the races of mankind. We are fighting this war not just for ourselves, but for all peoples."

Now, this seemed specific enough; too specific apparently for Mr. Churchill. For almost immediately after his return from the Atlantic meeting with President Roosevelt, he pointed out to the House on September 9 that, "At the Atlantic meeting we had in

in their respective national policies after the war. The two statesmen met on board ships in the harbour of St. John's, Newfoundland. The Charter was signed on August 14, 1941; it declared that neither power would seek territorial or other forms of aggrandizement from the war, and it affirmed the right of all peoples to choose their own form of government. The document later became the basis for the formation of the United Nations.

1   Clement Attlee (1883-1967) deputy premier in British government. Became head of Labour Party and succeeded Churchill as prime minister (1945-1951). Was a legal reformer and a socialist.

2   The West African Student's Union or WASU was established in London in 1925. By this time, African and Afro-Caribbean merchants and students from the emerging middle classes, sometimes sponsored by missionary societies, began travelling to Britain. Some of them became important theorists and activists in anti-imperialist movements, establishing newspapers, presses, and social and political organizations, WASU among them.

mind, primarily, the restoration of the sovereignty, self-govern-ment and national life of the states and nations of Europe now under the Nazi yoke ... so that it is quite a separate problem from the progressive evolution of self-governing institutions in the regions and among the peoples which owe allegiance to the British Crown."

So there it was. And all the Africans and Indians and Cingalese and Burmans and West Indians, and all the rest of the colonial peoples whose hopes had been raised by the announcement of the Atlantic Charter and the explicitness of Mr. Attlee's state-ment, were dumbfounded. When they had recovered from the shock they became more bitter than ever. First came U-Saw[1] from Burma to test the British attitude. Point blank he asked for a promise of self-government for Burma after the war, and point blank it was refused. While U-Saw as an individual was not par-ticularly important, he reflected the aspirations of the nationalists of Burma. There is no doubt, as we have been able to judge from subsequent events, that there was, as he said: "a small section of Burmese opinion which believes that to aid Britain win the war means to aid Britain to keep us in subjection ... There is another section which, while it cherishes no love for the Japanese, feels that if it is Burma's destiny to remain a subject nation, then it might prefer to be governed by a nation that is of the same blood and of the same religion."

Next, West African nationalists and intellectuals, watching these events very closely, addressed a cablegram to the Prime Minister through the leading Negro newspaper of Nigeria, *The West African Pilot*. It said: "Must we assume that the deputy premier's (Mr. Attlee) statement to the West African Student's Union, London, that the Atlantic Charter would benefit coloured races as well as the white race, is misleading and unauthorised? Are we fighting for the security of Europe to enjoy the Four Freedoms whilst West Africans continue to live under pre-war status? On behalf of the Protectorate and Colony of Nigeria, we request your clarification of the applicability of the Atlantic Charter regarding Nigeria. This will enable us to appreciate the

---

1 U-Saw was prime minister of Burma prior to and during World War II; he assassinated Aung San and five other Burmese nationalists in 1947.

correct bearings of 21 million Negroes in the sea of international politics."

This direct challenge from so-called "backward Africans" must have come as a shock and a surprise to the powers-that-be, and certainly was a most unlooked-for consequence of the simple question put by the West African student to Mr. Attlee in August 1941. What happened? The fundamentals of the question put by *The West African Pilot* were disregarded. Mr. Churchill replied through the acting chief secretary of the Nigerian government in the form of a letter, pointing out that:

> As explained by the prime minister in the House of Commons on September 9, 1941, President Roosevelt and the prime minister had primarily in mind the restoration of the sovereignty, self-government and national life to the states and nations of Europe now under Nazi rule. The declared policy of His Majesty's government with regard to the people of the British Empire is already entirely in harmony with the high conception of freedom and justice which inspired the Joint Declaration, and the prime minister does not consider that any fresh statement of policy is called for in relation to Nigeria or West African colonies generally.
>
> To suppose, however, that the statement which the prime minister made is incompatible with progressive evolution of self-governing institutions in Nigeria or elsewhere shows an evident misunderstanding of words, and any suggestion that this Empire's fight against Nazi tyranny is a fight for the freedom and security of the European race alone is a suggestion which he feels confident all His Majesty's loyal subjects in Nigeria and elsewhere would unite in condemning.

And that is about all that the Atlantic Charter means to the colonial peoples within the British Empire: That the regime of exploitation and colonial fascism under which they now exist is to continue after the war; that the system of imperialism is to run on indefinitely.

Events in the Far East have taught the British imperialists nothing. Had they enunciated the Atlantic Charter for the colonial peoples of the Empire as well as for the diverse European nations now under Nazi domination, it is probable that the debacle which has occurred would have been averted. There would certainly not have been so much apathy among the native peoples, nor such active support given to the enemy in certain places.

N: I think that most of the British public would agree on that score. And also on the point that this continues to be a war full of contradictions. For instance, recent speeches by leading statesmen of Britain and of the United States have contained statements which people of colour may bear in mind hopefully when the reconstruction of the world begins. Mr. Eden,[1] our foreign secretary, said at Edinburgh on May 9: "If there are unemployment and malnutrition and animal standards of life and poverty that can be remedied and are not remedied, in any part of the world, you will jeopardise peace." Let us underline "*in any part of the world*." Continuing, Mr. Eden declared: "Our purpose in developing our colonial Empire must not be to gain colonial advantage for ourselves, nor to exploit transient material opportunities." How will that fit in with colonial conditions if they remain as they are now, and have been for decades, after victory is won?

Then Mr. Henry A. Wallace,[2] vice-president of the United States of America, said, in the course of an address to the Free World Association:[3]

> Peace must mean a better standard of living for the common man, not merely in the United States and England, but also in India, Russia, China, Latin America ... No nation will have the God-given right to exploit other nations. The older nations will have the privilege of helping the younger nations to get started on the path of industrialisation, but there must be neither military nor economic imperialism.

---

1   Anthony Eden (1897-1977), first earl of Avon. British statesman, champion of peace, internationalism and the League of Nations. Became foreign minister in 1935; resigned in 1938. Became secretary of state for Dominion Affairs in 1939. In 1955 became prime minister.

2   Henry A. Wallace (1888-1965) was agricultural secretary under Roosevelt and Vice-President from 1941-1945. A controversial politician, he advocated extensive social reform and friendship with the USSR.

3   Not specifically identified.

Those who write the peace must think of the whole world. There can be no privileged peoples. Fundamentally there are no backward peoples, lacking in mechanical sense. Russian, Chinese and Indian children all learn to read and write and operate machines as well as your children and my children.

These are very fair words; I mean, they voice intelligent, progressive and scientifically sound sentiments. Has Mr. Wallace looked ahead, I wonder, at the working-out, the putting into practice of these concepts? These, and many other men of state that I could quote, aver in their speeches that ALL the peoples, ALL the races of the world must benefit of the great reconstruction. Now, will the people of colour be taken into account on the same level as those of white blood?

P: While we welcome the expression of these lofty, human and warm sentiments, they are not enough. First of all—do you not find it significant that Mr. Wallace, while talking of Indians, Russians, Chinese and Latin Americans, omits to make any mention of Negroes? These coloured citizens of the United States form a tenth part of the whole population: they now total 13 million people. Why does Mr. Wallace not urge his country to set its own house in order first? A few months ago there was a lynching in Missouri. More recently, a Negro servant was shot dead by a white policeman in Arkansas with no justification. Let Mr. Wallace get the Navy chiefs to allow Negroes into the service in positions other than those of mess-men or menials. Negroes of the United States would certainly be willing to fight for the democracy of which they hear so much if they could enjoy some of its "benefits." When discrimination against them is ended, when they are permitted to work in war industries and factories side by side with, and on the same footing as white Americans, and when all the Jim Crow,[1] that is to say colour bar, customs are done away with, and also the flagrant discrepancies between senti-

---

1   Jim Crow laws, late nineteenth-century statutes passed by the legislatures of the southern US states, were named for an antebellum minstrel show character. These laws created a racist caste system, segregating blacks and whites, and reserving inferior services for blacks.

ment and practice, then there will be more belief in statements such as these.

N: One remembers that President Roosevelt made an executive order banning discrimination in defence employment. That in itself shows how great is the prejudice against employing Negroes despite the tremendous urgency of the war situation. A revealing study by the chief of the Production Board, Robert C. Weaver,[1] who is coloured, in the June number of *The Atlantic Monthly*, gives us some figures. A survey was made in September, 1941, of employment prospects for Negroes in selected armaments industries. Sixty-nine point eight percent of aircraft production did not at that time employ coloured workers and did not envisage employing them; 24.3 percent did not employ any, but expressed willingness to do so in future; and only 5.9 percent had coloured workers. "Significant progress," the article concluded, "has been made since this survey was undertaken."

That the Negro is indispensable, that prejudice is intense, but that it is also recognised as a menace caused the setting up of the Committee on Fair Employment Practice.[2] And here is an interesting fact. Before America came into the war an investigation showed that out of 3,900,000 unemployed twenty percent were coloured, although the coloured form ten percent of the total population. Federal Security Administration in twelve months found work for 97,617 people but of these only 853 were coloured. Negroes used to be barred in the constitutions of twenty-four national unions and the American Federation of

---

1   Robert C. Weaver (1907-?) African-American statesman who held several offices concerned with mobilizing black labour during World War II. He later became the first African-American to hold a cabinet post: in 1966 Lyndon B. Johnson appointed him head of Housing and Urban Development. He published several books over the course of his life, including *Negro Labour: A National Problem* (1946) and *Dilemmas of Urban America* (1965).

2   Committee on Fair Employment Practice (US). Created by Roosevelt in 1941 after lobbying by A. Phillip Randolph (1889-1979), a black trade unionist and civil rights leader, co-founder of *The Messenger*, and president of the Brotherhood of Sleeping Car Porters. In the late 1930s and early 1940s, Randolph organized around the question of black employment in the federal government and in industries with federal government contracts. Roosevelt barred discrimination in the defence industries and federal bureaus, and created the Committee to oversee this legislation.

Labour[1] has always evinced the greatest prejudice against coloured labour.

On the other hand, the C.I.O. (Congress for Industrial Organisation[2]) the other great labour body in the States, has always admitted Negroes to its unions. A Negro, Willard S. Townsend, is president of one of these—the United Transport Service Employees of America—and is a member of the C.I.O.'s National Executive Board. President of the C.I.O., Philip Murray,[3] recently made him a member of the committee set up "to investigate and study the entire problem of equality of opportunity for Negro workers in American industry."

P: Yes, there is more hope in the field of labour now than in the past. Startling developments are occurring, and the C.I.O. is playing a big part in this. For instance, The United Electrical, Radio and Machine Workers of America (a C.I.O. union, one of the largest) cancelled its last national convention which was to have started on Labour Day in Indianapolis because local hotels refused to accommodate the Negro delegates working in basic war industries. This union, which has over four hundred thousand members, protested to the city officials and hotel management as follows: "This union is not only one hundred percent opposed to such discriminatory practices, but is making in the plants and shops of our industry a big contribution to the whole fight against this and other forms of fascism."

Then there has been the Seventh Annual Convention of the United Auto Workers' Union, the largest body of organized workers in America, which endorsed a resolution demanding full democratic rights for the 13 million Negroes in the U.S.A. The

---

1 American Federation of Labour was founded in Columbus, Ohio in 1886 during a period of widespread strike action on the part of workers seeking an eight-hour day. The AFL welcomed groups with different political orientations; it began with fourteen thousand members and by 1900 had one million members. The AFL merged with the CIO (see below) in 1955.

2 The Congress for Industrial Organization is also (like the AFL) an organization of trade unions in the US. The CIO provides members with assistance in a broad spectrum of programs including education, lobbying, research, and civil rights.

3 Philip Murray (1886-1952) was an American labour leader, born in Scotland. He was president of the CIO and of the United Steelworkers of America from 1942-1952.

Convention, held in Chicago, urged Congress to give the Fair Employment Practices Committee enforcing powers. It asked for a probe into Ku Klux Klan activities, the engaging of Negro women workers in war industries, employment of coloured workers in war plants where none so far were engaged, and inauguration of mixed regiments in the army.

N: Obviously the C.I.O. is the Negro's most powerful ally in the United States.

P: To return to the subject of our talks—if I understand you rightly they are to centre round: "What should be done for the coloured and native peoples in Britain's colonies?"

N: Yes.

P: Well, this must be said first and foremost: they are no longer satisfied with just the expressions of goodwill and the suggestions of better things in the by-and-by. I find it rather remarkable that no responsible colonial official has made any statement about the future of colonial subjects. No promises have been made in this war as they were in the last. Perhaps that is only to be expected; the promises were not kept last time; would they be believed now? No, the colonial peoples do not want promises; they want action, and not of a post-dated kind. What they demand is an immediate translation of the ideals, such as those expressed in what you have quoted, to the concrete institutions in their respective countries. There are glaring contradictions in so many of the statements made.

For instance: Mr. Eden talks of ameliorating the conditions of the subject peoples. The foreign secretary, however, envisages a post-war world still in the terms of Empire and imperialism. This constitutes the fundamental conflict with our point of view. We want not only the end of Nazism and of fascism, but also the end of Empire and "democratic" imperialism. The colonial peoples have clearly demonstrated their antagonism and their resentment against the Empire by their attitude in Burma, Malaya, etc. Furthermore, we consider that there can be no solution of the economic and social problems of the world, nor any permanent and lasting peace, while the system of imperialism continues to function — even within the most democratic political structure.

N: This is the very thing I have come to hear you talk about. Could you formulate some of the reforms that you think the different native peoples would themselves choose?

P: What we envisage as an ideal solution of post-war reconstruction is the *application of clause three of the Atlantic Charter to all peoples, regardless of the state of their social development. The organisation of the economies of all colonial territories should be made for the benefit of the peoples there under their own direction and control.* Furthermore, we would like to see the collaboration and co-operation of all the lands which now comprise the British Empire put on a federal basis, evolving towards a socialist commonwealth. Such a federation should have as one of its aims co-operation with the peoples of Europe, of the Americas, and other countries of the world.

N: Give me a concrete example of how this should work in one of the colonial territories.

P: We'll take the West Indies first. There is no fundamental racial or religious antagonism which stands in the way of any immediate advance there. *Politically* the West Indies have reached the stage where reforms could be instituted at once. Democratic institutions, based upon universal adult suffrage, including fully representative institutions and *responsible* administration should be set up. This is the form of administration which should be the basis for local self-government in the different islands. The islands should then be federated to form the United West Indies. The federal administration would assume responsibility for governmental services applicable to all the territories concerned. *Economically* the natural resources of all the various territories should be nationalized so as to provide a basis for carrying out needed social reforms to be evolved by the respective self-governing units. Such a programme can be applied during the course of the war without impeding the war effort. Rather would it serve as a stimulus to the population by giving them something concrete to fight for as the first step towards the realisation of the new order in their territories.

N: Anyone who has been to the West Indies realises at once that the coloured people, who form an overwhelming "national majority" over the whites there, are indeed "Europeanised" or "Westernised Africans" as they have been called. How could it be otherwise after the three centuries of their transplantation from Africa, and because of their constant contact and mingling with the white Antilleans? But what of Africa? Would you institute the same kind of reforms there immediately?

P: With respect to West Africa, a similar approach could be made. The various political institutions should be democratised as speedily as possible. The principle of self-government, territorially as well as municipally and in the villages, should be based on elected councils reflecting the interests of the people in place of so-called indirect rule, which is a form of administration imposed upon the African communities from above. As soon as this foundation has been consolidated, the four units—Sierra Leone, Gambia, the Gold Coast, Nigeria, which now constitute West Africa—should be federated along the lines suggested for the West Indies.

The apparatus of government, both locally and at the centre, should be transferred to Africans, because they can learn the art of government only by practicing it. As it is, while the executive and directive authority in the colonies is in the hands of white men, as heads of government departments, the actual performing of the routine work of administration and the running of daily life are already done by native Africans. This applies to all branches: judiciary, constabulary, civil service, post office and communications, press, transport, education, church, food-distribution, medical service and nursing, health and municipal services, and all the learned professions. In every walk of life Africans constitute the representative elements.

N: As do coloured West Indians in the British Antilles. Now I should like to hear about the opposition to these reforms.

P: I would say, briefly, that it is this: the ruling class in Britain, especially those with colonial interests, is afraid that if the political machinery of government is transferred to the natives, even to the middle-class section of the indigenous population, the way will be open for the more progressive political elements, who are the champions and defenders of the working class, to get control and introduce legislation furthering its economic and social interests. It is this fear which is at the base of the Crown Colony government.

N: I have seen some of that fear myself, a very ugly thing besides causing at times quite ridiculous situations. How does Crown Colony system operate?

P: It reserves to itself the right to a majority in the legislature. This majority preserves the economic and imperial interests of the rulers and can hamstring legislation to which they object. In the words of Lord Moyne:[1] "The supreme authority of the governor must be preserved, and it is essential that he should have the necessary powers of 'certification' and 'veto' ... It is an essential feature of non-self-governing colonies that the Executive Committee is purely advisory to the governor and that matters which come before the governor in council are not settled by vote, and that the governor is not bound to accept the council's advice." Here, then, is the reason for all opposition to reforms, and particularly to any reform leading to *responsible* self-government.

N: What is the feeling in the colonies about the present forms of government?

---

1 Walter Edward Guinness, Lord Moyne (1888-1944) member of the wealthy Guinness family. Served as secretary of state for the colonies and leader of the House of Lords prior to his appointment to Churchill's war cabinet in 1942. While working to broker peaceful arrangements between Palestinians and Israelis during the establishment of the state of Israel, he was assassinated by a Zionist organization for interfering with Jewish immigration.

P: At the present moment there is widespread agitation through-out the Empire, or, to use a Whitehall[1] expression, "the non self-governing sections of the Empire," for constitutional reforms. This should be welcomed, for it indicates political maturity on the part of the subject peoples. You see, *politically* self-government is the necessary pre-requisite for bringing about *social* and *economic* amelioration.

N: That is very interesting. Many people hold that the first reforms should be along economic lines. They lay emphasis on the progressive economic measures symbolized by the new Colonial Welfare Development Scheme put forward by the Colonial Office, which has the support of those concerned with the welfare of colonial peoples.

P: No; we want constitutional, that is, political, reforms first. Because unless we have control of the machinery of government in our own hands we shall never be able to institute the necessary new social and economic measures, and what is more, see that they are carried out. Just so long as the carrying out of such reforms as are promulgated is left in the hands of others there is no guarantee that they will be implemented.

In our next talk I will make some comparisons between the government of Ceylon, which has the most advanced form of colonial government, and that of the other colonies.

Chapter II How Britain Rules

N: I have been thinking since our last meeting that there is one question to be answered most particularly by those of the coloured races themselves, and it is this: Would you say that colour prejudice has decreased in England since the war began?

---

1 Whitehall is the name of a street in the City of Westminster in London that runs between Charing Cross and the Houses of Parliament. It also applies to the collection of shorter streets, squares and government buildings adjoining Whitehall Street. White-hall has been the site of the principal government offices since the establishment of the royal court at Whitehall Palace in the 1530s.

P: No, I would not. I could quote you some instances in which very marked prejudice has been shown against coloured people, Negro and Indian, by people in Great Britain.

N: Even with the fact that such a number of coloured airmen and soldiers can be seen in the King's uniform, to say nothing of the regiments of Indians and of African Negroes fighting in North Africa, whose prowess there, as also in Ethiopia has been repeatedly praised in the newspapers and officially commended in Parliament, and the number of African seamen participating in the war effort and its dangers, and the West Indian and African mechanics and technicians doing valuable work in Britain's war factories?

P: Even so!

N: Where did we leave off last?

P: I was saying that I am in favour of full self-government and complete autonomy for the colonies in their internal administration. This would take the form of fully elected representative councils based upon universal adult suffrage free from any restrictions by way of social or property qualifications. Candidates for membership should likewise not be subject to property qualifications. The veto powers of government should be completely abolished. The elected members of the councils should be not only *representatives of* the people, but also *responsible to* them. This is what I am advocating for all the colonies. But all are not yet themselves asking for this; they have not all reached this stage as yet.

N: What about Ceylon, the most advanced form of colonial government?

P: There the form of government is fully *representative*, but it is not yet *responsible*. Ceylon is now asking for the latter form, and that the veto powers of the governor be abolished. Jamaica which we may call the second type of colony, has been asking for both *representative* and *responsible* government. The Colonial Office is prepared to grant one form only — representative. It says it will give Jamaica what Ceylon has. But Ceylon and also Jamaica, to my mind, should be granted both forms. Looking back — the Donoughmore Commission,[1] which was sent out to Ceylon in 1927, made certain recommendations in connection with the new constitution; these were watered down by the Labour government, that is, by Lord Passfield,[2] when it was promulgated in 1929.

N: And how does West Africa, which is the most advanced section of the British colonies in the Dark Continent, compare with Ceylon and Jamaica?

P: What West Africa is asking for is not even representative government. All that is asked for is universal adult suffrage, a majority of elected members to the councils; the introduction of municipal government, and the abolition of indirect rule. Let me quote a recent discussion in the House of Commons in which Mr. Reginald Sorensen[3] embodied the demands and aspirations of West Africa. Mr. Sorensen asked:

> Whether the under-secretary of state for the colonies will, in view of the relevant clauses in the Atlantic Charter, announce plans for the more rapid democratisation of West

---

1 The Donoughmore Commission was sent to Ceylon in 1927 by the British government to examine the Ceylonese constitution and to make recommendations for its revision. The commission's recommendations were reluctantly accepted by the Ceylonese political leaders, and served as the basis for a new constitution in 1931.

2 Sidney James Webb, 1st Baron Passfield (1859-1947), a prominent British economist, historian, and socialist. Webb was a civil servant from 1878-1891, and became a member of the Fabian Society in 1885. Together with his wife, Beatrice Potter, Webb helped establish the London School of Economics in 1895, and in the early part of the twentieth century, they played a key role in the formation of the Labour Party. Sidney Webb was elected to parliament in 1922 and in 1929, he was elevated to the peerage, representing the Labour Party in the House of Lords. Webb also served as secretary of state for the colonies from 1929-1931.

3 Reginald Sorensen (1891-1971), a British MP who chaired a special South African Committee to publicize concerns about apartheid developments in South Africa. A socialist, Sorensen was an associate of the radical black intelligentsia living in Britain in the 1930s and 1940s, including figures like George Padmore and C.L.R. James.

African institutions including the native authorities; whether he will frame proposals to establish adult franchise, to eliminate official majorities on legislative councils, to appoint at least six Africans to the governor's executive council in each colony and ensure that a majority on municipal councils should be Africans; and whether African democratic organisations and personalities will be consulted to this end?

This is the answer that Mr. Harold Macmillan,[1] undersecretary for the colonies, gave him: "It continues to be the policy to introduce representative institutions in West Africa as the local populations become ready for them. But His Majesty's government could not lend themselves to the pretence of framing proposals for establishing adult franchise in communities where that system can have no reality." There were already nominated African members representing local communities on the legislative councils "well qualified to advise the governors on constitutional questions." Mr. Sorensen then said: "Does the right Hon. Gentleman appreciate that his reply will not give satisfaction to West Africans?" The proposals which had been put forward for West Africa had the support of representative Africans, and was it not necessary that the government "make some great endeavour to impress West Africans with our determination to assist their political progress?" But Mr. Macmillan replied that it was "very difficult to deal with the matter by question and answer," and "it requires much more general discussion of the large number of important problems which arise from the question."

This is the kind of thing that goes on in the supreme forum of the British Empire! West Africans are denied adult suffrage because it is felt that this would have *no reality* in their communities! However, Lord Moyne, whom I have already quoted, is less ambiguous: "The supreme authority of the governor must be preserved, and it is essential that he should have the necessary powers of 'certificate' and 'veto'" — these are his words.

---

1 Harold Macmillan, Earl of Stockton (1894-1986), British prime minister from 1957-1963. In 1924 he was elected to the House of Commons as a Conservative; he served until 1929 and again from 1931-1963. During the second world war, he was active in Churchill's cabinet, serving as undersecretary of state for the colonies in 1942, among other roles.

N: What is the difference between the governments of Ceylon and of Jamaica—the two most advanced colonial methods of administration?

P: The legislature of Ceylon is called the state council and is composed of five members. Forty-three are elected by universal adult suffrage and the other ten are nominated by the governor and are either government officials or representatives of vested interests. Jamaica has at present a council of fourteen elected members and fourteen nominated by the governor; some are officials, some unofficial, or business men. The proposed reforms would increase the fourteen elected members to twenty-eight; the nominated ones would be reduced from fourteen to ten.

Other colonies such as Trinidad, Gold Coast, Nigeria, etc., have constitutions composed of three types of members: (1) councils composed of official members nominated by the governor as heads of various government departments, known as "nominated official members" (2) nominated unofficial members (3) elected members.

N: What sort of people are they generally?

P: Club associates of the governor. You see, the governor comprises in his person a kind of trinity. As representative of the king, he is viceroy; as head of the legislature, he is prime minister; when he sits in the legislature, he is the Speaker. He is, as it were, omnipotent, and his right to nominate members is unquestioned. So in the legislature you will find the Planters' Association, the Bankers' Association, the Merchants' Association, and the Shipping Association. If, within the territory, there is a minority of any importance, its representatives are also there. Now, in the council the members sit round a horseshoe-shaped table. The official members face the governor; on his right sit the unofficial members, and on his left are the elected members, mandated on a restricted franchise.

In Africa a certain number of native chiefs sits among the Europeanised African members. However, of the four West African Colonies, Gambia has no elected members. In the East

African colonies there are neither elected or nominated Africans in the legislatures. The governor usually nominates some missionary or retired official to represent the Africans. In Malaya, until the British were "run out," as General Stillwell[1] put it, the British ruled through native sultans. This was a form of indirect rule, a form widespread in Africa in territories known as "protected areas." In Singapore there was a legislative council of eleven members nominated by the governor, both official and unofficial. There were only two elected members and they were Europeans representing the European chambers of commerce of Singapore and Penang; that is, the interests of the rubber planters and business men. Among the nominated members may have been a Chinese member, to represent the rather large Chinese population.

N: Now, after hearing about Crown Colony I should like you to tell me about "indirect rule." How does it function?

P: Indirect rule is the mode of government carried out through local chiefs under the supervision of British officials. Its origin is most interesting, particularly as its apologists are silent as to how it was built up from beginnings forced upon its innovator, Lord Lugard,[2] from sheer expediency. They hold it up as an example of British genius in not disturbing native institutions while guiding them towards responsible self-government. This view is sheer nonsense, as the facts will demonstrate.

In 1900 the Royal Niger Company, an organisation of merchant adventurers, relinquished the charter it had been granted in 1885. The Foreign Office took over and sent Colonel Lugard to develop British power in the hinterland as a means of stopping French and German encroachments on the northern parts of Nigeria. With a native army recruited from the Hausa people,

---

1 General Joseph Stillwell was Commanding General of the US Armed Forces in Burma and China during the second world war.

2 Frederick John Dealtry Lugard (1858-1945) British colonial administrator. Became governor of Nigeria in 1912-1919, where he developed the doctrine of indirect rule which allowed the British to exercise control of the subject population through traditional native institutions. Great Britain subsequently adopted this practise in many of its African colonies.

Lugard marched northward and completed the conquest of the Mohammedan sultanates of Kano and Sokoto. This was at the beginning of the century, when the home government was busy with the Boer War and in no position to send him reinforcements to quell hostile tribes and guerrilla bands. Faced with the immediate problem of establishing some form of administration to maintain "law and order" Lugard was obliged to improvise. It had been the British custom to banish chiefs once they had surrendered, but Lugard was forced to make use of them. He invested them with administrative powers, promised to respect their religion and customs, but made it clear that they were responsible to their British over-lords — who, in the words of Margery Perham[1] (lecturer at Oxford on colonial administration) were now "over all."

So, in making a virtue of necessity, Lugard introduced "indirect rule," which, with many amendments, has become the favoured means of British rule in colonial territories. In practice, a diffuse native bureaucracy has been superimposed upon the old feudal and tribal systems. The chiefs are no longer subject to the democratic control of their people, but derive their powers direct from the government by whom they are controlled and supervised.

Indirect rule was soon discovered by British officials in Nigeria to be a cheap method of governing wide stretches inhabited by primitive peoples. The experience and views of the earlier political officers were collected and later rationalized into a new philosophy of colonial government. The present complex machinery of administration has been elaborated out of the first crude makeshift. Native administration has political powers of a most limited kind, but powers of function which make it the cats paw of the imperialist rulers, and the scapegoat for all forms of misrule and despotism. To "maintain law and order," administer "justice," collect taxes, and supply forced labour, are its principal functions. The native administration is presided over by a paramount chief, who is assisted by a council of sub-chiefs and headmen whose

---

1 Margery Perham (1895-1982) was a historian who travelled extensively in Africa and who became one of Britain's best known commentators on colonial policy, particularly on political and administrative problems in Africa. Perham regarded Lugard as something of a mentor and later as a friend. See Appendix A.

composition is subject to the approval of the central government. Connecting links between African administration and central government are the British officials, the residents, provincial and district commissioners. Directed by the advice of these men, the chief is in a position to exercise the greatest despotism.

N: Would it be correct to think that, of the two, Crown Colony and indirect rule, the former system contains more scope for democracy?

P: I am opposed to both systems, for they are simply methods of achieving the same end: the maintenance of imperialist domination. However, apologists for imperialism make out that indirect rule is a conscious policy instituted to induct backward peoples in the art of self-government. But, as already explained, under this system the chiefs are merely pawns in the hands of the colonial administration. All intelligent and progressive elements are opposed to it. Margery Perham, its official apologist, who is always extolling it as democracy's gift to backward Africans, has been obliged to record the criticism levelled against it. "Most educated Africans," she writes in *Africans and British Rule*, "especially in West Africa and the Sudan, criticize and strongly condemn indirect rule. They say that it gives power to uneducated chiefs and elders instead of to the educated; that it strengthens tribal feeling and so continues the disunity of the country. It is, they say, part of the old policy of "divide and rule" by which an imperial power keeps its subjects weak and prevents their advance towards self-government." That is very succinctly put and exactly describes the growing attitude towards this form of imperial misrule.

N: Then, obviously, a change of governmental form is necessary?

P: Most certainly. But apart from the necessity of having a council and responsible government in order to institute plans for the amelioration of the conditions of the peoples generally, *constitutional* control of the apparatus of government would enable us to revoke and rescind all obnoxious legislation of a semi-fascist kind, such as: colour bar, pass laws, forced labour regulations, child labour, direct taxation in the form of hut and poll levies, etc. All of these have come into being as legal forms following legislation. Quite lately there has been introduced into Kenya the regulation making forced labour compulsory for all males from sixteen to sixty-five. This has been provided by enactment of the governor-in-council in order to afford a plentiful supply of the cheapest kind of labour for the planters of the colony.

N: There are colonies, protectorates, and mandated territories. What is the difference between colony and protectorate?

P: The names are arbitrary divisions only.

N: And what about mandates?

P: They are the same as colonies; they have governors and councils. The only difference is that when the governor writes his annual report for the Colonial Office, he makes an extra copy which is sent to a committee sitting in Geneva. That is all it amounts to in the way of difference. For instance, for government purposes the Cameroons is incorporated in Nigeria and subject to exactly the same legislation.

N: Are governors subject to revision from London?

P: In theory, the governor and his council can legislate for the territory under his jurisdiction. Legally-enacted legislation may be rejected by the secretary of state for the colonies in London, who has over-riding powers to throw out any Bill which the colonial legislature may pass.

N: Have all measures to be submitted to Whitehall?

P: No. Only when opposition in the colony is reflected through the council and they appeal to the colonial secretary, who is called in to arbitrate the issue. Let us presume that a quarrel has arisen between some of the council and the governor. The secretary of state may then say: "Your Excellency, I think this measure should not be passed." But normally, when the governor intends to introduce a new law, it is usually discussed in the executive (not the legislative) council; all Bills must be proposed by the governor. The executive council is the governor's cabinet, as it were, but is advisory only and he need not accept its advice. When the Bill has been agreed upon in the executive the governor has the text of it drawn up by the attorney-general, who then reads it in the legislative council; there may be three meetings to discuss it there, but members have no power to throw it out. If they feel strongly against it they may send representations to the Colonial Office. Although it has been passed into law the governor will not operate it as yet, and so what you might call "a constitutional crisis" arises.

N: How are representations made to the Colonial Office?

P: They cannot be sent direct; and although the conflict is with the governor they have to be sent through the governor. It is a good thing to forward a copy to an English M.P. at the same time. The governor adds his own marginal notes, and the secretary of state, on receiving the grievance, takes the advice of the under-secretary of the department concerned (a permanent official qualified as an expert), and a reply is drafted. This comes to the governor, who reports it back to the legislative council. That is the way it works. Like appealing from Caesar to Caesar.

So once more you see that if the legislature were in the hands of the people's representatives and controlled by them such legislation would not come up. The fundamental question is, therefore, control of legislation.

N: One of the arguments against this is that in many colonies "the natives are not yet ripe for it."

P: It is quite true that in the Colonial Empire as a whole there are sections which are much more advanced than others. The West Indies have reached a higher degree of civilisation because of their longer contact with Western culture and its assimilation. The people there, as a whole, are Christians, their mother tongue today is English; ways and customs, virtues and vices of Europe have become their own. These people are Westernised Africans.

On the African continent the process of assimilation has not reached the same stage. However, in certain parts, especially in Sierra Leone, and in the Gold Coast, Nigeria, Gambia, there are Europeanised African communities. What applies in general to the West Indies is also applicable to Ceylon, Mauritius, British Guiana, British Honduras, the Bahamas. In all of these exists an intellectual élite, the native bourgeoisie, which is the class constituting the vanguard of the progressive political movements. It is nonsense to say that such people are incapable of managing the affairs of their respective countries. For they and their sons have studied at American and European universities and, represent, in the main, several generations of culture and political consciousness.

In the less advanced areas, such as the hinterland territories of Africa, generally known as protectorates, in the Fiji Islands, Malaya, and other parts where tribal or semi feudal social institutions still persist, thanks to imperialism, which does everything to foster and maintain them, there are not such large Europeanised communities. However, despite all the obstacles and difficulties put in their way, the inexorable laws of human progress are taking shape, and from the younger elements emerges a class of natives which is dissatisfied with the status quo and which is demanding access to wider and fuller social conditions. The advent of these could be hastened by democratising the political institutions which exist there — a policy which British imperialism shows no desire to follow, war or no war.

N: The policy of keeping people backward, and without education at all, is a conscious one. For the last 150 years imperialism has been governing these colonies, and in India there are still eighty percent who are illiterate. By the way — do you remember a remarkable book, *How About Europe*? It is by Norman Douglas[1]

---

1 Norman Douglas (1818-1952) British travel writer and man of letters who was also a close friend of Cunard. After his death Cunard published a memoir titled *Grand Man: Memories of Norman Douglas, with Extracts from his Letters* (London: Secker and Warburg, 1954).

and in it many startling facts about Europe and India are contrasted. Of India he says: "There are about 229,000,000 people who can neither read nor write. The peasants living in 750,000 villages belong to this class." A little further he adds:

> Critics of Hindu illiteracy should not forget that British rule is largely responsible for it. By the Institutes of Manu,[1] the parent was obliged to place his child at school in his fourth year. At the beginning of last century there were schools in every Indian village; in sweeping away the village system we have simultaneously swept away the schools. John Bright complained, in 1853, that while our Government had almost wholly overthrown the universally existing native education, it had done nothing to supply the deficiency. Ten years ago only one penny per head was spent on education in British-ruled India whereas Russia was spending between seven pence and eight pence.

He then quotes G. T. Garratt's *An Indian Commentary*.[2] "One cannot fail to deplore the rapid decadence, probably more rapid than the official figures show of independent educational institutions."

This book was published first in 1928, so the "ten years ago" was 1918—yet even then Russia in her first year of liberation from the Tsarist regime and in the midst of the struggle was spending seven and eight times as much on education as British-ruled India!!! Imperialism is nothing if not well thought-out! Incidentally, as we are on the subject of India—I have just re-read two admirable books: Leonard Woolf's *The Village in the Jungle*,[3] about Ceylon, published in 1913, and

---

1 Institutes of Manu or Laws of Manu, the English designation for *Manava Dharma-sastra*, a Sanskrit compendium of ancient sacred laws and customs, written in verse. Manu, a mythical survivor of the flood and father of the human race, is held to be the author of these sacred laws.

2 Geoffrey Theodore Garratt (1888-1942) is the author of several books on India and British Colonial rule. *An Indian Commentary* was published by Jonathan Cape in 1928.

3 Leonard Woolf (1880-1969), historian, political essayist, critic, husband of Virginia Woolf and co-founder with her of the Hogarth Press; Woolf spent a number of years as a civil servant in Ceylon (now Sri Lanka) before marrying Virginia Stephens; *The Village in the Jungle* (1913) was a work of fiction based on the time he spent there.

E. M. Forster's *A Passage to India*,[1] which appeared in 1924, both of which have gone into innumerable editions. When you have read these you feel you have learned a good deal, that is, you have a start on the whole Indian question. I have never been to India, but knowing the West Indian colonies and something of the poor Indians of Trinidad I can see it all well. Both these authors were in the administration for years, so they know what they are writing about, and as each is very honest besides being a fine artist the reader is confronted with a whole new world of truth. One puts down Woolf's beautiful tragic book with a feeling not short of abysmal despair — that is, if things are to go on like this for ever. And Forster's remarkable ironic tragedy one ends with a sense of the utter futility, sadness, and ridicule, too, of race relations as here depicted. I mean, once more, if none of this is ever to change.

I should like to know just how the difficulties the Russians encountered at first in the adjustment of their great new social system among their so-numerous race groups compare with the monumental scale of the racial complexities of India. Or are these not really so inherently great, but built up by us? I would bet on the latter. And I am sure the Russians would tackle all this very well. Don't imagine for a moment that I think the British *incapable* of that. Oh, no. I have a great belief in the British. But *which* British? Let me tell you. The kind I have in mind are like the young engineer I know, and his fiancée, who is a schoolmistress; both are about twenty-four years old, studious, thoughtful, constructive, specialized in their own vocations, hating all race complexes, full of initiative — and also full of fun. We cannot do much that is good without putting a bit of love into things (as the French say), and a bit of humour. You will notice that these are qualities one may call those of "human values." There are many people like these, mainly but not only young people, in Great Britain, the dominions and the colonies — everywhere. They don't get much of a hearing as yet. But what is "after the war" for if not for people like this? People like this are very concerned

---

1 E. M. Forster (1879–1970) English novelist, associate of the Bloomsbury group. *A Passage to India* (1924), which remains his best-known work, depicts some of the tensions in colonial relations among the British, Hindus and Muslims in the early days of Indian nationalism.

indeed about our colonies; they want, and intend, to know them, to go and study there, some of them to work there for the welfare of the different regions as a whole. All of them say that we must have a wide exchange of Colonials, coloured and white, coming over here to us, just as we, technicians of different kinds, should go over to them. I will write a series of articles about this one day soon! However, this is a digression. So back to imperialism, and backwardness!

P: There you are—backwardness is an economic question. The conscious policy of imperialism is to keep colonial economies backward and colonial peoples ignorant. As long as such countries remain mere agrarian appendages to the "mother country," that is, sources of raw materials and also markets for manufactured commodities, there is no need to educate the people. Imperialism cultivates a small section of native intellectuals to man the lower offices and functions of the civil service and of commerce. If the countries were industrialised it would be essential to increase education, since it is impossible to carry on industry with uneducated workers. And here one can pay a tribute to the missionaries—despite the fact that they were largely instrumental in bringing the territories under white domination. Were it not for the missionaries the percentage of illiteracy would be even greater, for they were the pioneers of such organized education as does exist. Only within very recent years have colonial governments granted subsidies for missionary education work, and only here and there have they provided elementary and secondary education. Much can be read about this in Norman Leys'[1] book, *The Colour Bar in East Africa*.

This takes me back to my original premise. Unless the natives have control of their government, that is, of their finances, this educational problem can never be solved. Those who now control parliament know this problem, but it is against their interests to solve it. Now, consider this: Hitler went into territories where the people had a high civilisation, a high degree of literary cul-

---

1 Norman Leys published a number of books on Kenya in addition to this study of race-relations under imperialism in East Africa. *The Colour Bar in East Africa* was published by the Hogarth Press in 1941.

ture, with schools, universities and academies. What are the Nazis doing there? "De-literatising" them. They are closing the cultural and educational institutions, because an imperialist power can only rule an ignorant, oppressed people. Wherever an "advanced" people is found, for the purposes of imperialism it must be "de-enlightened."

When Britain went into Africa and India she found illiterate peoples with no organized education and she decided to keep them as they were. This is the only way to maintain imperialism, as must be clear. It does not necessarily flow out of evil intentions; for imperialism can be run only according to certain fundamental laws. At certain stages it can be more cruel, ruthless and brutal than at others. After the régime is set up and stabilized certain relaxations can be made. I am sure that British rule in Ceylon is more humane and more enlightened than it was a hundred years ago because it is more secure. As rule becomes more secure it is not afraid of internal enemies. But when insecure—that is when a Hitler or a Mussolini comes upon the scene.

N: There is also economic backwardness. In what proportion, I wonder, is this due to lack of initiative of the people themselves?

P: Well, let us take as an example the Gold Coast, which produces cocoa, or Nigeria, which produces palm oil. These are two raw materials which, given certain ingredients, would allow the natives to manufacture margarine, oils, soaps, etc. This would provide a new industry and thereby relieve the congested rural areas, improve the economic conditions of the industrial workers, and incidentally, their cultural condition. An internal market would come into being thus for manufactured commodities. But what prevents all this? Let us see—Is it money you want? Form a co-operative, say 50,000 members, each paying £1 in the course of one year. That is £50,000. Machinery is then bought in England or America; the factory will be set up. But in order to do this permission must first be obtained from the governor. How are you going to get permission from a legislature which is composed of vested interests? Not that a direct refusal will be given. Oh, no; that would make things much too obvious. But the conditions imposed would be found most difficult to comply with—as simple as that.

Or let us suppose that the council gives its consent, that conditions are not too onerous and that the factory is established. Soap is going to be made, and will be sold at a price that suits the people's pocket. What happens? The soap monopoly way back in London finds that its sales are falling off. The Nigerians are buying their own local product, which is cheaper. What does the soap monopoly then do? How much money, it asks, have Nigerian manufacturers put into their business, £50,000? Over go large consignments of soap which are distributed free to the people. And the local factory, unable to sell its supplies, unable to draw in more capital is obliged to close down.

N: A Cingalese gave me a beautiful example of this. There was a local cigarette in Ceylon selling at three a penny. "Elephants" they were called, and everybody began to smoke them. Brands from England were left on the shelves. What happened then? Over came the well-known makes from England—but not at their previous price, no. Now they were sold at six a penny! And what happened to "Elephants?" They just disappeared.

P: These things raise the question of monopoly capital. Under the present system it is all-powerful. Indigenous industries cannot possibly grow in such circumstances, and because they would compete with those of the metropolitan country everything is done to obstruct their establishing and growth. If the colonial peoples had control of the legislature laws could be passed to protect the native industries, laws which would prevent them from being systematically thwarted by monopoly interests.

N: What examples of the fate of local industries! This kind of thing must figure largely among the foremost grievances of indigenous colonial peoples. We have not yet examined the principal grievances. I should like you to outline them in brief, and, at the same time, with a little detail.

P: Yes, gladly, and I will do this when we have our next talk.

Chapter III A Charter for the Colonies

N: We were talking last about the effects of monopoly capital and you gave concrete examples of this. But there are many other grievances, and also not a few books that examine them, with varying degrees of solution, such as Lord Haley's [sic] *African Survey*,[1] and works by Buell,[2] Norman Leys and Leonard Barnes.[3] Tell me something about the principal grievances in Africa.

P: In Africa grievances are racial, economic and social. The economic ones are closely associated with the land problem. In East and South Africa the natives have been dispossessed of their land by the European colonists, and concentrated into special areas known as "reserves." Then they are subjected to direct "levy" in the form of hut and poll taxes. This has the effect of forcing them out of their reserves to seek employment on the plantations or in the mines; all of these are in the hands of private settlers or of joint stock companies. To get the money for their government-imposed tax the Africans are literally forced to accept whatever wages are offered, either by the individual employers or the companies. In most of the areas I am speaking of it is illegal for them to combine for collective bargaining. Especially is this so in the Union of South Africa, which is under Dominion administration.

In the East African colonies trade unionism has been legalized since 1940 but the rights remain largely on paper. The employer class, closely identified with the official class, has found ways of getting round the carrying out of the new trade union laws. Then, apart from the lack of land and the prevalence of very low wages, Africans are subject to special racial regulations known as "Colour bar." In South Africa there is a particularly harsh form of Colour bar.

---

1 William Malcolm Hailey, Baron (1872-1969), conducted this study under the auspices of the Royal Institute of International Affairs. *An African Survey: A Study of the Problems Arising in Africa South of the Sahara* was published by Oxford University Press in 1938.
2 Raymond L. Buell (1896-1946) an American academic whose published works include *The Native Problem in Africa* (1928).
3 Leonard Barnes (1895-1977) a journalist and writer on African affairs; lecturer at Liverpool.

N: Let me read you some lines out of Professor W.M. Macmillan's[1] booklet, "Democratise the Empire," published in 1941. He is a member of the Advisory Committee on Education in the Colonies, an expert on Africa, and also on the West Indies — as shown in his excellent "Warning from the West Indies" (in Penguin edition). Of South Africa he writes:

The Union of 1910 made no extension of native franchise. Instead, a long series of legislative measures openly defensive of white privileges, and repressive at least of black aspirations, culminated in the Native Franchise Act of 1936. In this act Cape influence prevailed only to the extent that native interests are now directly represented by a maximum of seven Europeans, elected on a separate register to a parliament of approximately two hundred members. The South African Union is therefore a dominion of a white democracy over a politically powerless black majority.

P: That speaks for the political side! And you know there is a law which prohibits the native from engaging in skilled or semi-skilled work.

N: What is the attitude of the white workers to this discrimination?

P: It is unfortunate, but true, that the white workers in South Africa were largely instrumental in placing Colour bar regulations on the statute book. In 1924, the Nationalist Party — the political organisation of the agricultural section of white South Africa, which is largely Boer — contested the general election under the leadership of General Hertzog.[2] Chief opponents of the Nationalists were those of the South African Party, the organ of

---

1 William M. Macmillan (1865-1974) wrote extensively about Africa, especially South Africa. *Warning from the West Indies: A Tract for Africa and the Empire* was published in 1936 by Faber and Faber.
2 James Barry Munnik Hertzog (1866-1942) South African military and political leader. Commanded a division of Boer forces in the Boer War (1899-1902). Organized the National Party, aimed at independence from British Empire. Formed a coalition government with Labour in 1924 and was prime minister until 1939.

the industrialists and mining financiers, who are mainly British. The leader of this party was then General Smuts.[1] Incidentally, this is why Smuts is such a favourite of the City of London. In order to strengthen their chances of success, Hertzog and the Nationalists made an alliance with the South African Labour Party, led by Colonel Cresswell. As the price for the support of Labour, Hertzog promised that this government would introduce racial legislation to protect white labour against the competition of coloured labour. This coalition, Nationalist-Labour, did win, and among the first Bills introduced in the South African Parliament after the 1924 general election was the Colour Bar Act, which laid down that the mining companies must employ only Europeans in all the better-paid jobs. As a result of this discrimination the European worker has been guaranteed a minimum rate of twenty shillings a day, while the average wage of a Negro miner is one shilling, six pence!

Colour bar regulations spread to other industries; to-day they cover all forms of occupational vocation in which white workers are engaged, such as dockers, railway men, etc. Similar legislation exists in Southern Rhodesia, which, unlike the Union of South Africa, is under Dominion Office supervision as far as legislation affecting Africans is concerned.

In March, 1932,[2] the Kenya Government, with the approval of the Colonial Office, legalized forced labour for plantation purposes, and in the East African colonies Colour bar exists in practice. Africans between the ages of sixteen and fifty-five are now liable to be called out for work on the white settlers' plantations in the Highlands for an average daily wage of three and a half pence. This may be implemented up to seven pence a day where rations are provided by the employer.

Since the loss of Malaya and its tin resources, similar laws have been introduced in Nigeria. Here natives between eighteen and forty-five are liable for forced labour in the tin mines. Generally speaking it can be said that the land problem here, in West Africa, is not as acute as in South and East Africa.

---

1 Jan Christian Smuts (1870-1950) South African statesman of Boer descent but a British subject by birth. Instrumental in the creation of the Union of South Africa (1910).

2 There is a handwritten note in the margin of the pamphlet suggesting that the date should read 1942.

Do not think that this is owing to any particular virtue in imperialism. Nothing of the sort. It was a dispensation of providence! It had its origins in the devitalising climate of the West Coast and the fact that prophylactics did not come into use until fairly recently. You remember how this part of the Dark Continent was always referred to as "The white man's grave." And since Europeans did not migrate in any number to West Africa there has been little alienation of land for plantations. This circumstance it is which has made these territories the "model" colonies in Africa. Not the kind-heartedness of imperialists but the mosquito has rescued 28 million natives of Nigeria, Gold Coast, Sierra Leone and Gambia from the worst effects of European colonisation. There are only about nine thousand whites in West Africa, mainly traders, officials, missionaries, commercial agents, etc.

Generally speaking then, the land in West Africa, or at least what is on the surface of it, has not been alienated, and the African native races, most of whom have access to more of it than those in any other part of the whole continent save, possibly, Uganda, are responsible for the carrying on of agriculture. However, they have been induced to restrict their production to commercial crops, to the virtual exclusion of food crops. This has received official sanction. Consequently, all necessities such as milk, rice, flour, sugar, meat and even fish are imported in canned form!

Land tenure of course varies. In the northern provinces of Nigeria, for instance, all land is controlled by the government and the peasants are tenants-at-will of the Crown. The Egba chiefs, of whom you will doubtless remember the Alake of Abeokuta,[1] are its custodians in Yorubaland and other Southern Provinces. In their capacity of native administrators, they allot sections of it to the people in accordance to their needs, these allotments being worked in conformity with traditional usage. Under the Native Lands Acquisition Ordinance of 1917, land may not be disposed of to non-members of a tribe. In many places, however, tribal custom has broken down, as in the regions around the capital,

---

1   Oladipo Samuel Ademola II, 7th Alake [Chief] of Abeokuta (1920-1948). Abeokuta is
    a Yoruba city-state; currently capital of Ogun State.

Lagos, and many chiefs and influential natives own large cocoa properties worked by hired labour. Similar native landlordism is developing in the Gold Coast — an inevitable development wherever a money-economy is introduced.

N: Taking it by and large, would you say that West Africans have avoided the worst features of colonisation?

P: No subject people can escape the depredations of imperialism. They are bound to feel them one way or another. If West Africans have not suffered widespread alienation of their land, nevertheless they are as badly exploited as their brothers in East and South Africa. In their case, not as agricultural labourers, but as producers for the foreign market. While left in possession of their lands because of climactic conditions, they have been encouraged by the British Government to cultivate almost exclusively commercial crops, as I have just said. Gold Coast and Nigeria are the two largest cocoa-producing areas in the world. Nigeria and Sierra Leone are great exporters of palm oil and palm kernels, while Gambia produces ground nuts (peanuts). Production is carried on by native farmers with the assistance of their families, usually on small lots. *But the marketing of these crops is in the hands of the monopoly combines.*

Among these, United Africa Company, a subsidiary of Unilever, has perhaps the widest tentacles. Its ramifications absorb the whole of West African economy. There is nothing too small or too large for this millionaire concern; it spurns nothing in which it sees profit. In the Gold Coast it has united with the large chocolate firms, J. Lyons and Co., Cadbury Bros., and others, to form a "pool." At the beginning of harvest this "pool" fixes the prices it will pay the natives for the season's cocoa crop. Working hand in hand with the local banks, shipping and insurance companies and the West Africa section of the Liverpool Chamber of Commerce, the "pool" strangles the African farmer.

Besides being buyers, these large companies are also sellers. They own and control the sale of food, clothing, tools and all the manufactured commodities which the African farmer is obliged to buy at their stores. They fix their own prices, and receive back from the natives any moneys they have paid to him as purchasers of his crops.

In 1937-38, the farmers of the Gold Coast held up their crop, and at the same time the entire population carried out a boycott of British goods. This was the only direct means they had of opposing the "squeeze" that the monopolies were working on them. Of course, a Royal Commission went out and made its report, and then came the war—no settlement was reached. Now the British Government buys the cocoa crop at a fixed price agreed upon by the chairman of the Cocoa Board at the Ministry of Food, who, not by chance, I'm sure, turns out to be Mr. John Cadbury.

The situation with the palm industry in Nigeria is practically the same; only, in this case, United Africa is alone in the field. Since 1924, the price has been depressed to such a level that the Nigerian farmer finds it almost impossible to live. Ground nuts maintain economy in Gambia. Without this crop the colony would be bankrupt, since the export-tax on the product is almost the sole source of revenue.

N: All of this certainly gives an idea of how it is with agricultural matters in Africa. Now tell me something about industry.

P: Exploitation in the mines has reached a considerable degree of intensity, especially in the Gold Coast and the northern part of Nigeria. Around these mines are centred large industrial populations completely divorced from the soil. Here conditions approximate those in South Africa as far as wages and labour are concerned. There is no Colour bar as in the Union of South Africa, for the simple reason that there are no white workers. Most of them are Africans, and as mining develops there is a growing tendency to squeeze the peasants off the land. Tin and coal are the minerals chiefly mined in Nigeria; gold, diamonds, and manganese in the Gold Coast; and diamonds and iron ore in Sierra Leone.

In Nigeria the mineral rights belong to the government, who took over from the Niger Company in 1900. This company has now merged into United Africa Company, which has a ninety-nine-year lien on more than half of the mineral rights. Coal mines at Enugu are operated by the government, while private companies have been granted concessions to work the tin mines of the Bauchi plateau. In Sierra Leone mineral rights are also vested in the government, which makes concessions to companies working deposits. A monopoly to exploit diamonds for ninety-nine years was secured by the Consolidated African Election Trust in 1934, at a fixed annual rental of £7000. The Sierra Leone Development Company, a British concern, works the iron ore at Marampa, one of the largest iron mines in Africa.

Under the Ashanti Concessions Ordinance of 1903, mineral rights in the Gold Coast remain with the native authorities, but negotiations in connection with concessions are supervised by the European district commissioners and the government has control over all money derived from these sales. The concessions are not worked on a royalty basis but at a fixed rental, often as low as £50 and nowhere exceeding £400 a year.

Natives employed in these mines form the largest proportion of industrial workers in West Africa. Wages are incredibly low, and despite constant demands for increases to meet the rising cost of living, as well as recommendations from various commissions, there has been no increase. In the government-owned coal mines, rates vary from five shillings, eight pence to fifteen shillings, five pence *a week* for the different grades, and it is estimated that a married surface-worker with a wife and two children spends, say, two shillings in rent and seven shillings in food, against a wage of five shillings, eight pence. In the privately-owned tin mines the average weekly wage is three shillings, six pence for regular labour. Casual labour is paid as little as two shillings, eight pence. Women and children employed at the coal mines receive even less than the men.

N: Just as they do in the cane-fields and cocoa woods of Trinidad, although the women do the same kind of work and certainly have the same expenses in the way of food as do the men. What sort of general conditions are there in these mining centres?

P: The all-round conditions are as pitiful as can possibly be and social legislation is practically non-existent.

N: And what about the prosperous class that exists in West Africa?

P: The more well-to-do of the farmers have been able to send their children to better schools or to provide them with higher education either locally or abroad. These educated or "Europeanised" Africans constitute the intelligentsia of the West African colonies. They represent the vanguard of the national and progressive movements which to-day are voicing increasingly the political and economic aspirations of the African people. This is a natural development.

Among all subject peoples, whether in Africa, India or the West Indies, it is always the middle-class intellectuals who form the most articulate section of the native races. And as industrialisation, such as it is—mining and small-scale factories—begins to develop, a working class, as distinct from the peasantry, is brought into being.

N: Is it possible for this prosperous class to open up in an industrial way?

P: Well, it can buy property and become relatively rich as landlords. But as for opening mines and the like, no; it is handicapped by impossible conditions. Imperialists are not in the colonies to further the fortunes of the native bourgeoisie. In East Africa, for instance, where copper and other minerals are found, the rights belong to the South Africa Company, which allows financial interests to work the minerals for an annual royalty of something like £500,000. This is the case in Northern Rhodesia, where, before anything else, this sum is set aside for payment to share holders outside the colony; all it gets back is one or two shillings in the pound income tax. As the companies are registered in London, their income tax is due there. Hence the colony is poor. So you see it is all a vicious circle.

N: Then how to get out of the vicious circle?

P: It is one of the greatest problems of our time. I can see no hope of solving it, of improving the condition of the native peasantry and proletariat—in Africa, India, West Indies, and in other Colonies—of civilising them, raising the level of their culture, education and physical situation in general, under the present system. If the progressive sections of the British people realise that there is no forward march for them under the existing system, how much, how very much more is this so in the colonies! Only a very radical and complete change will better the conditions of the colonial peoples. I have already said what I firmly believe to be the solution: *full political representation, economic security, the widest social and educational reforms.*

N: This seems to me the very point of our talks. I would like to hear you expand this "Charter for the Colonies."

P: A Charter? If you like. Anyway, the application of clause three of the Atlantic Charter. Now, thinking of the colonies individually, I would suggest the following measures:

For the African Territories:
(a) Economic, political and social equality, in all colonies, protectorates and mandated territories. (b) Abolition of forced labour. (c) Abolition of indenture, apart from labour contracts with the government for the prosecution of the war. (d) Abolition of Pass Laws, Colour bar and all racial disabilities (a matter which at the end of August was being debated in South Africa). (e) Censorship to be restricted to matters of military importance. (f) Freedom of assembly. (g) Limitation of company profits.

For South Africa:
The events in Libya have had striking repercussions in South Africa, especially as they affect inter-racial relations and the "civilised" labour policy. It was largely the South African Army which was eliminated in North Africa by von Rommel,[1] most of it being either killed or taken prisoner. Consequently, since there has been opposition to Smuts's proposal that black South Africans should be called up for military service, and owing also to the increased demands of industry, there is a marked shortage of semi-skilled and skilled labour. In these circumstances Colonel Reitz,

---

[1] Erwin von Rommel, German Major General famous both for his victories over the British and Commonwealth armies in North Africa during World War II, and for accusations of complicity in the attempt on Hitler's life in July 1944; he committed suicide rather than stand trial.

Minister of Native Affairs, has taken action to "ease up" the application of Pass Laws, to be replaced by what is known as the "Registration Certificate," and he now has to wear down the strong opposition raised against his proposal.

The Dutch Reformed Church passed a resolution putting on record its objection to the arming of the black South Africans. This said, in part:

> The principle of arming non-Europeans is contrary to the constitution and principles of the Word of God which is based on racial separateness and the principles of trusteeship on the part of Europeans against non-Europeans.
>
> The arming of non-Europeans would be contrary to the best traditions of the Afrikaner people. The policy of Christian governments in the Union, when involved in war, has always been to use the services of natives and coloured races in subordinate and menial capacities.

It warned the government against arming the natives and asked that a speedy declaration be made by government on this subject, and ended by saying: "The government should see that non-Europeans will be used only in subordinate and menial capacities."

The Dutch Reformed Church is the largest religious body in the Union. While many thousands of South African natives are serving at present with the divisions in Egypt and the Middle East in the British Imperial Ninth Army under General Sir Maitland Wilson, in the Union of South Africa they are only in labour battalions, in transport and in ambulance service. They may not bear arms and are under white commissioned and non-commissioned officers. Well, the shortage of white labour caused by this implacable stand of the whites has resulted in numbers of blacks being introduced into work which was previously strictly reserved for European workers.

These circumstances must have a far-reaching effect on the future of inter-racial relations in the Union; once more we have the illustration of how time *does* march on and that it is historic events which condition progress, even in the face of the most adamant reaction.

For West Africa:
Widening of franchise and extension of municipal government to all townships on a basis of local democracy. Extension of education and social services. Replacement of monopoly-control of West African trade by producers' co-operative organisations working in conjunction with the state. Release of the native spokesmen imprisoned for their activities in attempting to ameliorate social conditions.

For Kenya:
All land now held by European settlers and not actually cultivated by them to be taken by the Crown for free distribution among the African natives. The same applies to Crown lands.

For the West Indies:
In view of the findings of the last Royal Commission it is clear that the problem here is fundamentally economic and social, centring round the need for the redistribution of land and more intensive development of the economic resources of these territories. To convince the people that these reforms were genuinely intended, power should be transferred from the present Crown Colony bureaucracy to the elected representatives of the people, on the following basis: universal adult suffrage; removal of property qualification for membership of councils; people's control of expenditure.

For India:
In India machinery exists to make full self-government immediately practicable. There is no evidence that the opposition of the Muslim League to the National Congress is shared by the mass of the Moslems. The evidence of the elections is, indeed, decisively to the contrary. And if we needed further proof, during the troubles last July and August not even the Tory press reported communal riots.

A provisional government with a Congress majority should be set up, pledged to respect minority rights; this should be done as soon as possible. No action that has been taken by the British

Government, nor any move it may make, short of securing national control of the full machinery of government, will change the basic situation. Fundamentally the Indian problem remains one of agrarian reform. If any appeal is to be made by the leading national figures to the millions of illiterate peasants they must have something concrete to offer them, and this they can only do if the direction of affairs be in their own hands.

Have we not seen by the action that the British Government has taken that imperialism's final resort is to force? What can this solve? Nothing, I think. Gandhi[1] was the one person who could have kept the masses in leash; without him there is danger of the people rushing ahead. This kind of action by the British can only turn a festering into a running sore; any time the Japanese decide to attack they will meet a population not merely apathetic but actively hostile to the British.

At the beginning of the war I put on paper some of the suggestions I have just made. I said then and I say again now: In a conflict which purports to be one of free peoples against brute force and dictatorship, nearly 500,000,000 British subjects have direct interest, but as yet no incentive to participate wholeheartedly in a life and death struggle. *If the people of India and the colonies are to be asked to throw their full weight into this conflict they must be given that incentive. For what driving force is there comparable to that which animates free peoples in the struggle to maintain their liberty?* What is wanted, therefore, is a declaration granting to Britain's colonial subjects all the social and political rights for which the people of Great Britain are fighting.

And so, in the interests alike of colonial peoples and of victory over Nazism, we ask for the immediate declaration of a policy which is in itself just, and consistent also with the Atlantic Charter. Whenever, before the war, the question of colonies and their transfer to some other power arose in the House of

---

1 Gandhi, Mohandas (1869-1948) Indian nationalist leader. Trained as lawyer in England and worked in South Africa for several years, attempting to gain rights for immigrant Indians. Returned to India in 1915 and became a leader in the nationalist resistance to British rule. Developed a creed of passive resistance against injustice, *satyagraha*, or truth force. Assassinated the year following the independence of India and Pakistan.

Commons, government and opposition speakers alike emphasised that no transfer would be considered *without the consent of the people concerned*. We ask, now, simply that this implied right of self-determination be accepted in all its implications.

I would say to the people of Great Britain: The advantages of such a policy are incalculable. The relationship between the indigenous populations and the army in India, and the scattered forces in the colonies at present occupied in policing those regions against revolt and civil disturbance would undergo a complete change. These forces would no longer be regarded as the instruments of alien operations, but rather as friends and allies. A comparison: the Australians have welcomed the American contingents who have reached their shores.

In this changed atmosphere the vast man-power of India could be drawn upon. Industrial and agricultural resources would be exploited in a new burst of energy having behind it the full force of political movements which are to-day operating against England. The world would be electrified by a change of policy which would turn the slogan of "democracy" into a living reality — into the struggle of free peoples, regardless of race, for their common rights against a menace felt equally by all. Thereby, also, would be nullified the activities of Nazi and Fifth Column agents. Do not forget: Rome abandoned her colonies to save herself, losing both herself and her colonies. Yet Britain, by freeing her colonies, can save both herself and them and lay the foundation of a new Commonwealth of Nations, bound together in equal partnership.

I would say to the colonial peoples: The age of imperialism must end, but this will only prove true if we can defend our new rights against a new and ruthless enemy: Nazism. It will not serve you to lose a British master to find instead a German or a Japanese one. Freedom is for those who can defend it; and it will take all the force of the Allied powers and your force as well, all your energy and sacrifice, to defeat those who would build *their* empire upon the ruins of the old.

If this great change, this new policy for the colonies should come, my message to them would be: "Let Britain know that you are with her, that you accept and respond, that you will fight to the death against the Nazi and the Japanese peril, that you will keep your word to Britain as long as she keeps hers to you."

London, 1942.

MISCEGENATION BLUES

BLACK MAN AND WHITE LADYSHIP

Her Ladyship

AN anniversary is coming and that is why this is printed now, and the reason for its having been written will, I imagine, be clear to those who read it. By anniversary I am not, indeed, referring to Christmas, but to the calendric moment of last year when the Colour Question first presented me personally with its CLASH or SHOCK aspect.

I have a Negro friend, a very close friend (and a great many other Negro friends in France, England and America). Nothing extraordinary in that. I have also a mother—whom we will at once call: Her Ladyship. We are extremely different but I had remained on fairly good (fairly distant) terms with her for a number of years. The English Channel and a good deal of determination on my part made this possible. I sedulously avoid her social circle both in France and in England. My Negro friend has been in London with me five or six times. So far so good. But, a few days before our going to London last year, what follows had just taken place, and I was unaware of it until our arrival. At a large lunch party in Her Ladyship's house things are set rocking by one of those bombs that throughout her "career" Margot Asquith, Lady Oxford,[1] has been wont to hurl. No-one could fail to wish he had been at that lunch to see the effect of Lady Oxford's entry: "Hello Maud, what is it now—drink, drugs or niggers?" (A variant is that by some remark Her Ladyship had annoyed the other Ladyship, who thus triumphantly retaliated.) The house is a seemly one in Grosvenor Square and what takes place in it is far from "drink, drugs or niggers." There is confusion. A dreadful confusion between Her Ladyship and myself! For I am known to have a great Negro friend—the drink and the drugs do not apply.

---

1   Margot Asquith (1864-1945), known for her wit, married Herbert Asquith who was British Prime Minister from 1908-1918, and was made Earl of Oxford in 1925. Margot Asquith published a number of rather indiscreet autobiographies.

Half of social London is immediately telephoned to: "Is it *true* my daughter knows a Negro?" etc., etc.

It appears that Sir Thomas Beecham,[1] in the light of "the family friend" was then moved sufficiently to pen me a letter, in the best Trollope[2] style, in which he pointed out that, as the only one qualified to advise, it would, at that juncture, be a grave mistake to come to England with a gentleman of American-African extraction whose career, he believed, it was my desire to advance, as, while friendships between races were viewed with tolerance on the continent, by some, it was … in other words it was a very different pair of shoes in England especially as viewed by the Popular Press! This letter (which was sent to the wrong address and not received till a month later on my return to Paris) was announced by a telegram "strongly advising" me not to come to London until I got it adding that the subject was unmentionable by wire! I was packing my trunk and laid the telegram on top—time will show…. We took the four o'clock train.

What happened in London?

Some detectives called, the police looked in, the telephone rang incessantly at our hotel. The *patron* (so he said) received a *mysterious message* that he himself would be imprisoned "undt de other vil be kilt." Madame wept: "Not even a *black* man, why he's only *brown*." Her Ladyship did not go so far as to step round herself. The Popular Press was unmoved. This lasted about a month and I used to get news of it daily, enough to fill a dossier on the hysteria caused by a difference of pigmentation.

The question that interested a good many people for two and a quarter years (does Her Ladyship know or not?) was thus brilliantly settled.

But, your Ladyship, you cannot kill or deport a person from England for being a Negro and mixing with white people. You may take a ticket to the cracker southern states of U.S.A. and

---

1 Sir Thomas Beecham (1879-1961) was a prominent English conductor and opera impresario with a long and distinguished career. In 1906 he founded the New Symphony Orchestra; in 1908 he founded the Beecham Symphony and began presenting contemporary operas and symphonies. In 1932 he founded the London Philharmonic and in 1933 became artistic director of Covent Garden. A long-time friend of Maud Cunard, he was believed to have been her lover.

2 Anthony Trollope (1815-1882), the Victorian novelist, was well-known for social satire.

assist at some of the choicer lynchings which are often announced in advance. You may add your purified-of-that-horrible-American-twang voice to the Yankee outbursts: America for white folks — segregation for the 12 million blacks we can't put up with — or do without....

No, with you it is the other old trouble — class.

Negroes, besides being black (that is, from jet to as white as yourself but not so pink) have not yet "penetrated into London Society's consciousness." You exclaim: they are not "received!" (You would be surprised to know just how much they are "received.") They are not found in the Royal Red Book.[1] Some big hostess gives a lead and the trick is done!

For as yet only the hefty shadow of the Negro falls across the white assembly of High Society and spreads itself, it would seem, quite particularly and agonisingly over you.

And what has happened since this little dust-up of December last, 1930? We have not met, I trust we shall never meet again. You have cut off, first a quarter (on plea of your high income tax) then half of my allowance. You have stated that I am out of your will. Excellent — for at last we have a little truth between us. The black man is a well-known factor in the changing of testaments (at least in America), and parents, as we all know, are not to be held responsible for the existence of children.

Concerning this last I have often heard Her Ladyship say that it is the children who owe their parents nothing. But I am grateful to her for the little crop of [trivia][2] that has flowered this year: Mr. George Moore[3] — (at one time her best friend and thence my first friend) whose opinion I was interested to have on the whole matter, which I obtained by the silence that followed my frank letter

---

1 Webster's Royal Red Book is a social register for British courtiers and fashionable society; it includes listings of London streets and members of the British nobility.

2 The copy text reads "trivalia" and the first printing reads "trivialia." Unable to decide between Cunard's neologisms in this case, I have elected to amend the word to read "trivia."

3 George Moore (1852–1933), the Irish novelist, poet, and playwright, was Maud Cunard's lover prior to Beecham. Nancy published a memoir about him after his death, *G.M.* They were quite close when Nancy was young, and he encouraged her writing endeavours. At one point, Nancy suspected he might be her father; when she asked him, Moore denied it.

to him—was said to have decided not to leave me his two Manets[1] as he intended, but has subsequently contradicted this....

Her Ladyship's hysteria has produced the following remarks:

that —no hotel would accommodate my black friend.

that —he was put out of England (exquisitely untrue, for we came, stayed and left together after a month.)

that —she would not feel chic in Paris any longer as she had heard that all the chic Parisians nowadays consorted with Negroes.

that —I now wrote for the Negro Press. (One poem and one article have appeared in *The Crisis*,[2] New York.)

that —where would I be in a few years' time.

that —she does not mind the Negroes now artistically or in an abstract sense but ... oh, that terrible colour! (I invite Her Ladyship to send in writing a short definition of a Negro in the *abstract sense*.)

that —she knew *nothing at all of the whole thing* till Mr. Moore read her my letter.

Now, to be exact: my letter to Mr. Moore was written January 24 whereas Her Ladyship severely put through it several friends of mine in the preceding December, and had her bank signify to me on January 21, 1931, that owing to the exigencies of her Income Tax.... I suspect Her Ladyship of having conveniently forgotten that what seems indeed to have struck her as a bomb exploded before many witnesses in her own house. (This is very interesting and I don't doubt the psychologists have many such cases on their books—the washing of hands, let us add, by the main party.)

I am told that Her Ladyship was invited to a night-club, saw some coloured singers, turned faint and left ... yet at least one paid coloured entertainer has been to her house.

I am told that she believes all the servants in a London house gave notice because a coloured gentleman came to dinner.

---

1 Edouard Manet (1832–1883), French impressionist painter.

2 African-American magazine published by the NAACP (National Association for the Advancement of Coloured People) and edited for some time by W.E.B. DuBois.

AND I AM TOLD

that Sir Thomas Beecham says I ought to be tarred and feathered!

It is now necessary to see Her Ladyship in her own fort, to perceive her a little more visually.

I will ring up the curtain on a typical scene. *Petite* and desirable as per all attributes of the nattier court lady she is in militant mood over the contents of a Book on Beauty which is just out. She figures in it, pleasantly enough—a few words endow her with the brightness of the canary and the charm of the Dresden shepherdess. Other beauties, more or less descriptively, have been compared to Madonnas, Bacchantes, Robot women and nippy, flat-chested messenger boys. Her Ladyship has just thrown this twenty-five shillings-worth of modern history into the fire and with a poker holds it down. A beautiful, but Roman Catholic lady is present. This alarms her greatly, for there is a photograph of her in the book too, and for oneself to be burned, if only on paper … a malaise comes at the thought of the little wax effigies. Her Ladyship swears such things ought to be put down—she is *not* going to be a Dresden shepherdess—at least not in that copy.

But the memory of it cannot be put in the fire. What is the matter with people these days? Bolshevism is going on too, England breaking up. As for that rich young couple in the Labour party … she really doesn't want them in her house though she *does* invite them. And why does Mr. S, when she asks him point blank what he thinks of the British Aristocracy, answer "I really know nothing about it"—what does he *mean*? The die-hards come and tell her they alone can "save the country." Meanwhile she is worried enough saving her skin—from the authors, for they have discovered her and come to meat. And after due gestation…. Well, she will never speak to *them* again, says she—to the sly edification of the next lot. Boiling point in often reached. Her Ladyship may be as hard and as buoyant as a dreadnought but one touch of ridicule goes straight to her heart. And she is so alone— between these little lunches of sixteen, a few callers at tea, and two or three invitations per night.

Some of the afternoons are for the Art game or Picture racket. This consists of being *done*. Done by dealers and galleries in the

peculiar ramifications of interchange. A good or a valuable painting is traded for a questionable one — then two doubtfuls against
a decidedly bad one. After receiving the hesitating criticism of the
habituées this last passes quickly into the wedding-present zone.
A Marie Laurencin[1] costs three hundred pounds, but Her
Ladyship's walls, besides six or seven real ones, show two excellent
"in the manner of" executed expressly at thirty pounds each.
Meanwhile a Braque, a Masson, a Picasso[2] drawing have gone
their way. "And nobody ever tells me." It is impossible to tell Her
Ladyship anything. A variant of the Art game is the Jewel racket.
(Same system, same result.)

In the *Sunday Express* of November 22, 1931, can be read in
detail of how Her Ladyship spends a fortune on clothes she never
wears. "I have not the faintest idea of how much I spend on
clothes every year — it may run into thousands. I have never
bothered to think about it. But that is because I do not have to
bother about money." (Which tallies interestingly with her bank's
statement concerning the exigencies of her Income Tax — see
previously.) ... "I want to tell you candidly why it is that so-called
'Society' women spend so much on their clothes. It is not that the
cost of each garment is so very large; it is simply that we won't be
bothered."

The Market may be going on at any time, and generally is.
Others play it but Her Ladyship plays it best. Rich Mrs. XYZ
will be "taken out" if she guesses or takes the hint that she is to do
her duty by ... (the object varies). No sign of the hint ever being
administered. But the participants are well-trained, each is looking for what the other can supply, and each felicitously finds.
Many results have been come by in this excellent manner.
Snobbery opens purses, starvation fails.

Her Ladyship's own snobbery is quite simple. If a thing is *done*
she will, with a few negligible exceptions, do it too. And the last
person she has talked to is generally right, providing he is *someone*.
The British Museum seems to guarantee that African art is art?

---

1 French modernist painter (1885-1956); friend of Apollinaire and Picasso; Gertrude
   Stein was the first to purchase one of Laurencin's works.
2 Georges Braque (1882-1963), French Fauvist/Cubist painter; André Masson (1896-
   1987), French surrealist painter; Pablo Picasso (1881-1973), Spanish Cubist painter.

Some dealers, too, are taking it up, so the thick old Congo ivories that she thinks are slave bangles are perhaps not so hideous after all though still very *strange*; one little diamond one would be better ... though of course that is different.

Her Ladyship likes to give—and to control. It is unbearable for her not to be able to give someone something. But suppose they don't want it—what does this *mean*? Her reaction to being given something herself generally produces the phrase that people shouldn't do such things! Yet the house is full of noble gifts.

Her ladyship has a definite fear of certain words. Some days she will even shy at the word "lover." But as for the tabooed subject of pederasty it is frequently introduced and worried like a fox in death-throes by a whole pack of ... allusions. An unsafe enough topic in this milieu but made positively, imminently hot by the hostess' concern to hear about something she still can't quite believe.... "You know, those dreadful people who ... well, you know those horrid ..." and in a whisper "I'm told he got a loathsome disease, *an old man's disease*, like that." The homosexuals present grin. "Just her way." One or two, a touch uneasy, confides to her privately his unrequited passion for some woman. The blind does its work.[1] And the subject goes on merrily —sometimes unwittingly. "We all say now _____ is a fairy, he is so ... unreal, so ... inhuman— yes-he-is-like-a-fairy, he-is-a-fairy-don't-you-think?" Wilde's case is really too *on*pleasant to be discussed. Of course the classics ... it is different—what didn't they do in those days? But oh dear me, no-one who may ever have had any trouble that way will ever be spoken to by her again. He will be spoken *of*. And how.

Another time it is Communism. "You don't mean to say those people you talk of are communists? they couldn't be, no-one as intelligent, as intellectual as they are.... You can't know people like that," etc.... And away with the troubling thought. Her Ladyship is the most conscientious of ostriches and when she comes up again she hopes the *on*pleasant thing has disappeared. Perhaps it doesn't really exist. She is also a great cross-questioner and all her ingenuous ingenuity is seen at work on the picking of

---

1 [Author's note: I have been *proposed* to in Her L's house by a noted member of the cult—pretty half-heartedly—still it was part of the shield.]

brains. As those she puts through it are generally less quick in defence than she is in attack, and as she has a fantastic imagination she generally arrives at some result. Look out! as in the farce, evidence will be taken down, altered and used against you. It will make quite a farce in itself. She is a great worker for she is never content to leave things as they are. In digging away she may turn up some startling facts. She is shocked. She is suspicious. All is not as it should be. She does not recognise ... there may be no precedent—why it may even be scandalous ... it *is* scandalous! it is unheard of!! WHAT is to be done? Why, talk about it! What do people say? A mountain is thrown up by this irreducible mole. There—of course it is *monstrous*! It cannot be true ... and, though it is she who has informed the world, she is astounded presently when it all gets out of hand and falls back on her in anything but gentle rain.

Her Ladyship is American and this is all part of that great American joke: l'*inconscience*. Here she is, ex-cathedra at the lunch table, here she is telling some specimen A-1 illiterate of the greatness of the last great book, here—wistfully puzzled by some little matter everyone knows, here—praising rightly, praising wrongly, making and missing the point all in one breath. Generous to the rich, trying always to do the right thing (serve only the best champagne, the food is always perfect). One day the footmen have frayed trousers. The butler has taken a leaf from Her Ladyship's book and explains that *no good enough* ready-made trousers are procurable in London, and that the tailor being dear, and slow ... he falters. There is a scene. The interior economy is impeccable.

All this is the lighter side and to one who can stomach its somewhat suspect fifty-seven varieties it may prove an acceptable entertainment not lacking in style. But let him look to his possible enemies that also frequent the house—should one of these, how easily, impress Her Ladyship that for any reason he is undesirable he will find the door shut. He may get through it again if someone considerable enough puts in a good word—then, like to like, he may do the same to his detractor. The wheel turns. Is it an amusing atmosphere? *It is a stultifying hypocrisy.* Yet, away from it it has no importance; *it is, yes it is unreal.* There is no contact, the memories of it are so many lantern-slides. They move and shift together in a crazy blur of *dixhuitième*[1] gold-plate and *boiserie*[2] topped with the great capital C, Conversation, rounded off with snobbery and gossip. The company has got mixed up with the background and the *savonnerie*;[3] it all makes waves for a moment in the wind of this distant and real place where I find myself suddenly wondering if it all still goes on....

Then—Her voice went cold on the telephone—"You mean to say my daughter does know a Negro and that you know him too? Well, don't speak of it to anyone—nobody knows anything about it. *Good Bye.*"

[The Black Man][4]

Consider the following extract of what happened. From 1619 to after the middle of the 19th century hundreds of thousands of Negroes, men, women and children, were sold, stolen and torn out of Africa. They were herded into boats at one time specially built for their transport. The trade prospered; more profits were made at it, and more quickly, than at any other trade in history. Its apex, in number of slaves shipped from Africa to the New World, was the last two decades of the 18th and the first two of the 19th centuries—about the time there was most agitation for its abolition. An estimate puts the figure at over one hundred thousand slaves a year. On the special boats the slaves were manacled to each other two by two and to the ship itself; a space of six feet by one foot, four inches was allotted each on deck for the many weeks of the voyage. At night they were stuffed into the hold. Many would be found dead in the morning. Those that looked for death from starvation were forcibly fed—many hanged themselves, leapt overboard, died of the flux and of despair. They were made to jump up and down in their irons after eating; this was called "dancing," to obtain exercise. They were flogged, tortured

---

1   Eighteenth-century design.
2   Wainscotting.
3   A type of carpet.
4   To Cunard's consternation, the subtitle "The Black Man" was omitted in the second printing of her pamphlet. See "A Note on the Text," p. 70.

and maimed. After three or four such passages the slave ships had to be abandoned—having become unusable from filth. The stench of them spread some four miles out at sea. Once landed the slaves were sold by auction. Everyone knows how things went for them till 1863. Two hundred and forty-four years of slavery in America, and Charles Lynch existed—a Virginian Quaker. From the World Almanac figures—*admitted official* figures—3,226 Negroes have been lynched in U.S.A. between 1885 and 1927, an average of over six a month.

For the first six months of this year, 1931, thirty cases of Negro lynching are reported. Nine young coloured labourers are now in jail in Alabama (the Scottsboro case[1]) pending electrocution (for eight of them, and life-imprisonment for the ninth, a boy of fourteen) on a false charge of attempted "intimacy" with two white prostitutes who later stated they did not recognise the accused. After a first trial and condemnation the case has been postponed for re-trial in January next, but the possibilities are that the verdict will hold good and come into effect, unless the mob takes the law into its own hands and treats itself to a sight of "the quickest way"—lynching. The authorities take part in, often encourage the lynching. In the name of white American womanhood! Yet the fathers and mothers and ancestors of this superlative womanhood (as well as of the manhood that so superlatively "protects" it) were in a very great number of cases suckled at the black breast. I asked a Virginian how these two things can be accorded. He replied promptly "Oh d'black women 'r allright separately—but yu caun' go raoun' 'n tawk 'n all that with the coloured folks, yu jus' caun'—there's *tu many*. Yu caun' explain these things to 'n English person." I think one can explain the Virginian in two words: fear and jealousy. But d'black women 'r awlright, were very much alright for breeding bastards as new hands on the master's plantation. These were invariably treated worse than the rest. It is now legally laid down in some states that one-sixteenth of black blood constitutes a Negro. No wonder there are so many! The one hundred percent white Americans (and they are all one hundred percent he-males and one hundred percent supreme

---

1   See Cunard's essay on the subject, p. 209.

examples of white womanhood) go so far as to profess quite a friendly if distant feeling towards their long-suffering ex-slaves — only the damned niggers must be kept in their place and "yu caun go raoun' 'n talk with them an' all that because there's tu many." Why not send them all back to Africa? A little matter of between 12 and 13 million. Let us also scrap machinery and have the next war fought by representatives with stone canon-balls.

Now how does it seem to you put this way: several hundreds of thousands of whites have been torn from their country, chained in pairs to boats, flogged across the Atlantic, flayed at work by a nigger overseer's whip, hunted and shot for trying to get away, insulted, injured, thrown out, imprisoned, threatened with lynching if they dare ride in the black man's part of the train, their houses burned down, if, despite everything, they seem to get too prosperous, their women spoken of as "dirty white sluts" and raped at every corner by a big Negro buck, told there's no job in the office for anyone with a bleedin white mug and that their stinkin white bitches needn't go on trying to "pass" nor hope to send their white vermin to any decent school — three hundred years of it in all its different phases, substituting white for black all along the line. ... You would say Justice was strangely absent. You would say the hell of a lot more than that. Had this happened also to the white race as it has to the black one may well wonder which would have come out of it best.

I suppose if the Esquimaux had been more accessible the same as with the Negroes might have taken place. Only a less frightening miscegenation would have ensued — the white could have swallowed them quicker. Nothing to be alarmed about. But the Devil is a Black Man. Do you fear the Devil? Of course you do still — though God has gone by the board. You have the whimpering nursery mind in the age of fact. Or if the black man is Paul Robeson[1] ... ah then it is quite different, he becomes "the

---

1 African-American actor and singer (1898-1976), who graduated from Columbia University with a law degree in 1923. He began acting with the Provincetown Players in 1924 and was first acclaimed for his performance in Eugene O'Neill's *Emperor Jones*. He played the title role in *Othello* in London in 1930. Robeson's association with the Communist Party led to difficulties during the McCarthy era; he moved to England in 1958, only returning to the US in 1963.

noble Moor." Yet you may think yourself too good to sit with him at supper after the play.

For Louis XIV on the other hand it was an honour to entertain and make presents to a royal black man. Negroes were invited, fêted, sought after in the salons of 17th and 18th century France. In the realm of war black Haitian Christopher[1] was Napoleon's successful and unsubdued antagonist. From even the briefest study of colour-prejudice it would seem that this is based on economic reasons, it can be traced back to these.[2] Many people of different classes have no race or colour prejudice whatsoever. In France it is non-existent. It is not a problem but a glory to have so many black subjects. When in Montmartre some Negroes shot in self-defence a bunch of drunken Yankee sailors who had attacked them the French took the Negroes' side. A French person experiences no difficulty in shaking hands with a black man; the Negro is not excluded from commercial enterprise and competition, from social contacts, from social functions. Segregation as a word would have to be explained. The same with Germany to an even greater extent.

Not so with America. Its inconsistencies, too, are flaming.

When the American gold star mothers[3] were sent over at government expense to visit the war graves the Negro gold star mothers were segregated in a special ship (many refused this highly questionable honour). But this year General Pershing,[4] and other American notables including the ambassador, presided at a banquet given in a very smart Parisian restaurant at government

---

1 Henri Christophe (1767-1820) one of Toussaint L'Ouverture's lieutenants, and later one of the rulers of Haiti; Toussaint led the slave revolts in Haiti that led to its independence.

2 [Author's note: Walter White's admirably clear book *Rope and Faggot* and Professor Scott Nearing's equally fine *Black America* are the best approach to this subject.]

3 Founded in 1928, American Gold Star Mothers were incorporated in Washington, D.C. and granted a federal charter by Congress in 1929. Mothers who had lost sons in World War I created a mutual aid society that also sought to give care to veterans, and commemorate those who died in combat. Families who had lost a loved one in war hung gold stars in their windows, hence the name. In 1929-1930, Gold Star Mothers went on pilgrimages to the graves of US soldiers who had died overseas during World War I.

4 General John J. Pershing (1860-1948), commander of the American Expeditionary Force that led the Allies in World War I. After the war, in recognition for his service, Congress created a new rank for him: General of Armies of the United States.

expense to these same Negro mothers who had every right to consider themselves particularly insulted by the differentiation made in their transport and during their tour, the more so as they were no longer in white America. To have the Negro killed in war for "his" country is of course perfectly laudable—as well as indicated—but later to put the black mothers on a par with the white … an official banquet no doubt obviates the difference.

I believe that no fallacy about the Negroes is too gross for the Anglo Saxon to fall into. You are told they are coarse, lascivious, lazy, ignorant, undisciplined, unthrifty, undependable, drunkards, jealous, envious, violent, that their lips, noses and hair are ugly, that they have a physical odour—In the name of earth itself what peoples, individually, can disclaim any of these? The knave and the fool will out, the dirty will stink. But *all* Negroes are said to be thus, and all of it. The nigger Christy Minstrel[1] conception prevails—to be fair, mainly with the older generation—as does the Pip and Squeak[2] *Daily Mirror* children's page idea of the Bolshevik, all beard and bombs. So perhaps in London's high social circles of supposedly well educated arts-and-letters-appreciating aristocrats and hostesses it is a thing of age. It is certainly a thing of ignorance. These people simply do not know (and may be incapable of believing) that very great changes have taken place amongst the Negroes in America. (As the 12 million there are Anglo-Saxon by civilisation, education and speech, the greatest mass all together, as such, where it can be examined in the most advanced world-development conditions the American Negro is always taken as the case in point, the example, the leader.) Academies, colleges, schools, newspaper associations, busi-

---

1   As Cunard uses it, the term "Christy Minstrel" is synonymous with the stereotyped representation of blacks in black-face minstrelsy. In the1840s and 1850s, E.P. Christy founded a minstrel troupe in the US that came to be known as Christy's Minstrels. George Christy, who was one of the most famous minstrel performers, was part of the troupe. After that group disbanded in the 1860s, one of the former members created his own troupe and took over the name; that group toured England, and many subsequent minstrel shows in England called themselves Christy Minstrels.

2   Pip and Squeak were characters in a very popular 1920s comic strip published in *The Daily Mirror*. The strip was created by Bertram J. Lamb and Austin B. Payne, and the characters (Pip was a dog, Squeak a penguin) were named after Payne's World War I batman (in military terminology, an officer's attendant) who had been known as Pip-Squeak.

ness of most sorts, science, medicine, sociology, philosophy, research work of every kind, societies, art, music, drama, and a definite, definable intellectual and literary movement which has a great deal to show in as brief a time as the first thirty years of this century—all these entirely Negro—are the proof. The days of Rastus and Sambo[1] are long gone and will not return. The English prejudice gets a hard knock by the revelation that the pore ole down-trodden canticle-singing nigger daddy who used to be let out to clown for the whites has turned into the very much up to date, well-educated, keen, determined man of action (in all and any of these different fields) who is making it his business, for himself and his race, not to be put upon any more. In fact, the *real* freeing. Though the lynchings and other frightful abuses go on and on he will certainly achieve it.

Are intellectuals generally the least biased in race questions? Here are two reactionaries:

A little conversation with Mr. George Moore in Ebury St.

> *Self.* Yes, people certainly feel very differently about race. I cannot understand colour prejudice. Do you think you have it?
>
> *G. M.* No, I don't think so.
>
> *Self.* Have you ever known any people of colour?
>
> *G.M.* No.
>
> *Self.* What, not even an Indian?
>
> *G.M.* No—though my books are translated into Chinese.
>
> *Self.* Not even an Indian … such as might have happened had you met, shall we say, an Indian student. Don't you think you'd like to talk to an intelligent Indian or Negro?
>
> *G.M. calmly.* No. I do not think so. I do not think I should get on with a black man or a brown man. (*then warmly, opening the stops*) I think the best I could do is a yel-low man!

---

1   Names for black men or boys based on stereotyped notions of blackness. For example, in 1898 a Scottish woman named Hellen Bannerman published a children's story called *Little Black Sambo*; Rastus was the name given to the Nabisco Cream of Wheat chef.

Thus Mr. Moore—after a whole long life of "free" thought, "free" writing, anti-bigotry of all kinds, with, his engrossment in human nature, after the *injustice* of the Boer war, as he says himself, had driven him out of England.... There is no consistency; there is race or colour prejudice.

Sir Thomas Beecham's remark about the Negro making his own music left me puzzled, and I don't doubt, puzzled for ever. Her Ladyship was evincing a very querulous astonishment at the Negro (in general) having any achievements (in particular). I was informing her that for one, everybody knows the Negroes have a particular genius for music. At which Sir Thomas condescendingly remarked "They make their own music too." The tone of this pronouncement was so superior that I remained too dumb to ask whether at that moment he meant tribal or jazz. And Her Ladyship, far from being quieted became as uneasy as an animal scenting a danger on the wind.

This is all what's aptly enough called "Old stuff." What's actual since some twenty years is a direct African influence in sculpture and painting. None but fools separate Africa from the living Negro. But the American press is constantly confusing their civic nationality with their blood nationality; (the 12 million blacks are the loyalest, best *Americans*; a Negro in the States has written a good book, therefore he is a good *American* writer; the same of the coloured musician, the coloured artist, etc.).

"In Africa," you say, "the Negro is a savage, he has produced nothing, he has no history." It is certainly true he has not got himself mixed up with machinery and science to fly the Atlantic, turn out engines, run up skyscrapers and contrive holocausts. There are no tribal presses emitting the day's lies and millions of useless volumes. There remain no written records; the wars, the kingdoms and the changes have sufficed unto themselves. It is not one country but many; well over four hundred separate languages and their dialects are known to exist. Who tells you you are the better off for being "civilised" when you live in the shadow of the next war or revolution in constant terror of being ruined or killed? Things in Africa are on a different scale—but the European empire-builders have seen, are seeing to this hand over fist. And what, against this triumph of organised villainy had the black man to show? His own example of Homo Sapiens on better terms with life than are the conquering whites. Anthropology gives him priority in human descent. He had his life, highly organised, his logic, his customs, his laws rigidly adhered to. He made music and unparalleled rhythm and some of the finest sculpture in the world. Nature gave him the best body amongst all the races. Yet he is a "miserable savage" because there are no written records, no super-cities, no machines—but to prove the lack of these an insuperable loss, a sign of racial inferiority, you must attack the root of all things and see where—if anywhere—lies truth. There are many truths. How come, white man, is the rest of the world to be re-formed in your dreary and decadent image?

"THE AMERICAN MORON[1] AND THE AMERICAN OF SENSE— LETTERS ON THE NEGRO"

HERE are examples of some of the wild letters received by me at the time I was in Harlem, New York, collecting part of the material for this book. The American press, led by Hearst's[2] *yellow sheets*, had turned this simple enough fact into a veritable racket. Despite all the "liberal attitude of progressive whites" and the recent "New Negro" movement[3] whereby Americans learnt with incredulous amazement that there is a distinct Negro literature, any interest manifested by a white person, even a foreigner to America (such as myself), is immediately transformed into a sex "scandal." The American press method (one of America's major scandals), led by the world-famous "yellow press" of Hearst is to invent as vulgar and "sexy" a story as possible, to which any official denial merely adds another "special edition." The American public is intended to believe that no white person has ever stayed in Harlem before. But everyone knows that many thousands of whites actually live in Harlem, married to Negroes, or domiciled there.

No chance is ever missed by the American press, and the type of American that believes it (vastly preponderant), to stir up as much fury as possible against Negroes and their white friends. To do this the sex motive is always used. As in the South it is always the lie of the "rape" of white women by black men, so in the North it is always the so-called "scandal" of inter-racial relations. The Hearst publications *invent* black lovers for white women. A reporter goes round to try and bribe the hotel people into saying that such and such a Negro is staying there—communicating

---

1 [Author's note: The American widely used term for idiotic, cretinous or degenerate.]
2 William Randolph Hearst (1863-1951), newspaper publisher.
3 Also known as the Negro Renaissance or the Harlem Renaissance, the New Negro movement refers to a burgeoning of literary, artistic and socio-political activity by African-Americans circa the 1920s. Alain Locke (1886-1954), who is generally credited with coining the term, describes the renaissance in the foreword to his *New Negro* anthology (1925) as one of "those nascent movements of folk-expression and self-determination which are playing a creative part in the world today," marked by "a fresh spiritual" outlook and a "renewed race-spirit that consciously and proudly sets itself apart" (xvii).

rooms, etc. (This is the case in *my own* experience.) As of course there is not such a good "story" in scandalizing about plain coloured X, some well-known coloured star or personality is always picked (one instance of this was the late Booker T. Washington[1] himself, at the age of 60 or so). In that way the Hearst press hopes also to damage the star's professional reputation. If individuals persistently behaved in this manner amongst themselves, they would be locked up as criminals or insane; but what is to be done when this is one of the pillars of American society—the press? The equivalent to the jailing of individuals is of course the total suppression of the American press. An illuminating comment by Americans themselves on their newspapers is that journalists have got to write *something*—the papers have got to be filled every day, you know ...

It is necessary to explain to the English reader (I think?) that "Caucasian" in the U.S. is used as a self-awarded title of white man's superiority. It has no more to do, geographically, with the Caucasus than "Nordic" (same meaning) has to do with Scandinavia.

I should like to print all the raving, illiterate, anonymous letters—some are very funny indeed, mainly from sex-maniacs one might say—but what is to be done? They are obscene, so this portion of American culture cannot be made public.

Of course there were other letters as well—some four or five hundred—from Negroes and friendly whites, commending the stand I took and the making of this anthology. Of the anonymous threats, etc., some thirty. Most of them came in a bunch, just after the press outcry, May 2, 1932.

---

1 Booker T. Washington (1856-1915), author of *Up from Slavery* (1901) and founder of Tuskegee Institute. Washington was an important African-American leader whose base of support was particularly strong in the South; he advocated acceptance of racial segregation in the South while promoting black education, especially industrial education, self-help and racial pride in the hope that these might eventually have the effect of changing the political status quo.

Letters[1]

Mrs. Nancy Cunard take this as a solemn warning, your number is up. You're going for a ride shortly. You are a disgrace to the white race. You can't carry on in this country. We will give you until May 15th. Either you give up sleeping with a nigger or take the consequences. This is final. X 22. P.S. — We will not only take you but we'll take your nigger lover with you.

★   ★   ★

Miss Nancy Cunard repair to pay ransom 25,000 dollars will be demanding kidnaping H-B kidnaping inc.

★   ★   ★

Miss Cunard, this is one of the rare instances where we have found it necessary especially among intellectuals to deal drastically with those who would impair the fundamental principles of the Caucasian race of peoples. Since you have evidently found it expedient to disrespect your Aryan birthright and as we are conscious of that which might result from your present environment while in this country or your previous associations in Europe you will please be governed as below.

We shall call for you just as soon as the necessary plans have been completed for your reception.

The secretary of the second society of Caucasians of America.

★   ★   ★

Miss Nancy Cunard, you are insane or downright degenerate. Why do you come to America to seek cheap publicity? you have

---

1 Cunard prints the selected letters without either emending or highlighting grammatical and spelling errors. I have opted to follow her lead on the principle that the repeated use of [sic] would not enhance readability and that emendation would disguise telling features of these letters. The comments in brackets and parentheses are the author's.

not gained any favour but a whole lot of hatred. If I saw one of your publications I would be the first to suppress it. Furthermore I and a committee are appealing to the U.S. department of labour to have you deported as a depraved miserable degenerated insane. Back to where you belong you bastard. If you dare to make any comparison you had better look out for your life wont be worth the price of your black hotel room. You for your nerve should be burned alive to a stake, you dirty low-down betraying piece of mucus. [Here follows a sentence which might be considered obscene and which is not, therefore, printed.]

K.K.K. 58 W 58.
(I suppose this purports to come from the Ku Klux Klan, or possibly the writer only stole their "signature.")

Of the other side it is only fair to quote as well. There are *indeed* many white people who have a liking for Negroes; some are afraid to say so, others are not. (I must perforce exclude in this count entirely the followers of the Communist Party, with whom it is a *sine qua non* to stamp out all race "inferiority;" this has not exactly *come of itself* to some of those who have joined the Communists, and there have been cases of trial and exclusion of members who have been taken back into the Party after their admission of guilt in race-prejudice, and conditional on their eradication of it in themselves and in others.) This type of letter is from people who are presumably not yet aware that all race-prejudice has a distinctly economic basis, that the Negroes in America are looked down on primarily because they were once slaves; the more so in the South because these slaves were taken from them by the result of the Civil War in 1865. Though it is out of place nowhere when talking of the Negro and slavery to repeat that the vast bulk of Southern State Negroes are as enslaved as ever; the name only has gone, the condition is the same, and worse.

Letters

New York, May 2.

My Dear Miss Cunard,

It's with a great deal of pleasure that I read about you in today's papers. I might say also that I am proud of you when you come out and defend the Negro race. It has been my good fortune to know some very fine people of the Negro race. I went to public school with Negroes, they were no different than any other children, perhaps better than some others. I'm staying in New York tonight, so after dinner I went up to the Public Library at 103 West 135th St. to read a book by a Negro. I could not find any fault with the people there. In fact I found it a very pleasant place to be. The book I wished to read was looked up and obtained by a coloured gentleman. When I left the library at closing time I walked around for perhaps a half hour. Life there is no different than any other place in New York. I can enjoy looking at a pretty Negro girl just as much as at any colour. The so-called colour line in this country is often a big noise by people not near as nice as a great many of the coloured race. There is so much of good to say about the Negro race that it's useless for me to try and say anything. And I want to add that I am proud of you as a girl to come out and stand up for the Negroes, you certainly are a brave young lady. I surely would like to shake the hand of a real girl as you are a credit to your sex.

(This is a signed letter bearing an address.)

★   ★   ★

Dear Miss Cunard,

It is very gratifying indeed to know that in these trying days someone deserts the great make-believe world and devotes her time to a real problem dealing with humans. Your determination to do your OWN work in so noble a cause has inspired all of us who devote our lives to the service of others and we most sincerely congratulate you.

Out here in the mountains of South California we operate a small boarding school for boys. Our place is very beautiful and the setting is most inspiring. We would be happy to have you avail yourself of our hospitality and to come out and visit us at any time. You will find this a wonderful place for rest, quiet and study.

May success crown your every effort and may the example you have given the world be the means of creating interest in the conditions of the Negro in this country. Being a Virginian, the writer fully appreciates the status of the American Negro.

Best wishes to you, cordially.
(This letter is from a California school, from the Headmaster.)

I reproduce the following letter here as an example of the totally shameless and stupendous form of LIE that Southerners still hope to put over. This one comes from Rome, Georgia, and is anonymous:

Nancy Cunard, c/o Cooks, 587 5th Ave., New York, N.Y.

I would not worry too much about the Negro rapists in Alabama; it might spoil your complexion. Their "case" has now gone to the Supreme Court; and it is an internationally known fact that no judge is named for the federal courts—from the lowest federal court to the Supreme Court, the highest tribunal in America *unless and until* he has proven his bias in favour of the Negro race, *and unless and until* the Negroes have approved of him for the post. The president now in office has established this precedent as a permanent thing; it was never before the *only* requirement necessary—as is the case now. He dares not appoint a judge who does not fulfill this one requirement. So, don't worry: the Negro rapists will go free. In every known case where a guilty Negro's "case" has been carried to the federal courts he is *always* cleared and freed, because, by reason of the nature of his crime (if it is rape) he has become an *international* hero.

The grandson of a Negro rapist from Georgia (who, by the way, *was* lynched for his crime: white men were *men* in those days) has just been named vice-presidential candidate of the communist party subject to the November election. So, we are very apt to have a Negro vice-president *in fact* in a few more months. The Negro politicians rule the present regime *now*. Why not have them in office and let them rule *in fact*?

At the present time, it is such a common occurrence for a Negro beast to rape a white woman and murder her or leave her for dead, in the south, that it is no longer news. Sometimes it may rate a one-inch space on an inner sheet of the newspapers, but nothing is ever done about it. They are afraid it might offend "THE RACE." The victim is ignored and forgotten, while the bestial offender automatically becomes an international hero to be publicly acclaimed and rewarded by public honours, When I refer to "THE RACE" I am referring to their own name for themselves (see copy of *The Race*, published in Chicago).

As for the "dark" part of America — the south — Negroes control the south politically and economically: the president of our nation takes orders from them. Every federal position is open to them for the asking. Atlanta is the Negro capital of the south. It stands next to head in the number of homicides to the population: Memphis, another southern "dark" town, stands head. There are about ten Negro colleges in Atlanta, supported by misguided white people from afar, like yourself.

[Two lines, have had to be omitted here. They refer to two very well-known American official public figures whom the writer referred to as supporting "a Negro harem in Atlanta."]

So, I do not think you need lose any sleep, knowing that the little chocolate "brothers" in Alabama are all hunky-dory. Their "case" is with the Supreme Court, and all is well for them. *They* have nothing to worry about: so, why should you?

A Southern Woman.

It is really too patently stupid to comment on. Suffice it to say that the "Negro rapists" are the nine innocent framed-up Scottsboro boys[1]— that Federal Court judges are in no way

---

1   See Cunard's article, p. 209.

chosen for their lack of race prejudice and are as likely to be as determined "nigger-haters" as the rest of the general American population—that Negroes have no say whatever in their election to the Supreme Court (beyond their comparatively small vote of 2 million—the white American vote being 72 million—inasmuch as 4 million out of the 6 million Negroes who should vote are disfranchised in nine Southern States where two-thirds of the total Negro population of the U.S. live). "The president now in office" was Hoover, one of the worst presidents ever known where the Negro is concerned. "Vice-presidential candidate for Communist party" refers to James W. Ford, the first time a Negro has been chosen for such a position (thereby affirming the Communist theory of the abolition of all race "inferiorities") with the exception of Frederick Douglass[1] in 1872, in a very different kind of political campaign, however (see previously[2]). White women are not "raped and murdered," but this happens to black women, and Negroes are terrorised and framed-up every day. As for the political and economic control of the U.S. by Negroes—it would be impossible for one even totally ignorant of the whole state of things there to see how this could tally with the complete disfranchisement of all the coloured voting citizens in the Southern States, and the economic slavery, bondage and peonage to which they have been subjected for a very great number of years. (See statistics of the Negro vote.[3]) In a word this letter is the best example possible of the threadbare and vicious lies of the classic American race-hate.

Let me give some examples of the kind of "political control" the Negro has in the South. Intended to terrorise Negro citizens who might seek to vote in the primaries in Dennison, Texas, last

---

1 Frederick Douglass (1818–1895), foremost spokesperson for African-Americans during the Civil War and after, Douglass was also the most esteemed African-American man of letters in the nineteenth century. His *Narrative of the Life of Frederick Douglass, An American Slave, Written by Himself* (1845) was a key text in the abolition movement and an international bestseller.

2 James W. Ford (1893–?) was the head of the League of Struggle for Negro Rights and Communist Party vice-presidential candidate in 1932, running mate of William Z. Foster. Cunard here refers to a brief article by Ford describing Frederick Douglass's nomination for vice-president at a convention of the Equal Rights League in 1872. Ford's article, "Frederick Douglass, 1872," is reprinted in her anthology (*Negro* 22–24).

3 Cunard here refers to another item in her anthology, "The Negro Vote" (*Negro* 273).

week, handbills scattered throughout the town read as follows :

NIGGERS!
The white people do not want you to vote Saturday. Do not
make the Ku Klux Klan take a hand. Do you remember
what happened two years ago, May 9th?
(George Hughes was burned to death, the county courthouse destroyed) (*The Crisis*, Sept. 1932).

Albert White, editor of the Shreveport, Louisiana,
Afro-American, was last week driven from Shreveport by
enraged state and city police, forced to hide in outlying hills,
because of his activity in organizing a league of Negro voters. Unable to find White, the heavily armed constabulary
stormed the large Lakeside Auditorium where a mass-meet-
ing of the League of Negro Voters had been scheduled to be
held, stood guard before all entrances, threatened with death
any who dared enter. Shreveport's leading citizens declared
that the streets of their fair city would be drenched with
blood before Negroes would be allowed their right to vote.

(*The Crisis*, Sept. 1932)

Concerning the Scottsboro boys (see further[1]) this extract from
a (white) Alabama newspaper simply regrets that a lynching did
not take place. The expression "the shortest way out" signifies
precisely this, it is the *phrase used* for lynching.

The ugly demands … from outsiders that Alabama reverse
its jury decisions, and filthy insinuations that our people
were murderers when they were sincerely being as fair as
ever in the history of our country, is rather straining on our
idea of fair play. It allows room for the growth of the
thought that maybe after all "the shortest way out" in cases
like these would have been the best method of disposing of
them. (*Jackson County Sentinel.*)

---

1   Once again Cunard directs readers to other articles in the anthology, this time to her
    own "Scottsboro—and Other Scottsboros" (*Negro* 243-268) as well as Josephine Herb-
    st's "Lynching in the Quiet Manner" (*Negro* 269-270) and Theodore Dreiser's "Speech
    on the Scottsboro Case" (*Negro* 271-272).

THE RED AND THE BLACK

"SCOTTSBORO—
AND OTHER SCOTTSBOROS" (1934)

To bring out the absolute fiendishness of the treatment of Negro workers by the governing white class in America, more specifically but by no means restrictedly, in the Southern States, I am going to start with what may seem a fantastic statement—I am going to say that the Scottsboro case is not such an astounding and unbelievable thing as it must, as it certainly does, appear to the public at large. What? Nine provenly innocent Negro boys, falsely accused of raping two white prostitutes, tried and re-tried, still held in death cells after two and a half years…. It is unparalleled. It is not *primarily* a case that can be called political, as is that of Tom Mooney,[1] still held for 18 years in St. Quentin, a California jail, on an equally vicious frame-up because he was an active strike-leader; nor at first sight do the same elements predominate as in Meerut[2] and the murder-by-law of Sacco and Vanzetti.[3] But the same capitalist oppression and brutality are at the root—because every Negro worker is the potential victim of lynching, murder and legal lynching by the white ruling class, simply because he is a worker and black. No, this frame-up is not unparalleled, though the scale of it and its colossal development into what is now really a world-issue, are so. No previous Negro case has aroused such a universal outcry against the abomination of American "law."

Here are some other frame-ups, murders and lynchings of Negroes to compare it with, instances taken at random out of the huge record, quite recent cases only:

---

1 Tom Mooney was a militant labour leader who in 1916 was charged with bombing a pro World War I parade and killing 10 people. He was convicted of first-degree murder and sentenced to life in prison on the basis of false evidence. He spent twenty-three years in jail before being pardoned and released.

2 The Meerut trial (1929–1933) involved 33 men, 3 British, the remainder Indian, who were attempting to organize trade unions in India under the auspices of the Communist Party of India and the British Communist Party. Very harsh sentences were meted out, although they were later reduced in response to international agitation.

3 In 1920 Nicola Sacco and Bartolomeo Vanzetti, two Italian immigrants, were charged in a murder and robbery that occurred in Massachusetts. In this infamous case, the accused were effectively tried for their anarchist political activities; there was little evidence to tie them to the robbery. They were convicted and sentenced to death; Sacco and Vanzetti were executed on August 23, 1927.

1. Birmingham, Alabama. — Willie Peterson, a Negro war veteran, was arrested and charged with the murder of a white woman on the accusation of her sister, who had already "identified" two other Negroes previously; these were found to have been in Boston at the time of the murder. Yet on this woman's testimony alone, and against all the facts that clearly indicate the frame-up, Peterson has been condemned to death.

2. Norfolk, Virginia. — Charged with "criminal assault" on a white woman twice his age and size, Russell Gordon, *aged thirteen*, was arrested and held in jail several months until by mass protest and by showing up the thread bareness of the accusation (it was so dark at the time that the woman said she could not see the face of her assailant) lawyers of the International Labour Defence were able to bring about a dismissal of the case. Two points came to light — (1) that the woman chose this as a pretext to get her husband to change their home, and (2) that Russell Gordon was *unlawfully* charged and held, no person of thirteen being indictable of rape according to Virginia State Law.

3. Governor Blackwood of South Carolina thought an equivocation of words would save the State of South Carolina, famous for lynchings, actual and legal, from the blot of one more lynching. So he used the word "murder," denying that Norris Bendy, Negro, had been "lynched" by the gang of at least four men who broke into Clinton jail, dragged him out, beat and strangled him. Bendy was charged with having struck a white man. When his body was found in a churchyard near by, Sheriff Columbus Owens said he could not trace the lynchers "because they travelled in an automobile."

4. Alexander Lawrence escaped to Boston from a mob near Birmingham, Alabama, and brought the news that his mother had been lynched by a mob and their house burnt down. She had reprimanded white children for throwing dirt and stones at her. That was enough for the lynching. When Lawrence reported this to the county police the same mob re-formed and came for him.

For about two years the reign of terror in the "deep South" has stupefyingly increased. "Niggers have got to be kept in their place," which means exactly: that they are not to dare to ask for their wages, not to get together in any way with the white workers whose conditions are almost as miserable as their own. In some Southern State counties there has now been passed a measure which forbids any gathering of people, white, black or combined, to formulate any demands for better conditions, unemployment relief, protests against the ploughing under of the cotton crops (so as to keep up the price for the exploiting masters, a recent order which has brought even further ruin to the "poor white" and Negro croppers), etc. It is the association of black and white labourers, such as in share-croppers' unions, that the planters and authorities so much fear. A terrorisation of the Negroes ensues. And the favourite charge, the charge always brought whenever possible, is that of raping a white woman. For a Negro to speak even to a white woman is considered an insult, one that may be turned into an indictable offence. This is an old, old "crime," but it is being played up now as never before. If a white is found murdered the blame is put on some Negro. No proof? Proof is quite unnecessary.

5. Tuscaloosa, Alabama. — Vaudine Maddox, a white girl, was found murdered in a ravine. A white man who owed money to Dan Pippen, a Negro boy who had worked for him, went and said he had seen Pippen near the scene of the crime. That was sufficient. Pippen was arrested, and A. Harden and Elmore Clark, two other Negro boys, as well, for the simple reason that they were friends of his — not more. When Pippen's father and a fifth Negro testified that the son had been working with them all that day they too were arrested, the father for "obstructing the law," the other for no given reason. All were put in jail, Dan Pippen charged with murder and Harden as accessory to the crime. Some of the local personalities, frantically Negro-hating as they are, pointed out that it was more likely that Vaudine Maddox had been killed by a friend or an acquaintance, an "*equal*," a white therefore; they came to this deduction because it was shown that she had stood or sat chatting to someone on a log near the ravine,

and the pail of flour she was carrying was found standing by the log, undisturbed. Local attorneys were appointed to "defend" the accused, as prejudiced and determined terrorists of the Negro population as any outright lynchers, and who of course could be depended upon to get them convicted. The International Labour Defence[1] took up the case, although the boy's parents were later driven into making a statement repudiating the three lawyers it sent, and were made to read this statement in court, after beatings and threats. The fear of the southerners grows with every new exposure of frame-ups, and Irving Schwab, Alan Taub of New York, and F.B. Irwin of Birmingham, attorneys asked for by the accused and their parents, were actually denied access to the prisoners, although they showed the retainers signed by Pippen and by the other defendants' nearest of kin. More, they were threatened with lynching and taken out of the town. White authorities and those of the State College of Tuscaloosa (the latter anyway supposedly "cultured" people far removed from the "lower classes" on whom the blame for all race hatred and lynchings is always put) had got busy with the coloured ministry and made them sign a petition: "We feel that the fair-mindedness and Christian integrity of the citizens of this community will see to it that justice is given in these cases, and our conviction is that their defence should be left in the hands of competent lawyers." (Lawyers from the North, or even from other States, are called "agitators" in Alabama, and of course the "competent lawyers" signifies those appointed by the judge.) Most of the ministers and Negro population refused to sign. *The very next day Dan Pippen, A. T. Harden and Elmore Clark were taken out of the car in which deputy-sheriffs were driving them from Tuscaloosa to Birmingham Jail "for safer keeping," and lynched.* The bodies of Pippen and Harden were found riddled with bullets; Clark, or his body, had disappeared.[2]

As I write this a letter comes direct from the International

---

1   The International Labour Defence was the legal defence organization of the US Communist Party. In 1929 the ILD made the struggle for black rights its main priority. The Scottsboro campaign was key to the CP becoming a political force in Harlem, largely thanks to ILD involvement in the case.

2   [Author's note: Deputy-sheriffs are just anyone named such by a sheriff on the spot. There can be any number and they are vested with all legal powers to arrest, shoot, kill.

Labour Defence organiser in Birmingham, Alabama. Here it is:

Birmingham, August 14, 1933.

On June 16th these three Negroes were framed for the attack and murder of a white woman. They asked the I.L.D. to defend them. We sent in our representatives to Tuscaloosa, a distance of 60 miles from Birmingham and the seat of the state university. We procured the written request from the defendants and their relatives for us to defend them. On August 2nd, date of trial was set. Irving Schwab, Allen Taub (of N.Y.) and F.B. Irwin of Birmingham, three I.L.D. attorneys, went in to defend them. In the meantime the ruling class had worked up a sentiment against the I.L.D., had beaten the prisoners, threatened them with murder if they did not repudiate the I.L.D., and mobs had beaten the parents and made similar threats against them. Negro ministers were threatened and forced to issue a statement declaring that they did not want the I.L.D. in the case.

When our attorneys appeared on the 2nd they made a motion for continuance, which was granted. Then the question came up as to who represented the defendants. After placing the defendants and relatives on the stand (of course swearing against us *under duress* after the beating and lynch threats) the court ruled that we were out. Nevertheless we began an organized campaign to remain in the case and were gaining the sympathy of the masses.

I must relate the incident at the time of the trial. While the question of attorneys was being argued the judge received a telegram from W.L. Patterson (national secretary of the I.L.D. in New York) demanding the release of the framed-up defendants and the dismissal of the lynch attorneys, the ones appointed by the court. This so irritated the

Lynching mobs are often led by sheriffs and their deputies, who have nothing to fear from higher authorities, as these themselves, by their lack of action in bringing lynchers to justice and by their total indifference to the murder of Negroes, invariably prove themselves at one with the lynchers.]

judge that he read the telegram to the open court, and then in a frenzy said, "I will kill that son of a bitch if I have to go to New York." Two officers drew guns on Schwab and Taub and said, "We would like to begin with these two sons of bitches."[1] A short time later when they started to leave the court-room someone asked for an escort as their lives were in danger. A mob of four or five thousand had gathered and threatened to lynch the attorneys. They were brought to Birmingham under National Guard and escorted out of the city by police and told never to return. Incidentally the train was stopped on the way here, and uncoupled by another mob. After this incident when they saw the I.L.D. was still putting up a fight a lynch mob was prepared and the boys killed.

This whole attack is meant to drive the I.L.D. out of the South, and prepare to lynch the Scottsboro boys and the (Tallapoosa) share-croppers. If we cannot successfully fight this attack we will be given more severe ones. We are mobilizing all our forces, issuing thousands of leaflets, holding meetings, etc.

The blame for this lynching rests of course on the state authorities. Knowing perfectly well that mobs were forming to break into Tuscaloosa jail they directed sheriffs to transfer the prisoners to the large city of Birmingham. This was done without any kind of precaution (such as protection by State troops). Three deputy-sheriffs had the three Negroes handcuffed together in the back of a light car. They tried to excuse themselves later by saying they had taken a side-road to avoid the main road, which they thought might have been watched. But along this side-road all the same came two cars containing some twelve masked men with guns and pistols. The sheriffs were held up, and the prisoners taken away from them. The sheriffs told the *Birmingham News* that it was quite a novel experience. "Deputy Huff laughingly accused his companion, deputy Holeman, of swallowing 'a whole chew of my tobacco,' when the band of men surrounded the car."

---

1 [Author's note: Present in the Tuscaloosa court was William Brandon, formerly governor of Alabama.]

Deputy Holeman then just said that he "didn't get sick." "Deputy Pate, who was driving the car, said 'those Negroes didn't say a word from the time we left the county jail until the men took them from us. They certainly were quiet.'"

Such are the comments of the officers of the law, the accessories to lynchings. *After these lynchings the same sheriffs shot and killed a Negro.* A white Southern paper, the *Birmingham Post*, merely remarks: "Only one incident stirred the quiet of Tuscaloosa following the lynchings. Yesterday (the day the prisoners had been handed over by them) deputies Pate and Holeman shot to death a Negro who resisted arrest on a charge of disturbing the peace. The Negro came at them with a club, the deputies said. There was no connection between this shooting and the lynchings, the officers pointed out." What is the inevitable conclusion? That the sheriffs were glad to show the lynchers that they were not in the very least behindhand in their own killing of Negroes.

The judge's comment is equally illuminating: "Tuscaloosa county was willing to see the Negroes tried, and wanted to give them a fair trial, but some were not willing to have us go through another Scottsboro case." No more Scottsboros! *In the sense of the "quickest way out," a lynching.*[1]

The white terrorists, authorities, judges, sheriffs, ruling-class and press are often aided by such reactionary institutions and organisations as Negro colleges, universities and the National Association for the Advancement of Coloured People. A flaming example of the former was when the coloured institute of Tuskegee, in Alabama, turned over to the police two mortally wounded Negro share-croppers from Tallapoosa (Dec. 20, 1932), who had resisted eviction and had sought refuge with people of their own race. These "Uncle Tom Negroes," as they are called (the old-style, "white man's nigger" type) continue with monstrous hypocrisy to make assertions as to the probity of Southern courts. For instance, although they (and everyone else) know that a Negro is the innocent victim of that particular frame-up and has received the death penalty, they advocate lawyers who will urge

---

1 [Author's note: Since this was written the I.L.D. has made investigations which definitely show that the lynching mob was an invention of the sheriffs, who themselves shot the three prisoners, killing two of them.]

him to plead *guilty*, pretending that Southern justice may then extend the clemency of a life-term. (This is precisely what the N.A.A.C.P. attorney urged the boys to do at the initial trial in Scottsboro.) I have myself had to listen to a partisan of this organisation actually assert that had the Scottsboro boys pleaded guilty they might have got life terms, "and then they might have been set free, oh, some time later."[1] It is this odious and vicious treachery of the black bourgeoisie in America (as elsewhere), hand in glove with the lynchers and oppressors of black people, that makes the fight for their liberation doubly long, and bitter. It has been shown how world-protest and exposure of the Scottsboro trial scandal has won appeals and re-trials—partial victories only so far, but of vital importance not only to the innocent boys themselves but to the future of the whole Negro race in U.S. The N.A.A.C.P. is against mass pressure and protest; it does not believe in the solidarity of black and white workers and other militant sympathisers.

Recorded Lynchings For The First Six Months Of 1933

1. Harry Ross, shot and killed Jan. 3 by three white men, outside of Memphis, Tennessee. They reported they were taking him to the city to lay charges of "having made improper proposals to a white woman" against him, when he "tried to escape" from their moving car.

2. Fell Jenkin, twenty, was beaten to death by three white farmers at Aycock, Louisiana, Jan. 11. They said he had been trespassing on the property of one of them.

3, 4, 5. Three members of a family of fishermen were hacked to death on Tavernier Island, one of the Florida Keys, Jan. 19 by an invading gang of white men. All further information, including the names of the victims, was suppressed by the authorities.

---

1   [Author's note: In the case of Willie Peterson (see previously) the special prosecutor was Roderick Beddow, the same attorney who received $1,000 from the N.A.A.C.P. out of funds collected by them supposedly to defend the Scottsboro boys.]

6. Robert Richardson was shot to death in Baton Rouge, Louisiana, Feb. 2, while "attempting to escape" from a gang of twenty-five, headed by a deputy sheriff, which invaded his house on a report, given out later, that he had "annoyed a white woman."

7. Nelson Nash, twenty-four, hanged from a tree by a gang of men at Ringgold, Louisiana, Feb. 19.

8. George Jeter, died Feb. 18 from a beating administered by three white men, who later said he had "stolen their whiskey."

9. Levon Carlock, nineteen, beaten, tortured and shot to death by six policemen "out on a lark" in Memphis, Feb. 25. Police called on a white prostitute to say Carlock had "raped" her, at a time when he was sitting by his wife's sick-bed.

10. John Williams, lynched during the first week of May by a mob of seventy-five led by a sheriff. It was charged he had stolen a hog.

11. Will Kinsey, twenty-five, lynched May 12 by a mob of forty, following a dispute with his landlord in which his brother and the landlord were both killed. Kinsey, wounded by the landlord, was taken by a mob from a physician's office.

12, 13. Jerome Boyett and Harvey Winchester, both white, held on murder charges, were taken out of Huntsville, Tennessee, jail, and lynched by a mob of armed men.

(Taken from the International Labour Defence SCOTTSBORO weekly Press Releases, obtainable by writing to the Sec. International Labour Defence, Room 430, 80 East 11th St., New York City.)

This list, says the I.L.D., lays no claim to being complete, it is only the list of *lynchings reported publicly*. It does not take into account the growing number of police killings of Negroes that are increasing as substitutes for actual mob lynchings, which latter are more difficult to hide. The consolidating unity of white and black workers has forced police, sheriffs and other authorities to seek such methods of Negro terrorisation as will not attract such wide attention as formal lynchings which rouse more and more militant protests from workers of both races. Terror thrives best in the dark; it cannot stand mass exposure. Nor are any legal lynchings included in this list.

Here, however, from a later I.L.D. Scottsboro Release, is a list of murders *not counted* in the previous number of deaths:

List Of Negroes Murdered From January To July 1933

1. Charley Johnson, twenty, shot and killed last January by T.E. Christy for "disturbing a church service" at Shreveport, Louisiana.

2, 3, 4. Three Negroes were killed at Hazard, Kentucky, and a fourth wounded, when they refused to push a stalled car occupied by two white men and a white woman into town to a garage.

5. Emmett Gouche was shot and killed in the home of Lee Hill, white, with Hill's gun. Hill said Gouche "shot himself," though investigation showed the wound could not have been self-inflicted. Montezuma, Georgia.

6, 7, 8. Willie Washington, Tom Green, Emma Green, shot and killed by Harry Kinney and Robert Tilsey, both white, at Osceola, Arkansas, Jan. 19 when Washington failed to furnish them with a match they demanded. Mr. and Mrs. Green were murdered in an effort to destroy all witnesses.

9. Policeman A.J. Breedon shot and killed Harry Johnson, in Lumberton, North Carolina, Jan. 24, when he saw him coming out of a white man's yard.

10. William Heyward, shot and killed at Waterboro, South Carolina, by Louise Welch, white, when he got into an argument

with her brother while helping her to pull her car out of the mud.

11. Homer D. Mayfield, shot and killed by two Los Angeles policemen who said he tried to run away from them.

12. Richard Wells, murdered by Los Angeles police when a white man asked them to "catch him." It was later offered as an excuse that he had robbed a petrol station, but employees failed to identify him at the inquest.

13. Peter Miller, found murdered Feb. 9, after he had been threatened with death by the police for his working-class activities.

14. Jerry Miles, shot to death Feb. 28 by policeman A. Meadows, of Birmingham, Alabama, who said Miles "resisted questioning."

15. An unidentified Negro shot and killed by officers McCarthy and Phelps, March 2, because they saw him "climbing over a fence."

16. Harry Curtis, shot and killed by Douglas Weaver, a private citizen of Collinsville, Alabama, because he "resisted questioning," March 5.

17. Silas Drewery, 18-year-old Negro hotel porter in Birmingham, fatally shot by a policeman when he was unable to supply him with liquor demanded by the cop, March 9.

18. Cleve Horton, shot and killed by patrol-man Roy Eddleman in the washroom of a restaurant, in Atlanta, Georgia, March 24.

19. Reuben Ware, shot and killed near High Point, North Carolina, March 27, by John Harris, after the white man was accused of attempting to steal a cow from Ware's stepmother.

20. Joe Porter, shot to death in jail by two white men for whom

the door was left open by officials, April 24, Brinkley, Arkansas.

21. Jesse Davis, shot and killed on the streets of Birmingham, April 24, by police captain Eddie Lyons, who explained that Davis "tried to hold him up."

22. Jack Sutton, killed by deputy-sheriff Ira Suffit, at Sikeston, Missouri. Suffit said Sutton resisted arrest when picked up "on suspicion."

23. Gilbert Corbin, shot in the back of the head and killed by police detectives Bradley and Hitselberger of Baltimore, Maryland, in "self-defence."

24. Ben Singleton, sixteen, shot and killed by Charles Hintz, who said Singleton sold him a red bird which did not sing. New Orleans, Louisiana.

25. Lloyd Pinion, shot and killed May 1 in New Orleans police station after being arrested for being in the street early in the morning.

26, 27, 28. Louis, Joseph and Adam Cormier shot to death by sheriff Conner and deputy-sheriff Cole, of Welsh, Louisiana, when they resisted evictions from their farm, May 3.

29. John Davis, shot in the back and killed by special officer Jess Saunders, who said Davis "reached in his pocket for a gun." There was no gun in his pocket. May 7, Coalemee, North Carolina.

30. Percy Jones, shot in the back by policeman W. Bank, Washington, while driving a car, when he failed to halt on command, May 19.

31. Julius Daniels, shot to death by an unidentified white man when he retorted to abusive language. Buffalo, New York, May 24.

32. Fred Roller, suspected of stealing a car, shot and killed with a sawed-off shot-gun by detective Sima, Cleveland, Ohio.

33. Mrs. Scott, beaten to death with a hoe and a club in the presence of her two young sons, by Con Gamble, white landowner, when she threatened to move unless Gamble paid her wages. June 11, Harris, Louisiana.

34. Albert Dawson, shot in the back of the head and killed, in Wickliffe, Ohio, by policeman Harry Truex, who said Dawson, who was fifteen, had stolen a water-melon from a truck.

That is a six months' record—an under-estimate.

Not one of these crimes, by mob or individual, has been punished. On the occasions where an inquiry has followed, this move has been undertaken only to whitewash the authorities in an attempt at lessening the indignation of black and white workers, and to discourage the development of mass protests.

The I.L.D. report continues: "This survey is assumed to cover a fraction of one percent of the total number of such murders by police officers or by agents of the white ruling class who act with the endorsement and at the direction of the authorities. This endorsement is proved by the inevitable justification (of the whites) which ends every so-called investigation."

An exception to this rule is given now (I have had to search hard to find an exception), because of its bearing on the Scottsboro case in the sense of "one law for the white and one for the black." Keeping in mind the fact that the Scottsboro boys were arrested and condemned for a "crime" they did not commit and which was repudiated later by one of the alleged victims, and that they have been in the death cells for two and a half years, at times in most active danger of actual lynching, the sentence on the white murderer of a Negro must be sharply contrasted:

Asheville, North Carolina. July 27. Shouting vociferously in an open court room here recently that he would not try a white man for first degree murder, "regardless of how he killed a nigger," the District Attorney of this city succeeded in having a light two-year sentence passed on a white cold-blooded murderer of a young coloured woman. The outrageous court-room drama was the sequel to the murder of Mrs. Katherine Henry by a disreputable white man, Doff Garren. Reports state she was shot by him at a local street intersection "for using profane language." Garren was hailed into court, where he pleaded guilty of the murder charge. His trial lasted less than half an hour, during which the district attorney swayed Judge and jurors to heinous justice by his irascible prosecution. Garren received a two to three year sentence in the state penitentiary at Raleigh. (*Pittsburgh Courier*.)

It is monstrous to think that rape, even when actual, should be punishable by death. What is the opinion of many doctors? That it is extremely difficult to rape an unwilling person. The gravity of the sentence depends on the age of the "victim." Otherwise what is the meaning of the legal term "age of consent"? An offence, but a crime punishable by death … After all the evidence so overpoweringly in favour of the Scottsboro boys at the trial, brought to light even more at the Decatur re-trial, the evidence of the character of the two girls, the confession of one of these, Ruby Bates, that she had perjured herself in the Scottsboro court house at the first trial, there is no-one who believes any longer in the southern states, where they have been so determined to prove it, in the guilt of the boys. But that is not the point; the point is that Alabama "justice" will not relinquish any Negro victim; its "white supremacy" at all costs must be maintained.

Arrest Of The Nine Boys

Here then is the story of the Scottsboro case, the main facts of which, at least, are known to the world at large. On March 25, 1931, black and white hoboes were "riding the rails," hidden up and down the length of a freight train going from Chattanooga to Memphis, Tennessee. No money, no fares, setting out to look for work. Travelling in this manner is a frequent occurrence in

America. But such is the race hatred that white tramps even will object to the presence of Negro hoboes in the same wagon. Not for nothing has the white ruling class for decades been teaching the "poor white" that he can always look down on the Negro worker, no matter how wretched his own economic condition may be. So the white boys started a row and tried to throw the "niggers" off. The Negroes resisted them, and the whites did not get the best of it. All but one jumped off and telephoned the station-master at Stephenson to arrest the niggers who'd dared to fight with them. The train had already gone through this station, so was stopped at Paint Rock. Here sheriffs and excited citizens took nine Negro boys and three white boys out of separate parts of the train. At first all were charged with vagrancy and told to get out of that county as quick as possible. And then suddenly, while all were being searched, two of the white boys were discovered to be girls in men's overalls. So the sheriff got an idea; it wasn't possible for Negroes and white girls to be on the same train, in the same car maybe, without the question of rape coming in. The boys protested they had not even seen any girls; some of them had seen a fight, that was all. The girls denied that the boys had touched them. But some of the crowd were for an immediate lynching; authorities assured them the "niggers" would be properly dealt with and should not escape "justice." All were promptly locked up, the Negroes to be brutally beaten, the girls to be put through the third degree and forced into saying they had been raped. Both girls were known to be prostitutes; Victoria Price had a prison record, and impressed on Ruby Bates the utter necessity, now, of falling in with the authorities' views, so that they might themselves escape the law's punishment. The trial date was first of all fixed for April 1, but postponed till April 6, a fair-day in Scottsboro, one which would assure the largest crowd possible and enable the mob to witness the condemnation of what the local papers called "the Negro fiends."

Scottsboro is described as a sleepy little town of some ten thousand inhabitants in the northern part of Alabama, but on the trial day the presence of the military who had been called in to make a show of quelling the lynch spirit made it look like an armed camp. The authorities had deemed it necessary to send 118 soldiers to bring the nine boys into the town from Gadsden jail, where they had been held since arrest. Armed soldiers were on guard inside and outside the court house, to which only persons holding special permits were allowed entry after having been searched. Already by eight o'clock thousands had gathered from all over the neighbourhood, and by ten o'clock the crowd was estimated at ten thousand. The lynch spirit had been whipped up to such a point by the authorities that statements were going around saying that the "horrible black brutes had chewed off one of the girl's breasts." The doctor's evidence on his examination of the girls immediately they were taken from the train, showing they were unscathed, and which was public knowledge, meant nothing to the people of Scottsboro. The local newspapers tried to whitewash the presence of the agitated mob by saying that the crowd was "curious, not furious," and maintained it had gathered out of mere curiosity. The trial began on the 6th and was all over on the 9th of April—three days to convict and sentence to death nine Negro boys all under twenty years old, two of them thirteen and fourteen respectively. It is not difficult to see that the jury had made up their minds long before hearing any evidence, even before coming into court—verdicts on Negroes are automatic, it is always: guilty. There were no workers on this jury, nor white nor black. It was composed of local business men and neighbouring well-to-do farmers. Just before the proceedings began, Wembley, the legal adviser to the Scottsboro Electric Company, which controls the town, had walked through the mob and told them that "everything would be alright in a few days," and that his company had enough power to "burn up the niggers."

In court, the boys— with only a lawyer to represent them who had not, on his own statement, studied nor prepared the case (Stephen Roddy, member of the Ku Klux Klan, who told them to plead guilty), and another appointed by the court itself (Milo Moody), a member of the Scottsboro bar—without having been allowed to communicate with parents, relatives or friends (none of whom even knew, at this time, what had happened to them), yet maintained their innocence and told a straight story: they had not even seen any white girls on the train, they were riding the rails, some of them alone and in different cars, all had left home to go and look for work. During the proceedings the following evidence was heard:

Position Of The Boys On The Train

Willie Roberson, aged seventeen, hidden in one of the first empty box cars, where he stayed by himself, not seeing any of the white boys, or the girls who accused him.

Clarence Norris and Charlie Weems, aged nineteen and twenty respectively, both workers from Atlanta, who had got into a car together towards the end of the forty-nine trucks that made up the train.

Olin Montgomery, aged fourteen, who had got into an oil tanker by himself, going to Memphis to consult a free clinic for his bad eyes.

Ozie Powell, aged fourteen, also travelling alone in an empty freight car.

Roy and *Andy Wright*, brothers, thirteen and eighteen respectively, with *Haywood Patterson*, sixteen, and *Eugene Williams*, fourteen, childhood friends, all from Chattanooga, going to look for work on the river boats in Memphis.

Andy Wright testified that he had not seen any of the other defendants, save those he travelled with, or any white girls, until taken off the train at Paint Rock. He had seen a fight of some kind between white and Negro boys in another car and five Negro boys jump off; he had heard a white boy hollering and had gone to see what was the matter, and had prevented him from jumping off as the train was going fast. The testimony of all the boys was to the effect that some saw a fight and others did not, but that none of them saw or even knew of the presence of white girls on the train.

Testimony Of The Two Girls

Victoria Price, who was the main state witness and the chief plaintiff of the two because of the visible confusion and unwillingness of Ruby Bates in giving false evidence, stated that both of them had left their home in Huntsville together because there was no work for them in the cotton mills. They had hoboed their way to Chattanooga, but there had been no work there either, so they were coming back to Huntsville in the same manner the next day, March 25. They had been wearing men's overalls because it was easier to travel that way. First they had climbed into an oil tanker and then into a gravel car in which were seven white boys. They hadn't spoken to any of these. Then twelve Negroes had climbed into this from other cars and had begun to fight the white boys, "telling them we was their women," and holding them off with knives. (Anyone who knows anything about the terrorisation of Negroes throughout the South, and the whole of America for that matter, will see how unlikely it must be for any Negro to go deliberately and provoke a white man. His daily and constant preoccupation is to steer as clear of white people as possible.) Victoria Price continued, that having thrown the white boys off, twelve Negroes then proceeded to rape her and Ruby Bates (six each), that three of Ruby's customers had jumped off the train before it was stopped. Other evidence showed that Orvil Gilley had remained on it, the local papers claiming he had been forced to remain on it out of the viciousness of the Negroes, that he should witness the assault. The distance covered by the fast-moving train while these twelve attacks were alleged to have been going on was thirty-eight miles. The last boy, said Victoria Price, was in process of assaulting her when the train was stopped. She was positive that all nine of the Negroes in court had had sexual intercourse with her and Ruby. They had held knives at their throats, some of the boys had held her and her companion down while others ravished them; they had shot off guns five times. (No guns or knives were found on any of the defendants, save a small pocket knife on Eugene Williams.) She pointed out those who ravished her; she had to designate the attackers of Ruby Bates as well, for the latter could not and did not identify them.

Is it not astounding that there were no signs of struggle, no dis-arranged clothing, no hysteria on the girls' part, no guns or knives found when all this had supposedly been going on over that short distance of thirty-eight miles? And that Gilley was not bursting with indignation and desire to testify about his having been forced to witness it all? And that, for the first time in legal proce-dure, the victims of rape should have been locked up in the same jail as their attackers for ten days pending trial, whereas their homes were only a few miles away? And that if the Negroes had had any reason whatever to fear arrest they should not have jumped off the train? But most significant in this frame-up is the fact that on their arrest and questioning by the sheriffs both girls brought no charge whatsoever against any Negroes, and indeed refused to agree to the suggestion made to them that they had been attacked. This point, needless to say, was never brought up at the trial. The girls were not individuals with alleged wrongs, but had been transformed into part of the lynch machinery which "keeps niggers in their place" by such frame-ups, so that other "niggers" shall not dare to ask for their rights.

Evidence given by the two doctors who had examined the girls immediately they had been taken from the train should have been sufficient to clear the prisoners entirely. Doctor Bridges' tes-timony was that both girls had had sexual intercourse, he could not say exactly when. Its evidence suggested that it was several hours previous to his examination, perhaps as much as twenty hours or so. He had seen them as soon as the train was stopped (within a few moments, consequently, of the alleged rape). There were no lacerations or signs of force, etc. (such as might be expected if the rape story were true). They were not in the least hysterical, though they were extremely hysterical and crying when he saw them next day, after a night in jail. He had also examined Willie Roberson, who was suffering so acutely from a venereal disease that physical relationship would hardly have been possible.

(After later investigations made by the International Labour

Defence lawyers it was shown that the girls had both spent the previous night with two white boys in the "Chattanooga jungle," in the woods, and that it was nowise strange that Mrs. Callie Broochie (name of the woman with whom Victoria Price said they had stayed the night in Chattanooga) could not be traced, as no such person existed; "Callie Broochie" being the name of a character in a popular magazine and used by Victoria Price on the spur of the moment.)

There were no witnesses called for the defendants, nor did the prosecution put any of the white boys who had been on the train in the witness box, although all of these were under lock and key at the time of the trial, nor was Orvil Gilley, stated to have been an eye-witness, allowed to testify freely. The doctor's evidence was set aside, the prisoners had not been allowed to get into touch with parents or seek aid. The prosecution was content with the words it had put itself, under threat, into the mouth of a lying prostitute who proved herself smart enough in sensing what was wanted of her at the trial to earn public commendation as a good witness from the judge. Uncertain and confused Ruby Bates, who by the discrepancies of her evidence might have given the whole show away, was quickly silenced, while Victoria answered for her. So it was on the statements of this girl alone, that nine Negro boys and children, whose ages ranged from 13 to 20, were convicted and eight of them given the death penalty, the jury disagreeing over Roy Wright's case.

It took the jury less than two hours to return their verdict on the first accused, Clarence Norris and Charlie Weems. Spectators in court and mob outside as soon as this was known broke into frantic applause. The next day, Haywood Patterson was tried alone. After three hours the jury found him guilty. In the third case five of the remaining boys were tried: Olin Montgomery, Andy Wright, Eugene Williams, Willie Roberson, Ozie Powell. In the case of Roy Wright, aged thirteen, the jury did not agree, eleven being for death penalty, one for life imprisonment. This was an attempt at putting up some semblance of "fairness" in the sentencing of these Negro children. Several of the trial officials said later that he was "the worst of the lot." As a sop to outside public opinion the judge declared a mis-trial in this case; Roy Wright was sent to prison with the other boys, to await a further ordeal. The date set for the execution was July 10 the very first day possible after conviction, the law requiring ninety days interim for the filing of an appeal. The boys were then taken to Birmingham jail so that the mob in Scottsboro might not have the chance, even after the announcement of the verdicts, of trying to rob the State of its victims by an actual lynching.

Some Points In The Appeal

Up to the trial the victimisation of these innocent boys had been quite a local matter only, seemingly destined to increase the number of barely reported cases, amongst so many others, of death sentences passed on framed-up Negroes. But an investigator of the International Labour Defence had read of it — just the few lines there were — in a local paper, and had got in touch with the head office in New York. The I.L.D. took up the case immediately, one of its lawyers, Alan Taub, going to see the boys the day after the trial, on April 10. Notice of appeal was directly made, and all the false evidence and illegal procedure sorted out and studied.

Some of the main points in the Appeal to the Supreme Court of Alabama are as follows:

Defendants were prevented from having and did not have a fair trial.

The denial of the motion for change of venue was a reversible error.

The court overrode and disregarded the fundamental legal rights of defendants.

Mob spirit and hysteria dominated the trial, terrorised judge, jury and counsel, and denied to the defendants "due process of law."

The verdict of the jury was not sustained by the great preponderance of the evidence, and the guilt of the defendants was not proved beyond a reasonable doubt.

Material evidence newly discovered, which the defendants could not have procured and presented at the trial, should move the Supreme Court to grant a new trial.

Exclusion of Negroes from the juries denied to the defendants "equal protection of the law."

The circuit court of Jackson county (Scottsboro) had no jurisdiction to try and sentence the defendant Eugene Williams, a juvenile alleged delinquent.

Other points presented were that:

All of the defendants were without funds with which to pay for legal advice. They had not been allowed to communicate with parents or friends. A Chattanooga attorney, Stephen Roddy, had appeared at the trial stating that he was not retained, had not studied the case, had merely come "to investigate" the situation and was unprepared to appear for the boys, adding finally that he thought it would be better for them if he stepped out of the case entirely. As a purely official gesture, the court had appointed a member of the Scottsboro bar, Milo Moody, to represent the defendants. The trial had begun and Roddy had filed a petition for change of venue, but this had been overruled by the judge.

Not one of the white boys on the train had been called as witness for the State prosecution, although all of them were in custody at the time of the trial, except Orvil Gilley, who had been in the truck with the girls. He had given no testimony corroborative of their story and so had been dismissed, remarks being circulated about him such as that he was soft-headed, and "well, everyone knows what sort of woman his mother is."

On page 6 of the *Brief for Appellants*:

> When the court opened on April 6, 1931, a tremendous crowd, estimated at about 5,000, had gathered around the court house and were kept from entrance by the military force. At the end of the first trial, State *v.* Norris and Weems, when the jury announced the verdict of guilty, the spectators in the court room burst into applause, which outburst was taken up by the throngs outside and climaxed by a brass band bursting into such strains as "There'll be a hot time in the old town tonight." No safeguards were placed around the jury, who were allowed to mingle freely with the hostile populace, to read the hostile newspapers, and to witness the demonstrations.

Investigations made by Hollace Ransdell, of the American Civil Liberties Union[1] (*Report on the Scottsboro Case*) in May, 1931, took her to see the girls in their home in Huntsville. She found that both were cotton mill workers getting an average of about $1.20 a day, that is, the days there was work for them, for in the increasing trade depression many of the mills were laying off employees every other week. Small wonder, as many other workers did to eke out this miserable wage, that the girls had taken to prostitution. Both had bad reputations, especially Victoria Price. The Huntsville sheriff knew her trade but didn't bother her, because, he said, "she was a prostitute who took men quiet-like." But neighbours emphasised her drunkenness, the "violent and vulgar language" and the frequent association with Negro boys. They said she boasted about having "Niggers' day;" they signed affidavits for the I.L.D. attorney giving her a thoroughly bad and undependable character. Yet these things and many more of the sort were ruled out as non-pertinent by the trial Judge— although Orvil Gilley's character was pronounced against because his mother had the same reputation. Ruby Bates and her family lived in the coloured section of Huntsville in a house that

---

1 The American Civil Liberties Union was founded in 1920 by Roger Baldwin as a public interest law firm to agitate, litigate and educate around civil rights issues. Its mandate is to ensure that the individual freedoms entrenched in the American Bill of Rights are protected.

Negroes had inhabited; the social worker who led Hollace Ransdell to see them complained of "that nigger smell you never get
rid of," while Mrs. Bates, who is described as a modest and rather
orderly woman, murmured about "having well cleaned and
washed out the place." Talking to both girls and their families
made it very clear to Hollace Ransdell that the experiences they
alleged to have been through had not struck them as particularly
out of the ordinary. The publicity had impressed them very
much; that was all.

Other points made by the defence lawyers in the appeal were
the need for military protection on the trial days, testified to by
Major Starnes and the county sheriff, which gave proof of the
danger of lynching the defendants had been in. The jury had not
been, as they should have been, questioned as to whether or no
they bore any race prejudice. (This technical point strikes one as
bitterly ironic.) The local press had increased public hostility by
violent and inflammatory articles. An example of this, some time
after the case had begun to attract public attention and protest:

> The ugly demands of threats (sic) from outsiders that
> Alabama reverse its jury decisions, and filthy insinuations
> that our people were murderers when they were sincerely
> being as fair as ever in the history of our country, is rather
> straining on our idea of fair play. It allows room for the
> growth of the thought that maybe after all "the shortest way
> out" in cases like these would have been the best method of
> disposing of them. (From an editorial in the *Jackson County
> Sentinel*.)

It need not be explained that "the shortest way out" signifies
lynching. The brazenness of the lies and the hypocrisy of the
Southern white ruling class is without parallel. One is particularly
struck by this. For instance, State prosecutor Knight says there is
no race prejudice in Alabama ... Press and legal authorities are
always claiming that a fair, unbiased trial has been held ... The
only thing that the Southerners fear, as State law gives them full
power over, practically every conceivable legal matter without
there being the possibility of recourse to the Federal Government

of the U.S., which in the case of Negroes is hardly less prejudiced, is—exposure.

Entry of The International Labour Defence into the Case

Exposure of the Behaviour of The National Association For The Advancement Of Coloured People

On the day after the trial, April 10, an International Labour Defence attorney, together with the Southern representative of the I.L.D., interviewed the boys in jail, and after being retained as legal defence, at once issued notice that he would appeal for a new trial, as the boys were clearly innocent. On May 5th motions for a new trial were heard and denied by Judge Hawkins. At this hearing George Chamlee (former attorney general of Tennessee), I.L.D. lawyer, was present to plead for the boys. Roddy was not present. May 20th was set as the day for further hearing. On that day Hawkins phoned George Chamlee informing him that the hearing was postponed and set for June 5th. On June 5th the I.L.D. attorneys, Chamlee and Brodsky, argued motions for a new trial. Roddy and Moody were also present at this hearing. The question of the right of defendants to select counsel was raised by the I.L.D. attorneys and by Claude Patterson, father of Haywood, who was present to demand sole recognition for the I.L.D. attorneys, but judge Hawkins refused to make any decision on the point at that time. (From *Some Facts on the Scottsboro Case*, by Milton Howard, Labour Research Association, Jan. 15, 1932.)

After having been definitely retained by Claude Patterson to defend his son, George Chamlee examined the court record and discovered that Judge Hawkins had neglected to sign the order denying a new trial to Heywood Patterson. This technical point was seized on by Chamlee to demand a reopening of the case; out of fairness to the other defendants the same to apply to their cases. Motions for new trial were then granted and investigations that had meanwhile been made concerning the character of the girls, and actual facts in the frame-up, were now entered into the record of the appeal.

International Labour Defence representatives had seen all the boys on April 10, the day after their conviction, and had received from them authorization as defence counsel. In the next few days the same was received from the boys' parents and relatives, first orally, then in writing, and on April 14 the announcement of an appeal was first made by these attorneys. Yet immediately after these documents had been signed, Roddy, and two ministers of Chattanooga, asserted they had repudiations of the I.L.D. from certain of the defendants. It was shown that two of the boys had been coerced into signing these when told that I.L.D. lawyers were not fitted to defend them. This was the first attempt of the National Association for the Advancement of Coloured People to bring as much disruption and confusion as possible into the case. These repudiations were, however, immediately revoked by the boys. Because of the constant repetition of the mis-statement that the I.L.D. was not the sole organisation in charge of the defence, the boys and their relatives had to issue as many as six statements from May 1931 to January 1932 making the position clear. These were published in the press. Yet, persistently for many months, the N.A.A.C.P. continued to issue press releases and make publicity to the effect that it had control of the defence, despite the fact that the statements of boys and relatives were filed with the Alabama Supreme Court. The N.A.A.C.P. secretary, Walter White,[1] and sundry organs of the Negro press, at that time almost daily attacked the I.L.D., and in exact opposition to all facts continued to maintain that the boys had repudiated I.L.D. lawyers and were being defended by those of its own choosing. Thousands of dollars were meanwhile being collected by it for the defence on the basis of these statements. A very large retainer was paid to Clarence Darrow[2] (whom the I.L.D. had invited to

1 Walter White (1893–1955), author and chief executive of the NAACP from 1929–1955. Contributed articles to *Harper's*, *The Nation*, *The Crisis* and other magazines.
2 Clarence Darrow (1857–1938), American lawyer who practiced in Chicago and who, from his 1894 defence of Eugene V. Debs (the American socialist leader and president of the American Railway Union) on charges brought in connection with the Pullman strike, became known as a defender of the underdog.

help them immediately after the convictions but who had declined on grounds of advanced age). Darrow, "engaged" by the N.A.A.C.P., "retired" at the end of 1931 from the case, which, as the N.A.A.C.P. itself had no connection with it, he could on no account have been considered to be in. Confusion upon confusion was added by Walter White's diverse statements to press and public that his organisation had been represented at the trial by the same Roddy who had said himself at that moment that he was neither engaged nor ready to undertake the defence. And the climax in the scandal of the N.A.A.C.P.'s manoeuvres and squandering of funds came when its Chattanooga branch telegraphed headquarters, "Roddy has betrayed us," in May, a month after the trial, but Roddy continued to be retained.

The boys had been sentenced to die on July 10. Protests were pouring in from all over the world. Workers' organisations had signed by tens of thousands. The first mass manifestations to take place in Europe were outside the American consulate in Berlin; the militancy and anger of the German workers was supreme. Soon there were demonstrations in front of the American consulates in other countries; the legations were wiring to America for orders as to what attitude to take as these manifestations had great effect. Einstein, Thomas Mann, Wells, Shaw, Dreiser, Gorki[1] and thousands of other celebrated and lesser known intellectuals had protested. In America the I.L.D. called for the utmost co-operation in a Scottsboro United Front. It roused the entire country by countless meetings, gatherings and speeches showing up this attempt at legal lynching, Negro and white churches, clubs, societies, business concerns, etc., individuals of every shade of political opinion gave their support. But the N.A.A.C.P. ignored all invitations of co-operation while all the time pro-

---

1   Albert Einstein (1879-1955) Nobel-prize winning physicist known for the theory of relativity and for linking the practice of science with social responsibility; Thomas Mann (1875-1955) German novelist, known for works such as *Death in Venice, Buddenbrooks*, and *The Magic Mountain*; H.G. Wells (1866-1946) English novelist, journalist, historian, known for science fiction works such as *The Time Machine* (1895) and *The War of the Worlds* (1898); George Bernard Shaw (1856-1950) Irish playwright, socialist, supporter of women's rights, known for such works as *Major Barbara, Pygmalion*, and *Arms and the Man*; Theodore Dreiser (1871-1945) American writer, known for naturalist novels like *Sister Carrie*; Maxim Gorki (1868-1936) Russian playwright and fiction writer whose works represented the working classes.

claiming its desire for unity! This "unity" it demanded in the same breath as it denounced the I.L.D. on the allegation that the latter's only interest in the case was to make Communist propaganda!!

The I.L.D. *is a non-partisan organisation* which defends the cases of black and white workers alike; yet its slogan of "Legal Defence supported by Mass Protest" was distorted into "No Legal Defence—only Mass Action." A "red scare." The boys' parents were not spared this. They were told that the I.L.D. (solely identified with Communists) would lose the boys their lives. The legal capacity of the defending lawyers was also attacked by Walter White, although recognised from the start by Alabama courts. The public was also told that the I.L.D. were terrorists sending threats of death to the governor of Alabama, to the judge, etc. These, and the countless cables and messages from all over the world, were protests against the frame-up and legal mis-procedure in the lynch atmosphere of the courts, as much prevalent later at the Decatur re-trial as at Scottsboro. They are protests such as: "This organisation of ten thousand members demands that you stop this legal lynching and holds you responsible to stay the hands of the lynch mob." (Executive Committee, League of Struggle for Negro Rights.[1]) Yes, the "red scare" was what this disgrace to the Negro people, this insult to the Negro masses of America, the N.A.A.C.P., put forward as its own conception of United Front to Save the Scottsboro Boys.

Throughout that year and subsequently, pursuing its double-faced policy of trying to get the boys and their relatives to entrust the defence to its lawyers while completely ignoring the nation-wide demand for its collaboration, the N.A.A.C.P. actually refused to allow the Scottsboro parents to make appeals and to speak at its public meetings and in churches, etc., where it had influence. But the most vicious of its counter-moves to all the efforts made to gain public support is to be found in a statement by Walter White (published by several Negro papers) to the effect that *mothers were invented* at Scottsboro meetings: "When the sup-

---

[1] The League of Struggle for Negro Rights was created by the Communist Party in 1930 as part of its program on the Negro question. Langston Hughes was made the League's first president, and its central focus was lynching.

ply of mothers was inadequate to cover such meetings, substitutes were found" (Walter White, *Harper's*, Dec. 1931.)

The astoundingly hypocritical and treacherous bearing of the N.A.A.C.P. throughout the whole case, and up to the very present, when it is being called upon by the I.L.D., sole defence for two and a half years, to hand over all funds collected, which it has delayed again and again in doing, needs a word of explanation. It is a body financed largely by white "liberal" money; it is capable of raising large sums; it has branches all over America; it has existed since 1912; it is supposedly the representative body of the whole coloured race, pledged to its interests. Because of these very attributes and what it supposedly (but supposedly only) stands for, it could not afford to be out of the Scottsboro case, yet it has been sufficiently seen that it is virtually at one with the Southern lynch-courts by its assertions that the world-protests are only "a red scare," by its advocacy of letting the law take its course (lynch law), by its engaging of Stephen Roddy (lynch advocate), by its lies and frauds, insults and inventions against the actual defence. Here are just a few of the members on its executive committee or branches: Frank Murphy,[1] ex-mayor of Detroit, a party to police murders and attacks on the starving white and black workers outside Henry Ford's[2] factory in April 1931. Arthur Capper,[3] senator from Kansas, who made no sign of protest against the continuation of the Jim-crowing (segregation) of Negro Gold Star mothers[4] on their journey to French battlefields,

---

1 Unable to identify more specifically.

2 Henry Ford (1863-1947) was the American automotive engineer who designed cars and founded the Ford Motor Company (officially incorporated in 1903). Ford is equally famous for having introduced, in 1913, assembly-line production in his automobile factory. Ford also resisted early efforts at unionization, successfully in 1933, although by 1941 Ford Motor Company signed a deal with the United Auto Workers.

3 Arthur Capper (1865-1951) Born in Topeka, Kansas, Capper began his career as a newspaper reporter, then a publisher before entering politics; he became governor of the state of Kansas (1915-1919) and then US senator (1919-1949).

4 Founded in 1928, American Gold Star Mothers were incorporated in Washington, D.C. and granted a federal charter by Congress in 1929. Mothers who had lost sons in World War I created a mutual aid society that also sought to give care to veterans, and commemorate those who died in combat. Families who had lost a loved one in war hung gold stars in their windows, hence the name. In 1929-1930, Gold Star Mothers went on pilgrimages to the graves of US soldiers who had died overseas during World War I.

nor over the shooting down of black and white bonus-army marchers in Washington. Major J. Spingarn,[1] who advised the Negro soldiers to meekly accept the Jim-crowing in their regiments and forget about the lynchings of their people when the American imperialists needed their blood and bodies for the war, insulting them further with the lie that "full democracy" for the Negroes would come out of this very war. Walter White, promulgator of the monstrous lie the Scottsboro parents were impostors. Miss Nannie Burroughs,[2] educationist, who in print advised Eddie Tolan,[3] Negro, the world's quickest runner and American Olympic Games winner, 1932, to be content with his record and forget all about his "race-inferiority." The N.A.A.C.P. seeks to justify itself at the expense of the really militant and functioning organisations (such as the League of Struggle for Negro Rights and the I.L.D.), in the eyes of the whole Negro population, by which, however, it is becoming more and more openly discredited, as it becomes, itself, more morally and politically discredited.

After The Scottsboro Trial

Our legal procedure is a kind of map of our ruling-class mind. In the South, in a case where Negroes are involved, every white man is given the luxury of being part of the ruling class. You have to realise how physically and emotionally undernourished and starved the small tenant farmers, the small storekeepers, the jelly-beans and the drug-store loafers who make up the lynching mobs are, to understand the orgy of righteousness and of unconscious sex and cruelty impulses that a lynching lets loose. The feeling of superiority to the Negro is the only thing the poor whites of the

---

1   Joel Spingarn (1875-1939), a US literary critic who taught at Columbia University from 1899-1911. Spingarn, together with his brother Arthur and W.E.B. DuBois founded the NAACP in 1909, and he became chair of the board in 1914.

2   Nannie Burroughs (1879-1961), educator, civil rights advocate and religious leader. Burroughs founded the National Association of Wage Earners to draw attention to the plight of black women.

3   Eddie Tolan (19??-1967) was the first black man to win two Olympic gold medals. He broke Olympic records in both the 100 and 200 metre races at the 1932 Olympic Games in Los Angeles.

South have got. A lynching is a kind of carnival to them.

Reading the testimony of the Scottsboro case, you feel all that—the band outside the courthouse, the mob starved for joy and sex and power hanging around, passing from mouth to mouth all the juicy details of the raping. You feel that filthy prurient joy in the court room, the stench of it is in the badly typewritten transcript of the court procedure, in the senseless ritual, the half illiterate, poorly phrased speeches of the judge and the solicitor, the scared answers of the two tough girls, evidently schooled for days in their story, sometimes seeming to enjoy the exhibitionism of it. Evidently the court stenographer didn't take the trouble to put down what the colored boys said in their own words; what they said didn't matter, they were going to burn anyway.

Thus wrote John Dos Passos.[1] From this, from the investigations after the trial, from I.L.D. press releases you get a characterization of the Southern whites. There is not much in the whole case written down about the Negroes. The eight families of the boys are typical, most exactly so, of the oppressed black toilers on the Southern land. Ada Wright, Roy and Andy Wright's mother, is the granddaughter of a slave who in her time was sold for three hundred dollars. Black children were taken away from their parents then too, not by frame-ups and murders and the fact of being forced out by starvation at home to go hiking and bumming for work all over America in thousands as now, but by being sold on the auction block when who jumped highest under the lash fetched the most. The slave-driver has merely changed in name; nowadays he is any one of the bosses, landowners, authorities, sheriffs, etc. Some work is needed by the state—"niggers" are arrested "for loitering;" black man power, treated as that in African colonies, used the same way. "Niggers" have no rights. Andy and Roy's mother started working at twelve years old for a white family for her food and clothing, no wages. At seventeen

---

1   [Author's note: In *Contempo*.] John Dos Passos (1896–1970) was an important American writer, author of the protest-genre trilogy, *USA* (*The 49th Parallel* 1930, *1919* 1932, and *The Big Money* 1936) and founder of *New Masses* (1926).

she was earning seventy-five cents a week. Her husband was put in jail on a ninety days sentence, "forgotten" there for eight days longer by the warden. Andy began to earn a few cents as a rag-picker; then he had a lorry driving job. At the time her boys were arrested Ada Wright was cook to a white family. When they heard the news they gave her five dollars. "You must get a lawyer." But other whites said they would sooner throw money in the river because Negroes arrested for that could never have a chance anywhere in the South. But she managed to collect fifty dollars and put it in a lawyer's hand. Neighbours came and told her to "keep away from the Reds"—that was after the I.L.D. had taken up the case—but she saw "the Reds look like the only ones want to help us."

Such is the law's fiendishness that it was several months before the I.L.D. was able to force permission out of it for any of the parents to see their children, under death sentence. I heard one of the defence attorneys, Joseph Brodsky, describe in New York the long dragging journeys in rural trains that some of these parents had to make to be allowed finally to see and speak to their children in the presence of insulting, infuriated guards for exactly two minutes before being driven out of the jail again. An electric current was on top of that prison wall as extra prevention of escape. Inside there were bayonets, executions of other condemned Negroes the boys were made to witness, constant threats and violence. What did they do to little Roy Wright, aged thirteen? They offered him a "promise" of five hundred dollars and his freedom if he would turn state evidence and say the other boys had committed the rape. When he refused they knocked out some of his front teeth. Andy Wright was molested by the guards. Even when they should have been in other cells, during the different stages of the trials and appeals, they were, they are now, in death row. Most brutal of all, the wardens on one occasion at least withheld from them the news of the stay of their execution.

Here is a letter from Andy Wright to his mother:

Kilby Prison, Montgomery, Alabama, April 14, 1932.

Hello Mother Dear, how are you today. This leaves your son

not feeling so well. Mother I am trying hard not to worry but I really can't help but worry because I have got tired of laying in this little tight place. I wish they could have us moved back to Birmingham county jail so we will have room to walk around some, and maybe I wouldn't worry so much. I know for sure I wouldn't, but in this little tight place with nothing to keep my mind together, no enjoyment here at all to keep a person from worrying you can imagine how it goes with me. So Mother dear I will close now. Read and remember your son for ever. — A. Wright.

The series of execution dates and stays of execution has been going on now for two and a half years, and down this vista of torment is the threat of one of the most torturing deaths ever devised, electrocution. How did Beatrice Hastings (one of the many writers who has protested against this monstrous case) word it? "A human being boiled in his own blood, burned and scorched until death comes in from five to fifteen minutes."[1]

Protests And Demonstrations

The capitalist press has, of course, been silent on as many of these as possible. The first exposé of the frame-up appeared in the New York *Daily Worker* on April 2, 1931, the week before the trial. On April 24 the first protest cable from Europe arrived from the Berlin Transport Workers Union, and the first large Harlem Scottsboro Protest Parade was held and broken up by the police. Throughout the summer, the execution date having been set for July 10, there were meetings and manifestations not only all over America but in European countries outside the American embassies and legations. On May 1, 1931, the I.L.D. had organized over three hundred thousand Negro and white workers in 110 American cities. In Detroit alone there was a manifestation of ten thousand. In Cuba a militant meeting took place outside the American-owned *Havana Post*. Several deaths, smashed windows in the American Embassy and police fights marked the breaking

---

1 [Author's note: In *The Straight-Thinker*, September 1932.] Beatrice Hastings was the pen name of Emily Alice Haigh (1879-1943), author of *Defence of Madame Blavatsky* (Worthing: Hastings P, 1937).

up of a huge manifestation in Berlin. Protests poured in from the workers of the Soviet Union, of China, of Mexico. *L'Humanité*, in Paris, lists in one day, just before the execution was postponed by the appeal, the following protests:

40,000 Parisian workers. The Fédération Unitaire des Métaux. Jeunesses Communistes. Italian Section of the Red Aid.
15,000 members of the Paris Municipal Workers.
The Ligue de la Défense de la Race Nègre.

On receiving these protests the American legations cabled to the U.S. for instructions; the organisation of the International Labour Defence of each different country has mobilized more and more protests and manifestations with each successive move in the case.

In the Soviet Union the vice-president of the Academy of Science wrote, "that such things can come to pass is unbelievable and incompatible with the mind of a normal being. Of course anything can be expected from the U.S. where proceedings have been brought against Darwinians. But I do not understand how American science can remain mute on such scandalous sentences."

Later, in July 1932, when Mrs. Wright had come to England, amongst other public protests sent to the American Ambassador for transmission to Hoover[1] was one from the London School of Economics. Another from the University of London, signed by 274 of the students and teachers, by Professors Ginsberg, Martin, White, Hogben, Laski, Tawney and Eileen Power:[2] "We, the undersigned, emphatically join in the world-wide protest against the legalized murder of the Scottsboro Negro boys. We regard this travesty of justice, the result of the gravest race prejudice, as an

---

1 Herbert Hoover (1874-1964) US Republican who was president from 1929 to 1933.

2 Morris Ginsberg (1889-1970), British sociologist at University of London; Kingsley Martin (1897-1969), political scientist at London School of Economics and a member of the Fabian Society; Albert Beebe White (1871-1952) historian; Lancelot Thomas Hogben (1895-?), mathematician and member of the Fabian Society; Harold Laski (1893-1950) political scientist and socialist who formed the Left Book Club, published a left-wing weekly called the *Tribune*, and became chair of the Labour Party in 1945; Richard H. Tawney (1880-1962), labour historian (expert on early modern capitalism) and leading socialist; Eileen Power (1889-1940), historian at Girton College and London School of Economics, member of Union of Democratic Control.

intolerable abuse of the basic principles of civilisation, and demand immediate repeal of the sentence."

Some of the members of the Church to protest were: the Bishops of Durham, Worcester, Bradford, Rochester, Wakefield, Chichester, Southwell, Pella, Galloway, Dunkeld, Hexham, Newcastle, the Chief Rabbi, Dr. Hertz. Amongst writers, poets, artists and intellectuals: Dreiser, Sherwood Anderson, Sinclair Lewis, Professor Franz Boas, Ezra Pound, John Dos Passos, Edna St. Vincent Millay, Malcolm Cowley, Heywood Broun, Waldo Frank, Floyd Dell, Eugene Gordon, Lincoln Steffens, Langston Hughes, Mary Heaton Vorse, Mike Gold,[1] and all the American

---

1   Theodore Dreiser (1871-1945), American writer of naturalist novels like *Sister Carrie* (1907) and *The Genius* (1915). Sherwood Anderson (1876-1941) American writer, author of "Winesburg, Ohio" (1919), a collection of short stories about the people of a small town in Ohio (Clyde). Anderson began writing in 1913 after having served in the Spanish-American War, working as a copywriter in Chicago, and managing a paint plant in Elyria, Ohio. Sinclair Lewis (1885-1951), the first American to win the Nobel Prize for Literature. His concern with issues of gender and racial equality, and with the disenfranchised inform his work. Lewis was nominated for the Pulitzer Prize for *Main Street* and *Babbitt*, and won for *Arrowsmith*. Franz Boas (1858-1942), anthropologist at Columbia University best known for his work with the Kwakiutl Indians from Northern Vancouver Island and the adjacent mainland of British Columbia, Canada. Boas was a proponent of cultural relativism, the view that the differences in peoples were the results of historical, social and geographic conditions and all populations had complete and equally developed culture. This position represented an important counterpoint to the evolutionist view of Louis Henry Morgan and Edward Tylor. Boas and his students (among them Margaret Mead, Ruth Benedict, Melville Herskovits, Edward Sapir and Zora Neale Hurston) changed American anthropology forever. Ezra Pound (1885-1972), one of the poets responsible for defining and promoting a modernist aesthetic in English-language poetry. An American expatriate, Pound facilitated an important exchange between British and American writers, and played a key role in advancing the work of contemporaries W.B. Yeats, Robert Frost, William Carlos Williams, Marianne Moore, H.D., James Joyce, Ernest Hemingway, and especially T.S. Eliot. He remains best known for the encyclopedic epic poem titled *The Cantos*. John Dos Passos (1896-1970), important American writer, author of the protest-genre trilogy, *USA* (*The 49th Parallel* [1930], *1919* [1932], and *The Big Money* [1936]) and founder of *New Masses* (1926). Edna St.Vincent Millay (1892-1950), American poet and playwright known as much for her bohemian life-style as for her verse. First garnered attention for the lyric "Renascence," later published in *Renascence and Other Poems* (1917). *A Few Figs from Thistles* (1920) drew much attention for its controversial descriptions of female sexuality and feminism. She was associated with the Provincetown Players and lived in Greenwich Village. She won the Pulitzer Prize for *The Harp Weaver* (1923). Malcolm Cowley (1898-?), leftist American literary critic, known for works such as *The Dream of the Golden Mountains: Remembering the 1930s* and *Exile's Return: A Literary Odyssey of the 1920s*. Heywood Broun (?-1939), American columnist and champion of social justice.

John Reed (literary) Clubs.[1]

Outside America: Wells, Bertrand Russell, Middleton Murray, Aldous Huxley, Julian Huxley, Arthur Symons, Augustus John, Rebecca West, Virginia Woolf, Professor Malinowski, Priestley, Storm Jameson, Naomi Mitchison, David Garnett, C.R. Nevinson, Laurence Housman, Norman Douglas.[2] Outside

---

Member of the Algonquin Round Table writers, a group of columnists, essayists and drama critics who met regularly for lunch at the Algonquin Hotel in New York. Broun was a columnist for the New York *Tribune* and the New York *World*, and a regular contributor to the *Nation* and the *New Republic*. He also founded the American Newspaper Guild in 1933. Waldo Frank (1889-1967), a radical American writer, he contributed to socialist journals such as *The Liberator* and *New Masses*. In his novels Frank tended to advocate social and political reform. Books on politics by Frank include *Our America* (1919), *In the American Jungle* (1937) and *The Prophetic Island: A Portrait of Cuba* (1961). Floyd Dell (1887-1969) "The Scott Fitzgerald of Illinois," Dell wrote about the restlessness and disillusionment that characterized America in the years between World Wars I and II, as well as the lighter side of the Jazz Age. A committed left-wing journalist, he left his post as editor at the *Chicago Evening Post* for *The Masses* and then *The Liberator*. During the Depression, Dell was editor of special reports for the Works Progress Administration. Eugene Gordon was a left-wing African-American journalist who wrote for the *Boston Post* from 1919-1935, and who published articles in *New Masses*, *The Nation*, and in the late thirties, *The Moscow Daily News*. Gordon was a contributor to Cunard's *Negro* anthology. Lincoln Steffens (1866-1936), American journalist and author; wrote about government corruption in works like *The Shame of Cities* (1904) and *The Struggle for Self-Government* (1906). Langston Hughes (1902-1967), one of first writers identified with the Harlem Renaissance, Hughes remains one of the most important African-American poets, critics, and promoters of African-American letters. Known for his experiments with the blues form in verse in such collections as *The Weary Blues* and *Fine Clothes to the Jew*. Mary Heaton Vorse (1874-1966), American novelist and labour organizer who lived in Greenwich Village; associated with the Provincetown Players. Mike Gold (1894-1967), leading figure in communist writers organizations like the John Reed Club and its later incarnation, the League of American Writers; Gold was involved with *New Masses*, wrote for the *Daily Worker*, and published a number of books, including the autobiographical *Jews without Money*.

1   John Reed (1887-1920) was an American journalist who first won recognition for his articles on the Mexican revolution; he spent four months with Pancho Villa and published *Insurgent Mexico*. In the US he published in the left-wing magazines *New Review* and *The Masses* and became involved with strike organizing, an activity for which he was arrested numerous times. In 1917 he witnessed the Russian Revolution and published his eyewitness account, *Ten Days that Shook the World* in 1919. He died of typhoid in the Soviet Union. The John Reed Clubs were named for him and were a vehicle for organizing and supporting left-wing writers. Richard Wright became very involved with the John Reed Clubs in Chicago; they were his entrée to the Communist Party. After 1937 the clubs were replaced by the League of American Writers.

2   Bertrand Russell (1872-1970) British philosopher, logician, essayist and well-known advocate of peace; John Middleton Murray (1889-1957), influential literary critic, editor of *Rhythm* and later *Athenaeum*; husband of Katherine Mansfield; Aldous Huxley

England: Einstein, Gorki, Leo Tolstoi, Barbusse, Gide, Leon Pierre-Quint, the French Surrealist (writers) Group,[1] and tens of thousands of others in every land.

The total number of protests from all over the world is listed at some 10 million. In the face of all this (which is noted here as an

---

(1894-1963) English novelist and essayist whose satire on the role of technology in modern society, *Brave New World* (1932), remains his best-known work; Sir Julian Huxley (1887-1975) English biologist, first director general of UNESCO and a founder of the World Wildlife Fund; Arthur Symons (1865-1945) English poet and critic who introduced the work of the French Decadent poets to the British through translation and criticism; Augustus John (1878-1961) one of the best-known artists in Britain in the early part of the twentieth century, John led a nomadic, bohemian life and painted portraits of a number of prominent writers, including Hardy, Shaw, Lawrence; Rebecca West (1892-1983) English journalist and novelist involved with first-wave feminism; Virginia Woolf (1882-1941) one of stylistic innovators of modern novel, Woolf was at the centre of the Bloomsbury Group; her novels include *Mrs. Dalloway*, *The Waves*, and *To the Lighthouse*; her essay *A Room of One's Own* remains one of the central texts of first-wave feminism; Bronislaw Malinowski (1884-1942) British anthropologist whose methodological innovations contributed to the development of anthropology as a discipline: the field-trip, involving empirical research and detailed observation, was key to his method; *Argonauts of the Western Pacific*, about the Trobriand Islanders who were Malinowski's primary subjects, remains one of his most important works; J.B. Priestley (1894-1984), English essayist, novelist and playwright. *The English Journey* (1934), an account of his travels through economically depressed areas in England, preceded slightly George Orwell's *The Road to Wigan Pier*; Storm Jameson (1897-1986) left-wing English journalist and novelist; Naomi Mitchison (1897-1999), Scottish novelist and children's writer; David Garnett (1892-1981), English writer, associated with the Bloomsbury Group; C.R. Nevinson (1889-1946), English painter, a pacifist who opposed World War I and depicted the horrors of war in his painting; Laurence Housman (1865-1959), an English artist and writer best known for a series of plays about the Victorian era; Norman Douglas (1818-1952), British travel writer and man of letters who was also a close friend of Cunard.

1   Albert Einstein (1879-1955) German physicist and foremost contributor to modern understanding of physics, through his theory of relativity; Maxim Gorki (1868-1936) Russian / Soviet playwright and fiction writer, closely associated with the Russian revolution; Gorki was among the first to introduce proletarian characters into Russian literature, and his novel *Mother* (1907) is still seen as a prototype of the proletarian novel; Leo Tolstoi (1828-1910) Russian novelist and friend of Gorki; his works *War and Peace* (1869) and *Anna Karenina* (1877) are regarded as masterpieces of Russian literature; Henri Barbusse (1873-1935) French realist writer concerned with social change; his novel about the first world war, *Under Fire: The Story of a Squad* (1917), won the Prix Goncourt; Barbusse joined the French Communist Party in 1923; André Gide (1869-1951) French writer known for such works as *L'Immoraliste (The Immoralist)* (1902), *Les Caves du Vatican (Lafcadio's Adventures)* (1914), and *Les Faux-monnayeurs (The Counterfeiters)* (1925); Gide flirted with Communism in the early 1930s, travelling to the Soviet Union and later writing critically about what he saw; he won the Nobel Prize for literature in 1947; Leon Pierre-Quint (1895-1958) French literary critic who wrote critical

indication only of part of the volume of mass indignation) what is the reaction of the U.S. authorities? Both the President, at that time Hoover and now Roosevelt,[1] and Governor Miller[2] of Alabama have had it in their power all along to grant pardon or to order that the boys be freed. The attitude of American authorities is of course classic. They decline to comment, "know very little about the case," etc. Governor Miller, however, was surprised and disquieted by the number and militant tone of the cables and messages received. Voices from the entire world denouncing the condemnation of nine mere Negro working lads in Alabama, a thing of purely local issue, the sort of thing that had happened all the time "without any fuss" ... But no, it was no concern of Governor Miller. He saw then, he sees no reason now, to exert his powers.

A sidelight on the official American mentality, regarding the intellectual status of the Negro, is given by Comrade Garan Kouyaté[3] (a Bambara African) after going with a delegation to the American Embassy in Paris at the time of the U.S. Supreme Court Appeal in November 1932: "When we got there we were

---

biographies of Gide and Marcel Proust; The French Surrealists were an avant-garde group of artists and intellectuals who united (for a time) under the leadership of André Breton, author of the Surrealist Manifesto of 1924. Original members of the group included Breton, Tristan Tzara, Louis Aragon (Cunard's lover for a time), Paul Éluard, Antonin Artaud, Max Ernst, Raymond Queneau, Joan Miró, Michel Leiris, Benjamin Péret, Phillipe Soupault, René Crevel and others. A number of Martiniquais studying in Paris were also associated with the Surrealists: Jules Monnerot, Pierre Yoyotte, Étienne Léro, and Aimé Césaire. Excommunications, regroupings, and new manifestos followed into the 1950s. In the first surrealist manifesto, Breton defined surrealism as based on the principle that a higher reality, accessible through dreams, psychic automatism, and disinterested intellectual games, could revolutionize a moribund and corrupt society which, due to its over-emphasis on reason, was unaware of the sur-real. Anti-imperialist, and sympathetic to communism (several members of the group joined the Communist Party in 1927) the surrealists contributed a manifesto titled "Murderous Humanitarianism" to Cunard's *Negro* anthology.

1 Franklin Delano Roosevelt (1882-1945), American president from 1933-1945. Famous for the "New Deal," an economic and social program aimed at countering the effects of the Depression, which greatly expanded the role of the federal government.

2 Benjamin M. Miller (1864-1944) Democratic Governor of Alabama from 1931-1935.

3 Tiémoko Garan Kouyaté (c.1900-1942) From Soudan (now Mali) in French West Africa, Kouyaté lived in Paris for many years and was a leader in the struggle against imperialism, representing French West Africa at international conferences of Negro workers, and in the International Trades Union Congress of Negro Workers. A communist for a number of years, Kouyaté was also one of the forerunners of nationalism in West Africa, and a friend of George Padmore.

told the ambassador was out. The chargé d'affaires who received us admitted that deputations had been coming all day with the same object. His whole manner showed the utmost surprise at Negroes talking correct French. His astonishment turned to anger and mortification when we told him in plain terms that we held Miller and the President of America responsible for the lives and fate of the boys."

Ada Wright and J. Louis Engdahl in Europe

America brings pressure on all European countries to keep these agitations and mass protests out of the press. How much more so did this pressure operate, with the fullest concord of all the capitalist governments in attempting to debar Mrs. Wright and J. Louis Engdahl,[1] national secretary of the American I.L.D., when they came over in the summer of 1932 to tell the European workers of the Scottsboro frame-up and exploitation of the Negro masses. This tour comprised thirteen countries. In Hamburg and Berlin Mrs. Wright was forbidden to speak. Denied entry into Belgium, but smuggled across the frontier. Imprisoned, as was Engdahl, for several days in Czecho-Slovakia and Bulgaria, then deported. Acclaimed everywhere by huge crowds and manifestations they were constantly harried and held up by various national authorities. Denied entry into England. After a long delay, Engdahl being still debarred, Mrs. Wright was given just ten days here, during which she appeared and spoke at no less than seven meetings in London, and in Manchester, Dundee, Kirkcaldy, Glasgow, Bristol, with I.L.D. organizers. Ireland refused her entry. Engdahl and Mrs. Wright were later at the Amsterdam Anti-War Congress, all members of which signed a mass protest. Their European tour culminated in Russia at the moment of the celebrations of the Soviet Regime's fifteenth anniversary. It was here that Engdahl died, weakened and worn out by the incessant fight and organisation of the whole Scottsboro campaign. And meanwhile a child of eleven was speaking to huge audiences throughout the middle western states in America. This was Lucille Wright, sister of the boys.

---

1   J. Louis Engdahl (?-1932) was an ILD leader.

Alabama And Washington Supreme Court Appeals

On Jan. 21, 1932, the Alabama Supreme Court heard the Appeal. The case was argued by I.L.D. lawyers in presence of the biggest assembly ever held in the Montgomery court. Although justice John Anderson disagreed with the other judges, holding that the accused "did not get the fair and impartial trial required by the Constitution," the Appeal was dismissed and the death verdicts maintained on seven of the boys. Eugene Williams, second youngest, was granted a new trial on the grounds that, as a juvenile like Roy Wright, his case had been tried in the wrong court at Scottsboro. But neither of these boys' cases have been re-heard.

The defence had already announced that if the Appeal failed it would take all the cases to the Washington Supreme Court, the highest in the land. Appeal to this court was heard by nine judges, some of whom were said to be known "liberals." This took place on Oct. 10, 1932, while a large demonstration and picketing was going on outside, attacked by police with tear-gas bombs and clubs, sixteen being arrested and many clubbed. The judges deliberated, but their decision was reserved for one month till after the presidential elections. On Nov. 7 it was known that the appeal had been granted. That this came in no way from the abundant evidence of the boys' innocence and frame-up, nor from the numerous other factors of injustice during trial, is shown most clearly by the one ground on which the Appeal was allowed. As *The Liberator* wrote: "Only the fact that the boys *had not been properly represented by counsel* entitled them to a new trial. The crying evidence that the trial was held in an atmosphere of lynch law, that threatening crowds milled about the streets, the fact that Negroes were barred from the juries that tried the boys—all these facts the judges of the Supreme Court set aside as 'immaterial.' Such is the impartial justice of the highest court in the land."

Ruby Bates Repudiates The Rape Lie

About two or three months after this, while the I.L.D. was preparing the whole of the case anew for re-hearing, it became public that a letter written by Ruby Bates to a boy friend, in which she stated that she had lied about the "rape," had been seized and kept by the police. The defence forced this to be handed over to the court as evidence. Ruby Bates had written:

Jan. 5, 1932, Huntsville, Alabama.

dearest Earl, I want too make a statement too you. Mary Sanders is a god–damn lie about those Negroes, those policemen made me tell a lie. that is my stement because i want too clear myself that is all too if you want to belive me ok. if not that is ok. you will be sorry some day. if you had too stay in jail with 8 Negroes you would tell a lie two. those Negroes did not touch me or those white boys. i hope you will belive me the law dont. i love you better than Mary does ore any body else in the world that is why i am telling you of this thing. i was drunk at the time and did not know what i was doing. i know it was wrong to let those Negroes die on account of me. i hope you will believe my statement because it is the god's truth, i wish those Negroes are not Burnt on account of me. it is these white boys fault. that is my statement and that is all i know. i hope you tell the law; hope you will answer. Ruby Bates. P.S. this is one time that i might tell a lie but it is the truth so god help me.

The Decatur Re–Trial

March 27 had been set for the re-trial in Decatur, Alabama, although the defence had asked for change of venue to the large town of Birmingham as less likely to contain the lynch spirit so dominant in Scottsboro. Decatur is under forty miles from Scottsboro and as frantically, bitterly prejudiced. But change of venue had been denied. At this time prosecuting attorney Knight made statements to the press that the boys had had a fair trial and would have a fair re-trial. It has been seen how fair the first trial was. At this time also Knight opposed the defence lawyers when they asked that action be taken against the militiaman who had stuck a bayonet into Roy Wright's face in addition to the beating and torturing that he had undergone in the attempt to make him testify against the other boys. Knight said a Negro's accusation was of no value, and covertly opposed demands from the defence for private interviews with the boys prior to the trial; the presence of guards of course preventing prisoners from speaking openly.

On March 27 the trial opened. The chief figures in it are:

Samuel Leibowitz, defence counsel, a celebrated criminal lawyer from the North, who had never yet lost one of his very numerous cases.

Joseph Brodsky, chief lawyer of the International Labour Defence.

General George Chamlee, of Chattanooga.

State Attorney Prosecutor Knight, who had prosecuted the cases at Scottsboro, a Southerner of the rankest cracker type.

Judge Horton, the same who was later to hear the second Alabama Supreme Court Appeal.

Ruby Bates, one of the two white girls, who had repudiated her false testimony and whose letter to a white boy friend confessing she had lied had been stolen and kept for months by the police.

Lester Carter, one of the white boys on the train, who now came forward to testify to the Negroes' innocence and to denounce the frame-up.

Although all the boys were brought to Decatur only *Haywood Patterson* was tried. As at Scottsboro the crowd began to collect early; the court-room was jammed. There were soldiers everywhere, by the judge's desk, and outside, hedging in the courthouse with drawn bayonets. About four hundred people inside the court, of whom a third were Negroes. These last were of course in the separate Jim-crow pen, including the two Negro reporters from the *Afro-American* and the *Norfolk Journal and Guide*. To leave at the end of each session the Negroes had to wait seated until the whites had gone out first. Meanwhile the Southerners were proclaiming *there is no discrimination*. In the same breath they would say that men of dark skins are not "of sound mind." This idiocy was thrown into sharp relief by the courageous and intelligent testimony of a Negro plasterer from Scottsboro put on the stand by the defence the first day. At two o'clock a van rolled up with the boys from Birmingham jail, preceded and followed by squads with riot guns and tear gas. Olin Montgomery is nearly blind. He stumbled as he got out. A wave went through the crowd. They thought he'd been shot; they thought the shootings were beginning. That was the state of tension the townsfolk were in. As Roy Wright entered the court Leibowitz came and took him by the hand, to the angry stupor of court officials. By now the audience had increased to about six hundred, and half of these were Negro.

A Southerner, Mary Heaton Vorse, a white author, who was present throughout the entire trial, told me that the Negroes and whites were "perfectly friendly, fraternising even" everywhere except in court, where the tension was bitter, violent, at times positively frantic, so that you didn't know what mightn't happen. I find this "friendliness" too difficult to believe; one cannot see how this could happen, with the daily insults flung by Knight at the Negroes, with his appeals based on race difference and prejudice made continuously to the only-too-appreciative jury. I think her desire that it should be so made it seem so to her—as also her statement that Judge Horton was just and well-disposed ... a fact that I will come to presently proved it otherwise. We know there are degrees in the visibility of prejudice.

All through the day small organized bands of whites from surrounding communities such as Scottsboro, Huntsville and Athens kept filtering into the town, adding to the danger of "extra-legal" action, a danger to the boys, to witnesses called for the defence, to the defence itself. "There is no danger whatever to the prisoners," proclaimed the authorities. The jail the boys were kept in during the two weeks of the trial was so rotten and old it had been abandoned for white prisoners. "Why, you could break out of it with a spoon," said a sheriff—indicating unwittingly it could be broken into as easily.

The first proceedings were statements by defending counsel Leibowitz that *no Negroes had been employed on juries for forty years. This is illegal*; this is in exact opposition to the thirteenth, fourteenth and fifteenth amendments to the U.S. Constitution, which guarantee that Negroes shall serve. These amendments had to be made in 1865, for until abolition no Negroes had any rights, civic, legal or political. These amendments are systematically, unfailingly disregarded in all the Southern States, as Leibowitz proceeded to show when he called for the jury roll. There was not a name on it of any Negro citizen qualified to serve; not one had served within living memory. Knight refused to answer on this point. "Prove it," was his retort. And Leibowitz proved it.

An arc light was thrown on the cracker mentality when Benson, of the Scottsboro *Progressive Age*, was called in. Leibowitz asked him if he had ever known a Negro to be placed on the jury roll. "Never heard of one, never noticed one," answered Benson with apologetic glances at prosecutor Knight. "There are 666 Negroes of serving age in Jackson county [where Scottsboro is situated], were none of these qualified to serve as jurors?" continued Leibowitz. "Some of them are good Negroes as far as Negroes go," said Benson, "but they couldn't be said to possess sound judgment, they couldn't get round that clause and they all steal; they haven't been trained for jury duty" (!) "I might say the same thing about women—the Negroes haven't been trained, not made a study of justice and law, and such." The defence collected evidence showing that there were twenty-six Negroes at least who could have served in the Scottsboro trial.

No, it was not the trial of the nine boys, particularly during the whole first week in Decatur; it was the trying and proving guilty of the entire Southern manner of denying to the Negro his constitutional rights.

Meanwhile, and throughout the trial, and ever since, and without doubt in the future too, the Southern authorities, press, etc., proclaim that there is neither discrimination nor prejudice; and that these fiendish and scandalous trials were "fair." William Patterson, national secretary of the American I.L.D., himself a Negro, and a lawyer, analysing, commenting on the whole matter wrote: "If the authorities of Alabama had been or were in any way sincere in their claim to a desire to give the boys a fair trial and to prevent them being lynched, they themselves, through their organ the capitalist press, would issue a call for full social, political and economic equalities for the Negro, and expose the real reason why the Negro people are now in such a state of oppression, and why the Scottsboro boys are framed on faked charges. But this they cannot do, for capitalism would then no longer be capitalism."

The sheriff of Morgan county, in which Decatur is situated, needed thirty national guardsmen to "prevent the boys escaping;" the same troops which had beaten and mistreated them previously and were soon to do so again. It is a recognised provocation to lynch mobs to call in the aid of the National Guard; double provocation to call in, as was suggested, the federal troops.

On this first trial day, the judge, Horton, overrules the defence's demand that all the indictments be quashed on the ground of the absence of Negro jurors. Knight's cracker spirit begins to rise. He addresses the witness Tom Sanford, Negro plasterer, as "John," bullies and browbeats him. Leibowitz remarks sharply, "Call witness Mr. Sanford." "Not doing that," answers Knight. Then a lynch inciting pamphlet is discovered. It is being hawked about in the crowd. A battle opens between defence and prosecution; Leibowitz demands its suppression, Knight defends its right to be circulated. Finally the judge has it confiscated.

A day or two later Knight jumps to his feet clapping his hands during the declaration of a prosecution witness that the boys took a penknife from Victoria Price. Constantly there are little incidents of this sort, rabid pin-pricks of hatred studding the whole of the trial. The testimonies of state (prosecution) witnesses form an indescribable jumble of lies and contradictions, each more stupefying than the last. They are contrasted against each other by Leibowitz. For example: Price said she fainted after the "rape" in the train; but a state witness affirmed he saw her walking and talking. Another had seen a Negro prevent a white girl from jumping off the train—but the photograph taken subsequently from the spot where he stood showed that he could have seen nothing at all. Price's overalls, she said, were torn and stained; yet they were neither when produced in court. "And why were they not introduced into the first trial?" asked Leibowitz. Knight and the judge made objection to this query. Throughout, Price spoke mechanically, maintaining the whole of the rape story with its knives and guns, but only answered questions at the direct prompting of Knight. And the two doctors, Bridges and Lynch, called by the state, branded as false the story she told of being battered and bleeding. She was without any marks or wounds, save a few scratches which would be likely to come from clambering about on the train and from the gravel in the freight-car she'd travelled in. While she was being cross-examined a man got up in court. "Let's get Leibowitz now," he muttered. The soldiers seized and searched him for arms and put him out. Also were put out two others who had begun a struggle.

The lives of Leibowitz, Brodsky, Ruby Bates, Lester Carter and the boys were in constant danger from mobs or gangs forming daily, broadcasting their intention of lynching them. Well, it would have been too much even for the State of Alabama if four white people, the four chief protagonists in this case angrily watched by a universe, had been murdered. So all the time a handful of soldiers was set around lawyers and witnesses. They didn't know it perhaps, but at the time that Ruby Bates and Lester Carter were giving evidence two lynch-mobs had already started out from Huntsville and Scottsboro to get them. The militia posted along and across the roads outside Decatur turned them back. In keeping with the reiterated lie that nothing at all was going on, given out by the authorities, the press were asked not to mention this. But the press said they had come to send news and to take photos. "Send it only if something happens." Terrorisation or interference with the press was a strong feature throughout. Photographers were threatened at Paint Rock while taking pictures of the scene of arrest. A group of black and white people were arrested because found together in a Negro neighbourhood; charged with contempt of court (!) they were then brought before judge Horton. A white journalist, Fuller, had already been run out of the town because he was reporting for a Negro daily, *The Atlanta World*. As to Leibowitz, they called him "a Russian Jew Nigger who ought to be hung." But the attitude and spirit of the Negro population were stirringly militant. "If a mob comes we're not running," they said. They were told, of course, that the Communists were only making propaganda and that they did not care about the issue of the trials. "If the reds are responsible for all this," said the Negro workers, "then we are with them."

And the boys in the rotten jail you could break out of with a spoon…. A special correspondent went to see them. Thirteen iron steps and the shadow of the hangman's noose. So, for two years they'd been face to face with the electric chair across the passage in front of their cells and now they had the gallows to stare at in the electric light. On the last step was the trap-door to eternity — a painting of Christ at Gethsemane, done by some dead convict, above it. The correspondent looked at the gallows and the Christ. Then he saw the eye — the Scottsboro boys were looking at him. It was full of shadows in that place — jailors and guards moving about, the shadow of the actual noose, shadows of themselves shuffling round, straining ears for the rumble of mobs. They couldn't sleep; they were wondering all the time if they would die in Decatur, lynched, or be convicted again. Did they dare even to think of the possibility of acquittal? Vermin was on them, the cockroaches crept over the filthy cell floor; the bed bugs lived in their clothes, they couldn't get them out; jail gives no change of clothes. "What'll you do when you are freed?" asked the journalist. "Olin Montgomery seized one of the greasy bars and leaned against it, peering intently with his one near-sighted eye, 'Go home' he said simply. 'Oh boss, I wants to go home. I been here two years and nine days, two years and nine days.'"

Between the scenes in court, the gallows and the mob threats, the blood-lust outside and the agony, terror and despair within, the brutalities of the jailors and the thought of death that must never leave them, how is it that these boys did not go insane?

In court the "lantern-howled morons," as Leibowitz ended by calling them, are sitting and smoking, very informal. Plenty of them out of work in this impoverished rotting South always fifty years behind the times in everything. Hard eyes staring at judge and counsel. Only a whetting of the appetite so far to be sure, the death hunger will be sated alright, for haven't they been assured again and again that the boys won't get out of Decatur alive if the jury does acquit them? The Negroes sit apart, straining to hear and see, grim and silent. Other Negroes outside, trying to see into the court. Leibowitz and Chamlee keep Haywood Patterson between them. There's a photo in a French paper, Haywood Patterson is holding a horseshoe.... "Were you tried at Scottsboro?" "I was *framed* in Scottsboro." They try to force him to admit he pronounced a phrase they have invented themselves: "I told you if we had killed those girls we wouldn't be here." Knight has announced that he will simply *ignore* Ruby Bates' repudiation of her Scottsboro testimony, her admittance of perjury. A little later Knight says he'll have her arrested for perjury. Leibowitz tells the world that the Negroes are being framed up — he says he will fight like hell to save them.

"The Negroes Never Touched Me, As They Never Touched Victoria Price"

This is what Ruby Bates told the court. Though they had heard she was coming now to be a witness for the boys, and that she had publicly repudiated the rape lie, to hear this Southern white girl, one of themselves, utter this statement, made them aghast and convulsed them with fury. It is the first great crack in the old Southern structure of white supremacy. It will never be forgotten, it is a very high and splendid point in the history of black and white. Realise too that it needed very great courage, physical and moral, in these two young white Southerners, Ruby Bates and Lester Carter. With their testimony they were piercing the whole of the rotten Southern fabric of lies and race hatred, holding it up to the entire world, tearing it inside out.

Knight and other court authorities said Lester Carter and Ruby Bates had been "bought" by the Communists, pointed at the different clothes the latter was now wearing (most ordinary city girl's clothes). "We didn't dress Victoria Price up like a lily of the valley," vociferated the state prosecutor. Until her appearance in court Knight had been angrily shouting: "Produce Ruby Bates!" and saying it could not be done. She came in with Brodsky and Mrs. Jones, a social worker. "You have been asking for Ruby," said Leibowitz quietly, "here she is. I ask that she be sworn." An electric shock went through the court. An I.L.D.

Scottsboro release says: "Knight, who had been in the witness room preparing rebuttal witnesses, rushed back into the courtroom. Judge Horton called for order; an extra cordon of soldiers was thrown round the courthouse. Victoria Price was called in and stood staring at Ruby as she was asked to identify her as her companion on the trip."

Cross-examined by Knight with all the rancour and viciousness that one can visualise, she made a flat denial of the rape, could not identify Haywood Patterson, explained that she had lied out of excitement, ignorance, terrorisation by the police and at Victoria's prompting to escape jail. "The whole thing was a frame-up," she said. And it had troubled her so long that finally she had left her home in Huntsville in February 1933 and gone to New York, and seen Rev. Dr. Fosdyck, and he had told her to go back South and tell the truth at Decatur. She had not even known the meaning of the word "rape;" she had had to ask her mother what it meant; that was after the Scottsboro trial. No, the boys had certainly not touched her or Victoria.

Lester Carter, a tall blond Southern boy, gave evidence too. His conscience had been at him for two years, since the frame-up. Now, here, it was "like getting well from being dead." His story tallied with Ruby's; he had been on the train with the girls — he was very detailed. He'd met them both in Huntsville jail in 1931; he was then doing fifty days on a chain gang. Victoria was under sentence too. And Ruby had come to see her. After they'd got out they had met again and planned the trip. They'd spent that night in the Chattanooga jungle. The other boy who was along was married, so he hadn't accompanied them on the journey; he was going to follow later. On the train, he (Lester) had seen some white boys throwing stones at some Negroes; they'd shouted to him to come and join them, so he'd gone along. Then he jumped off the train when one of the Negroes took a swing at him. They did not have either knives or guns. He had been one of those who had notified the authorities about the fight. At Paint Rock, later, he'd overheard Victoria ask Orvil Gilley to pass as her brother, so that she would not be arrested for hoboing. And in Scottsboro jail, where they had all been locked up without knowing on what charge, he heard those two having a quarrel, Victoria telling Gilley he must keep to her story, and what did niggers matter anyway? let 'em all go to jail. But Gilley had said she was mad, and that "some time a nigger may have to testify to save your life." Of course the State interjected here that Carter had been coached to say all this. So Carter told how he had been in the Scottsboro prison for sixteen days and barred from testifying because they saw he wouldn't lie. After that he'd been so uneasy in his mind he had bummed his way to Albany in New York State to see Governor Roosevelt, who refused to see him. And finally he had heard that the I.L.D. in New York was defending the boys and had gone to them.

What did Knight do in the face of this testimony? He asked Lester Carter if he had syphilis! This attempt to damage his character drew an immediate protest from Leibowitz indicating that this astounding question was sufficient for a mis-trial to be declared. The judge overruled this, and Knight said, "I am not ashamed of the way I am treating this witness."

A gynecologist from Chattanooga, Dr. Reisman, had proved with charts and diagrams of feminine anatomy that it was not possible the alleged rape could have occurred at the time stated, backing up the declaration of the other two doctors. (It goes without saying that these doctors were also threatened by lynchers.)

Knight is now again browbeating Haywood Patterson. "Did you pick up Victoria Price and hold her over the side of the train? Who did you see raping the girls?" Patterson repeats he'd seen no girls at any time, admits freely to the fight when the white boys had attacked him and the others. And he tells his mother—she is sitting beside him, she hasn't seen him for over a year (they allow her to see him sentenced to death again), "I'm afraid of what'll happen if they free me."

Another mob formed; led by Ku Klux Klan men, two hundred of them were coming to the court house for Leibowitz. Sheriff Davis argued with and "cajoled" them (yes, that is the word used), but they wouldn't go away till they saw the soldiers were at the point of firing. This is when most of the press agreed to withhold news. The Klansmen however boasted of it, and the I.L.D. forced the truth of this and of many other incidents into the open.

As the trial went on five of the Negro boys were put on the stand by the defence. And then the very initial start of the whole thing came out. It was Eugene Williams who told how the white boys were climbing from one car to another and one of them had walked on Haywood Patterson's hand, and Haywood had asked him couldn't he be more careful ... and so the fight had begun. And then Haywood had pulled back Orvil Gilley as he was about to jump off. Why would he save a white boy's life to let him see a white girl raped afterwards? asked Haywood Patterson.

Victoria Price had said she'd never seen Carter or Gilley, but Dallas Ramsay, a Negro witness, had seen them all together on the morning of the freight-ride, when she had asked him when there was a train to Memphis. Both General Chamlee and a sister of the Wright boys, who live in Chattanooga, said how they had searched it for the Callie Broochie and her house where Price said they had spent the night, but in two years' investigation had never found either. Further "character testimony" was ruled out by the judge, who had allowed Knight to insult and attack defence witnesses as much as he pleased.

"That Black Thing"

Knight is shaking his fist at Haywood Patterson and calling him "that black thing over there." Leibowitz has made a four-hour summing up. Insults to Ruby Bates, Lester Carter, Leibowitz and Brodsky have been spat out by Knight and other prosecuting counsel. Leibowitz and Brodsky are "New York Jews, but jew money can't buy Alabama justice;" all four have received many death threats. And another of the prosecuting attorneys has made a lynch-inciting speech which has increased the number of fiery crosses (Ku Klux manifestations) that have burned nightly for over a week in all the surrounding villages. The ammunition stores report they are sold out, "but no cartridges sold to niggers."

The jury deliberates all night. Then they actually ask if they can give their decision based on the Scottsboro trial!! They don't want to take into account any of the Decatur hearing. Next morning the jury file in, many of them with broad grins. Horton reads out their verdict: "Guilty. We ask for the death penalty." The court empties in a flash; the news is shouted all over the town. The first case is settled, and now they can get on with that of Charlie Weems ...

One would like to engrave the entire report, the whole detail of these trial testimonies of both sides, the false along with the real, on some matter that would last as long as humanity; to record for ever also the moment of this cutting open of the plague of hatred, the exposure of Southern courts' "justice." The whole of the American Negroes' misery tightens into one phrase, into two lines written by one of their own poets:

> Oughta had mo' sense
> Dan to evah git born

That is by Sterling Brown.[1] And if it rings agonisingly defeatist so often it rings as bitterly true. But it is going to change. Five years ago the Scottsboro boys would have been just another locally heard-of case of nine more dead victims.

Aftermath Of Race Hatred

It was only two hours after this monstrous renewed death verdict was known that the *Amsterdam News* (Harlem's largest Negro paper) issued a proclamation asking for five hundred thousand protest signatures to be collected and sent to Roosevelt. In a few hours some fifty thousand had come in. And the I.L.D. immediately announced the "Free the Scottsboro Boys March" on Washington, which thousands volunteered for. Floods of protest telegrams came to Miller, governor of Alabama, Horton, Knight. The *Huntsville Times*, not content with the verdict alone, asked for the arrest of Ruby Bates. When Leibowitz, who had given his services in the case, arrived back in New York a crowd of some five thousand workers, mostly Negro, met him at the station and manifested their gratitude for the heroic fight he and the other defence lawyers had made.

---

1   Sterling Brown (1901–1989), an important poet and critic whose career began with the Harlem Renaissance. He drew on material from the rural south, and received favourable attention for his collection *The Southern Road* (1932).

A new development, the postponement of Charlie Weems' trial, came as a surprise to the defence, and was announced at the same time as the date of execution of Haywood Patterson was set for June 16. The notice of appeal already filed by Brodsky automatically suspends this.

Throughout the whole case there have been numerous acts of terrorisation in Alabama, opposition of all kinds in diverse parts of America. Here are just a few: General Chamlee's house broken into by a gang who tried to rifle a safe containing legal documents. L. Harper, Negro teacher, sacked from Birmingham for having given his pupils Scottsboro protests to distribute. Ted Richards, a Negro boy of nineteen, jailed for two years for speaking on Scottsboro, asking freedom for the boys, for organized action against evictions. Herman Carter, author of "Scottsboro Blues," held up and threatened by white hooligan motorists in Nashville, Tennessee. Two Negroes shot at and wounded in a Decatur street by "unknown" whites. The house of a Negro witness who was to testify in Charlie Weems' case burned to the ground, in Decatur. In other parts of America: June 1933, in Mount Vernon, New York State, the Ku Klux Klan covered the walls of an auditorium, where a black and white workers' meeting was being held to protest Scottsboro and Negro terrorisation, with messages, "The Ku Klux Klan has its eye on you" — the word "eye" being represented by the large and evil photograph of one. Leaflets frantically attacking black and white solidarity filled the hall. At the time of the Decatur trial the I.L.D. had issued a Scottsboro penny stamp to aid in raising funds. Although the Red Cross and other stamps go regularly through the mail the U.S. post office in New York attempted, but failed, to bar this stamp. A play given by the John Reed literary club in Los Angeles was broken up by a fascist police squad, books, paintings, documents destroyed, because they protested against Scottsboro and Negro oppression.

Today as I write, this comes fresh news from Birmingham, Alabama, that another Negro has been shot dead in the street by a gang at that moment making its third attempt to lynch yet another Negro.

There have been statements that the Scottsboro boys were

fighting each other in their cells, fighting the wardens. Attempts to show them up as callous criminals. Haywood Patterson was reported stabbed to death by Andy Wright. But an investigation by Brodsky showed that, as usual, it was the wardens who were mistreating the boys. One reads of the boys beating each other with leaden piping torn from the walls. Jailors struck the boys and forced some twenty other prisoners to start an attack on them; when they showed they would defend themselves they were starved. Brodsky, after seeing them, said their spirit was high, that they believed in their ultimate freeing by the weight of the mass protests.

The March On Washington

It took place from Harlem on May 6, when some five thousand, mostly Negroes, left in vans, lorries and trucks, some starting on foot. Rain drenched them. Police that accompanied them in heavy numbers had taken the precaution to mix oil with the gasoline of their motor-cycles; the workers marched in an atmosphere of burning, acrid smoke. On their way through Baltimore new contingents joined them. At the same time a different group, some of the black bourgeoisie also left New York for Washington, to tell President Roosevelt how fair Judge Horton had been despite the death verdict, and to assure him that they continued to have faith in the justice of Southern courts. This was an attempt at disrupting the Scottsboro United Front, their objective being of course to discredit as much as possible the I.L.D. and the defence. In this a large amount of funds collected for the defence was wasted by the N.A.A.C.P. and other reactionaries.

A Scottsboro Press Release says: "Ruby Bates marching at the head of the Scottsboro parade in Washington, May 8th, by herself gives the parade more significance than any other single unit. When she told Mr. Howe, secretary to the President, and Mr. Rainey, Speaker to the house, that the Scottsboro boys are innocent, she exposed the frame-up at the doors of the highest authority in the land." At the Capitol, William Patterson and a delegation of the marchers asked to see Roosevelt. Secretary Howe said it was quite impossible, the President was seeing no-one but foreign representatives and bankers. Patterson insisted that Roosevelt be informed of their presence and demands. Down the telephone then came Roosevelt's emphatic *No*, heard by all in that room. The marchers' objectives were to demand immediate freeing and safe conduct of the innocent boys, to protest against the death sentence, to leave with Roosevelt and congress the "Bill of Civil Rights for the Negro People" prepared by the League of Struggle for Negro Rights. This Bill states that the thirteenth, fourteenth, and fifteenth amendments must be made to function (right of Negroes to vote and sit on juries) and contains a clause demanding the death penalty for lynchers. A copy of this Bill was taken by James W. Ford[1] (Negro Communist leader and Communist candidate for vice-presidency in 1932) to Speaker Rainey, who pretended he knew almost nothing about the Scottsboro case, but who gave himself away by trying to browbeat Ruby Bates on her change of attitude. The Negro congressman, Oscar de Priest,[2] a millionaire landlord who is responsible for some of the bloodiest evictions of black and white workers, when confronted by William Patterson's demand that he present the Bill to congress, cut short the interview, replying that if anything needed to be said he would say it himself, no-one could tell him what to say.

The effect of the march was to greatly increase the adherence to the defence. The number of meetings has multiplied itself as time draws nearer for the October re-trial. Mother Wright, Ruby Bates and I.L.D. speakers are at this moment on a three-month tour; Mother Patterson, Lester Carter and Richard B. Moore,[3] a

---

1 James W. Ford (1893-1957), labour union and Communist Party leader. Wrote *The Negro and the Democratic Front* (1938); ran for vice-president of the United States in 1932.

2 Oscar de Priest (1871-1951), businessman and politician who became a significant political figure in Chicago. He garnered considerable popularity through his condemnation of the treatment of the Scottsboro boys, but he also had a reputation as a "Red hunter."

3 Richard B. Moore was one of the first African-Americans to join the Communist Party, after several years organizing in black nationalist groups. He was known as an effective street speaker in Harlem, and served as national secretary of the League of Struggle for Negro Rights for a number of years. He was also a field organizer for the ILD and a leading Party spokesperson for the Scottsboro movement.

dynamic Negro communist orator, are speaking in some hundred different places in the West and Middle West.

Alabama Supreme Court Appeal, 1933

A lot has been said and written about Judge Horton's "fairness." Yet the evidence presented him in the Appeal was precisely the same as that used in Decatur, and on which the jury had convicted Haywood Patterson. Nothing new had been added. Judge Horton had not set aside the jury's verdict; he had confirmed it. On June 22 Horton granted the appeal. If he was "fair" in granting it now in the Alabama Supreme Court, he had not been so in condemning Haywood Patterson in Decatur. The judge's decision, now that the evidence greatly preponderated in favour of the accused, sums itself up in his own words: "The natural inclination of the mind is to doubt and to seek further."

This decision has had the immediate effect of producing a new lynch figure: ex-senator Heflin, a leading member of the Ku Klux Klan, who has wired his "services" free of charge to prosecutor Knight. This is one more indication of the Southern ruling class determination to have the boys killed. A move to get the coming re-trial in October transferred out of Horton's court into that of Judge Callaghan, another well-known Ku Kluxer, has also been spoken of. Applications for bail for the boys were refused; the two youngest are still illegally held since the beginning, never having been tried in the juvenile court where their cases belong. Knight has made it clear throughout that he will do his utmost against these now fifteen-year-old boys, whom he calls "incorrigibles."

★   ★   ★

That, at present writing, is the state of the case. That the verdicts on all the boys will most probably be the same as that on Haywood Patterson is likely. This is one of those long periods, of which there have been many in the two and a half years since the frame-up was enacted, during which no fresh move takes place, no word about the boys comes out of America. Remember the apprehension that lives with you as your daily companion in a cell—the boys face this third trial in October, next month. Yes, the legal position is better for them now, two Appeals having been granted; but the lynching spirit was even fiercer at Decatur than at Scottsboro, prosecutor and jury as determined to convict. As the world's anger, the world's protests augment, so do the fury and mortification of Alabama mobs and "justice." The outcome of the third trial is by no means certain. One thing we know there will be, and that is a yet greater increase of hysteria, an increase of the danger of actual lynching. Despite state law it is *not* an impossibility, constitutionally, for the case to be tried out of Alabama, right out of the South. A word from President Roosevelt would be sufficient influence to bring this about. But the boys can rely only on the International Labour Defence. The I.L.D. has proved by its colossal legal fight and organisation since the beginning that world protests backing up the struggle to establish Negroes' legal rights can stay the hand of lynch law, can and do expose the criminal mistreatment of Negroes in America.

It is only by fighting that anything of major issue is obtained. In the way of justice, of aid and of good the black man in America until now has received from the white only what must be classed as the comparative crumbs of humanitarianism and philanthropy. We do not ask for our Negro comrades these tokens of guilty conscience, these palliative gestures. *We demand recognition and enforcement of the Negro's full rights, as an equal, as a brother, and an end to the oppression of coloured peoples the world over.* (Sept. 16, 1933)

"A REACTIONARY NEGRO ORGANISATION"

A SHORT REVIEW OF DR. DUBOIS, *THE CRISIS*, AND THE NAACP[1] IN 1932 (1934)

Was the article by Dr. W.E.B. DuBois that will be found immediately after this[2] written so long ago that conditions have entirely
changed for the Negro in America since its writing? No—for
since the abolition of slavery in 1863, though conditions have
become better for the individual Negro (where by perseverance
he has been able to go through college, enter certain professions
and evolve for himself the status of a bourgeois—in very small
proportion to the 12 million of his race—and where despite this
bourgeois status he is the victim of Jim-crowing or discrimination
throughout the entire U.S.) the Negro masses have been more
and more subjugated and dragged back to the conditions of slavery—with this difference: in many ways they are worse off now
than under slavery, for under slavery they were the valuable, very
valuable property of their owners; now they are the object of
unpunished lynchings, persecution, flagrantly unconstitutional,
prejudiced mis-trials in the courts and economically enslaved on
the land and by the coloured wage-scale. This condition is not
new; it is merely worse. Yet Dr. DuBois, in this general article on
"Black America," has not a word to say on any of this, which,
however, is the core itself, the intrinsic and foremost meaning of
the words "Black America."

It should here be noted that another coloured writer, as long
ago as 1897, D.E. Tobias,[3] in a pamphlet denouncing the

---

1   [Author's note: National Association for the Advancement of Coloured People.]
2   Immediately following Cunard's "review" in the anthology is a reprint of DuBois's
    famous essay "Black America," originally published in *America as Americans See It*, ed.
    F.J. Ringel (New York: Harcourt Brace, 1932), 139-155.
3   [Author's note: Quotations from this writer's pamphlet, *Freed but not Free*, further on.]
    Cunard reprints excerpts from Tobias's pamphlet in *Negro* (201-208) which she indi-
    cates was published in London in 1899 "by a young Negro whose father and mother
    were freed from slavery in S[outh] Carolina" (201).

Southern system of the leasing-out of prisoners, was far-sighted (and honest) enough to write:

> The problem of economics is the one vital problem of the hour; from every quarter of the globe comes important news as to the great unrest of the working masses that just measures be taken in order to settle the troubles between labour and capital is of paramount importance, and the right solution of this problem concerns all sorts and conditions of peoples. The problem of solving the evils which afflict the working man is destined to occupy the prior place upon the platform of all social and political reform questions of the forthcoming century, and there is no country in all Christendom where the question is likely to be handled with greater difficulty than in America.

Then, as now, Negroes were excluded from most of the labour unions. Dr. DuBois has not a word to say on the "last to be hired and first to be fired" policy which obtains everywhere in the States concerning the Negro.

Dr. DuBois is the editor of *The Crisis*, the official monthly organ of The National Association for the Advancement of Coloured People—a powerful organisation, largely financed by the money of the white "liberal" bourgeoisie and of the black bourgeoisie. Its supposed function, as its name implies, is to look after the interests of the whole coloured race in U.S.A. —to investigate lynchings, defend the cases of coloured people in court, and in general to protest, to fight against the million yearly outrages perpetrated on the Negro in America.

Yet, to name only one item, we find that the N.A.A.C.P. "counts as lynchings only those *actually investigated*" (London *Daily Herald*, January 13, 1931, italics mine) when giving out its yearly findings of lynchings. The year in question, as referred to by the *Daily Herald*, was 1930. Twenty-five "authenticated" cases of lynching were announced by the N.A.A.C.P. It does not take into account those other lynchings, shootings and murders in other forms which are exposed by such publications as *The*

Harlem Liberator, The Labour Defender, and which find a place in the numerous Negro newspapers, because it has not sent its agents "to investigate." The figure given for 1930 by the International Labour Defence was seventy-nine lynchings. In this are taken into account the deaths of Negroes at the hands of prejudice-maddened individuals as well as of mobs, but a death caused by any form of race-hatred that falls short of an actual burning or hanging by a maddened crowd is not listed by the N.A.A.C.P.

Since writing this I have come across further corroboration of precisely this point. The *Afro-American* of January 14, 1933, states:

> Charges that Tuskegee Institute[1] and the National Association for the Advancement of Coloured People followed a deliberate policy of suppression and deception in giving out statistics on lynchings for 1932 will appear in the *Labour Defender*, official monthly organ of the International Labour Defence.

The League of Struggle for Negro Rights listed thirty-seven instances of lynching, the N.A.A.C.P. reported eleven, and Tuskegee eight. The I.L.D. article will say:

> "Whenever a lynching is reported, the misleaders of the N.A.A.C.P. get into communication with government officials in the state. If these white officials can show that in the lynch-gang there was a man with the silver badge of a sheriff, or some other officer of the law, then the national officer of the N.A.A.C.P. is satisfied that the lynching was 'official.' That lynching is then stricken from the list.
>
> "We accuse the misleaders of Tuskegee and the N.A.A.C.P. of deliberately deceiving the membership of the N.A.A.C.P. and the Negro and white toiling masses generally as to the present lynch-terror; a deception which, if not exposed, would result in throwing the Negro masses and the militant white workers off their guard against the lynchers. We accuse them of omitting the lynchings led by officials in

---

1 [Author's note: An important Negro college in Alabama with a special branch of research into all racial and inter-racial matters.] See also note 4, p. 275.

order to prevent the Negro masses from recognising these state and local officials as the best assistants of the lynchings."

Proposed Aims Of The N.A.A.C.P.

In 1912 Dr. DuBois made a famous speech in Atlanta:

We plan an organization so effective and so powerful that when discrimination and injustice touched one Negro, it would touch 12 million. We have not got this yet, but we have taken a great step toward it. We have dreamed, too, of an organization that would work ceaselessly to make Americans know that the so-called "Negro Problem" is simply one phase of the vaster problem of democracy in America, and that those who wish freedom and justice for their country must wish it for every black citizen. This is the great and insistent message of the National Association for the Advancement of Coloured People.

It is, however, the International Labour Defence, a non-partisan organisation fighting for the rights of black and white workers alike, and undertaking the defence of such monstrous cases of race hate and class struggle as the Scottsboro case, that of Euel Lee, Angelo Herndon, the Tallapoosa Share-Croppers[1] and a great many others that have come up since, that has taken the very steps announced by DuBois in his Atlanta speech.

The coloured race is becoming increasingly aware of the true policy of the N.A.A.C.P. and its organ, *The Crisis*. One of the two

---

[1] Angelo Herndon was an eighteen-year old coal miner in Mississippi and a militant African-American communist. In 1933, an Atlanta, Georgia court found him guilty of inciting insurrection and sentenced him to twenty years in prison. The ILD stepped in on Herndon's behalf, holding rallies coast to coast, and won an acquittal. The NAACP was largely ineffectual. Cunard gives an account of the Tallapoosa share-croppers in "Scottsboro — and Other Scottsboros." According to her, the sharecroppers had resisted eviction from the land they worked and were severely beaten; they sought refuge at the Tuskegee Institute, but were turned over to police. Euel Lee was an African-American labourer who was charged with the murder of a family for whom he had once been a farm hand in a rural county of Maryland dominated by racist divides. The ILD got involved in the case and organized a defence campaign, although they were ultimately unsuccessful in preventing his execution.

most influential and widely read Negro newspapers in America, the *Baltimore Afro-American* wrote the following in December 1931, under the heading of "Say *Crisis* hid Relief Facts:"

The Crisis magazine, organ of the N.A.A.C.P., has been severely upbraided for the publication in its December issue of the statements of eleven city mayors who assert that in their cities there will be no discrimination in the application of relief.

More specifically there has been criticism of the release, said to have been sent out by the N.A.A.C.P., stating that "In general, the replies give assurance that there has been and will be no discrimination in the application of relief to coloured people."

While *The Crisis* printed these letters with little comment, it is pointed out that its editors are well aware of the fact that discrimination against the coloured jobless is carried on in all of the large cities, either openly or by various underhand or red-tape methods. In Buffalo, Syracuse, Rochester and New York City, coloured workers are systematically denied jobs at the city agencies.

In New York City women are forced to stand in Jim Crow lines. Cards printed by the New York State Employment Service list four branches in greater New York, one of which, in Harlem, is called the "Coloured Agency." Coloured workers say that when they apply to other branches they are advised to go to Harlem, regardless of their places of residence ... In California a sign over one relief agency reads: "We don't help Negroes." A charity organization in Los Angeles broadcast the same message over the radio....

The cities of the South segregate and discriminate openly and as a matter of course. Chattanooga forces the colored workers to come on different days from the whites, gives them the worst jobs and the fewest of these. Workers cannot get their relief in cash but may have only a small grocery order.

Dr. DuBois knows well enough the true state of the Negro's ghastly misery in America, knows it fully and covers it up. Now and again, in *The Crisis*, the truth of the wretchedness of conditions for Negro workers is allowed "an airing"—as, for instance, in the form of a review, with quotations and photographs, of John Spivak's *Georgia Nigger*[1]—a blazing denouncement and show-up of Southern Negro chain gangs, peonage farms and methods of the modern slave-drivers, which was published in October 1932. But in nearly each number of *The Crisis*, the swamping hordes of pictures of young college folks who are making good (*The Crisis*, "A Record of the Darker Races,"[2] is not primarily an educational organ which would account for this), the pictures and articles concerning proselytising missionaries, new churches, the samples of "Christian art" that infest its pages and begloom its covers, the baby competitions, and ever more and more colleges, the general humanitarian, philanthropic and patronising atmosphere positively stultifying in its bourgeois placidity, with a few elegantly acid *bon mots* from its atheistic editor on current events, all convey, and intend to convey, the impression that the millions of American Negroes (with perhaps a few Southern exceptions that are hardly mentioned) have all passed on and away from slavery, through beauty parlours, through culture, through the great white uplift itself.... It can also be put this way: more fuss would be made over a relatively slight race-incident, such as an insult encountered by some bourgeois Coloured luminary, than indignation, let alone protest, aroused by a series of mob attacks, police brutalities or grossly unconstitutional acts of mis-justice against the Negroes of *another class*—what to Dr. DuBois must appear an *alarming class*—the Negro workers. To dissociate itself completely from the main

---

1 [Author's note: See further on, "Flashes from Georgian Chain Gangs" and "Quotations from *Georgia Nigger*."] Cunard refers to her reprints of excerpts from Spivak's book (*Negro* 216-222) and an article by Spivak titled "Flashes from Georgian Chain Gangs" (210-216). Spivak was a journalist whose *Georgia Nigger* (1932), which mixed documentary reportage with fiction, depicted life on the chain gang for African Americans.
2 "A Record of the Darker Races" is the subtitle of *The Crisis*.

burdens and struggles of the Negro workers — that is the general policy of the entire N.A.A.C.P.

The N.A.A.C.P. and The Scottsboro Case

An exception to this is afforded by the Scottsboro case; let us review the way the N.A.A.C.P. dealt with this until it was superseded by the International Labour Defence, who intended to save the boys from electrocution.

To recall the words pronounced by Dr. DuBois in his Atlanta speech: "An Organisation so effective and so powerful that when discrimination and injustice touched one Negro it would touch 12 million...." After a lynching mob of ten thousand had milled round the court-house in Scottsboro in which the nine innocent boys, framed up for a false accusation of rape, were being represented by a rank one hundred percent "nigger-hating" lawyer who told them to plead guilty, after death sentence had been pronounced on eight of them (the ninth being under age, though none of them was yet twenty years old), the N.A.A.C.P. came on the field, and instead of thundering against this unconstitutional lynch verdict (in which Negroes had been debarred from the jury and kept out of court), instead of expending its uttermost abilities in providing the best defence possible, it sent a lawyer who placatingly asked for ... sentence of life imprisonment on all nine instead of the death penalty!

It is too much to expect such organisations, run mainly by white capitalist "charity" and controlled by individual personages such as DuBois, to take sides, even on such a vital occasion, against their own bourgeois interests, even to appear to recognise that the Communist Party has, provenly, the interests of the oppressed Negro race at heart, and in hand. But if the organisation in any way lives up to its aims, if the individual is honest, both will admit that the Negro has sufficient enemies in America without adding to these — there can be no need to wrangle as to who shall defend him.

Yet what happened? — a flood of insults and would-be obstructions from the N.A.A.C.P. directly it saw that the I.L.D. had convinced the boys' parents that it had the power to handle the cases with the maximum of militancy; the I.L.D. was accused of pocketing the funds that it was raising all over America to conduct these nine cases; efforts were made to confuse the minds of the boys themselves in their death-cells as to which faction of lawyers was to defend them in the re-trials insisted on and obtained by the I.L.D.; such phrases were broadcast as "the Communists are using the Negroes as a spear-head" (i.e. to make them bear the brunt of class struggle, of class propaganda) "and will then abandon them," etc.

The N.A.A.C.P. went further. While protestations were pouring in from all over the world from workers and every other class of society, the I.L.D. was holding mass meetings all over America to arouse the public conscience and the consciousness of the Negroes themselves against this outrage, and to raise funds. At some of these meetings appeared at least three of the parents of the different boys, Claude Patterson, Viola Montgomery, Ada Wright. Everyone in Europe knows of Mrs. Wright's voyage through some twelve different countries. She has been seen, and heard. But the N.A.A.C.P. found this to say, to damage as far as possible the chances of the Scottsboro defence: "Mothers popped up everywhere," the phrase ran like that, purporting that the Communists, "as a spear-head," of course, had *invented mothers* to "fetch" the sympathies of the general public.

In a public statement likewise, September 15, 1931, the N.A.A.C.P. said:

> The Communists were using the cases of these eight condemned boys as propaganda for their cause of world revolution, and to the cause of this propaganda it is indifferent whether the boys are saved or not.

It is necessary to say immediately, and this cannot be denied, that the Communists are the most militant defenders and organizers that the Negro race has ever had; they are *the only* defenders of the oppressed Negro masses. Time and again the white comrades have been killed for this; the white comrades go to jail, are beaten up, encounter every form of attempted terrorisation for their active attack on the persecution and lynchings of Negroes, and this terrorisation has never before reached the point it is at present. Between Communists and Negroes the race barriers are down for ever; at long, long last white and black stand united. To recognise this fact it is not necessary to be a Communist, but to realise and not admit it is perforce to be a liar.

The N.A.A.C.P., while it also, as well as the I.L.D., was handling the case in the first few months, had given Clarence Darrow[1] a large retaining fee. No one is likely to overlook, however, that the same Darrow defended and got off with one hour's imprisonment the two white upper-class American murderers of a young working-class Hawaiian in the scandalous Honolulu case last April, which shows clearly enough that Darrow's deference to class and to the maintenance of white American prestige outbalances every scruple of the merest justice. The N.A.A.C.P. had also collected funds for the defence of the boys, but it was a great many months before these were turned over to the I.L.D., who by then had brought the cases to appeal in the Alabama supreme court, and to the governor of Alabama, both of whom maintained the original death verdicts. The I.L.D. lawyers then carried the cases to the Supreme Court of the United States, the highest in the land, where the original verdict was pronounced invalid, thereby calling for a complete re-trial of the entire case. We see by this that we are at some distance from the life sentence asked for by the defending counsel of the N.A.A.C.P. in the Alabama court. There is a theory that no Negro once as deeply in the toils of the Southern "Law" as were the Scottsboro boys can be saved from it—it is not worth while trying, prejudice is too strong. The N.A.A.C.P., the supposed representative organisation of the Negro race, was of this opinion; yet we see what the I.L.D. has been able to accomplish: in face of all the said prejudice it has obtained judgment from the Supreme Court for a re-trial. The battle is far from over, but had the N.A.A.C.P. continued to mishandle the case the Scottsboro boys would have been long ago eight more framed-up black victims. They would have been dead.

---

1 Clarence Darrow (1857-1938), American lawyer who practiced in Chicago and who, from his 1894 defence of Eugene V. Debs (the American socialist leader and president of the American Railway Union) on charges brought in connection with the Pullman strike, became known as a defender of the underdog.

I do not believe there is one responsible editor of a Negro newspaper,[1] (of which there are some four to five hundred in the U.S., *The Crisis* and *Opportunity* being the only two magazines,[2] the organs of Negro culture) who by now does not realise in his treacherous heart that the Communists *alone* are determined, militant and capable enough to bring about the real freeing of the Negroes. Daily the facts to prove this are piling up; they cannot be, they are *not* ignored. The few thousands, perhaps tens of thousands, constituting the coloured bourgeoisie, split up as they are into non-militant camps of "democrat," "republican," "socialist," "New Negro," "intellectual," "religious," "race-conscious," etc., are not representative of the Negro masses; they are further from these masses than the white workers whose problems are the same essentially in the increasing struggle *to live*, except that the Negro's chances *to live* are even worse. It is the super-enslaved mass of Negro workers that counts — on the Southern land, and in industry, where, less paid than whites, they were allowed their "niggers' jobs" in every form of what American white supremacy wouldn't do and gave to these "niggers," till it too, starved, and consequently took these despised "niggers' jobs" for itself.

There have been two leaders of the Negro race in America: Frederick Douglass,[3] throughout the middle of last century, and Booker T. Washington,[4] from the seventies until he died in 1916

---

1 [Author's note: With exception of *The Harlem Liberator*, exception also to be made of the editor of the *Afro-American*, who has lately openly affirmed his appreciation of the Communist Party.] *The Harlem Liberator* was the official organ of the League of Struggle for Negro Rights; James W. Ford (Communist Party vice-presidential candidate in 1932) headed the organization after Langston Hughes.

2 Cunard oddly overlooks *The Messenger*, cofounded by A. Philip Randolph and Chandler Owen.

3 Frederick Douglass (1818-1895), foremost spokesperson for African-Americans during the Civil War and after, Douglass was also the most esteemed African-American man of letters in the nineteenth century. His *Narrative of the Life of Frederick Douglass, An American Slave, Written by Himself* (1845) was a key text in the abolition movement and an international bestseller.

4 Booker T. Washington (1856-1915), author of *Up from Slavery* (1901) and founder of Tuskegee Institute. Washington was an important African-American leader whose base of support was particularly strong in the South; he advocated acceptance of racial segregation in the South while promoting black education, especially industrial education, self-help and racial pride in the hope that these might eventually have the effect of changing the political status quo.

[d. 1915]—sons of slaves both. But whereas Douglass was a fighter, and therefore pure in spirit, Washington temporised. He said, also, as it happened, in a speech in Atlanta, "In all things that are purely social we can be as separate as the fingers, yet one as the hand in all things essential to mutual progress"—signifying that the theme of "so far but no further, black man," was acceptable to him.

The Negro Bourgeoisie

Dr. DuBois has often been discussed and described as the third leader of the Negro race. Yet we find him and other heads of the N.A.A.C.P. doing nothing whatever in the way of organizing to get their rights for the black people. We find *the Communist party only* (despite the up-to-a-point, *on paper,* somewhat similar programme of the misleading and hypocritical Socialist party), the Communist party alone fighting for the very things for which the N.A.A.C.P. supposedly came into being: equal rights. Equal social, political and economic rights; anti-lynching laws brought in *and enforced,* cessation of Jim-crowing. Only, the Communist party is going very much further, and we are curious to know what Dr. DuBois has to say about its demands for self-rule of the Negroes in the Black Belt,[1] with the land to belong to the black farmers, instead of the peonage of these black farmers as share-croppers, as it now exists. Perhaps, in deference to old custom, Dr. DuBois thinks this is flying too far in the face of soundly established Southern prejudice....

In 1932 the so-called leaders of the Negro race in U.S.A. are saying the Communist party is "using the Negro as a spear-head." Many things have changed since the days of Booker Washington. Certain Negroes have acquired the status of a financially comfortable bourgeoisie. They know where to go to eat without being insulted and thrown out; they have good homes; many have influential white friends, etc. Some are rich. If, *individually* speak-

---

1 The Black Belt was the name given to a region of contiguous counties stretching through eleven southern states from Virginia through the Carolinas, Georgia, Florida, Alabama, Mississippi, Louisiana, Tennessee, Arkansas and Texas where at least thirty-five to fifty percent and often more than fifty percent of the population was black.

ing, this is to the good (which is not to be denied, the more so as it is only just over seventy years since the slaves were liberated with exactly nothing to build their own "free" lives upon), it does not take them very far. For, south of the Mason and Dixon line,[1] just the other side of Washington, the coloured millionaire will, increasingly as he goes South, find himself crowed—crowed in all the public places and circumstances of daily life. He must, indeed, also pick his *milieu* in New York City and throughout the entire U.S.A. His own economic independence has in no ways set him at liberty to come and go as he pleases as a normal citizen in his own country. For the economically independent, segregation or semi-segregation replaces slavery. Yet the economically independent (and many that are not in that position) prefer the evils of the present system to even allowing that the Communist party is fighting for the most radical changes and is putting a new spirit into the Negro masses, is opening their eyes, and teaching them that they too must struggle for their own full rights.

But the Communist theory does not tolerate the riches of the individual against the poverty of the masses. The Negro bourgeois "leaders," along with the white bourgeoisie, are so afraid of this theory, which is being established more and more in the consciousness of black and white workers alike, and in some of the intellectuals of both races, that they will go to any lengths, denying and attacking their own race, to shelter from it. That is one precise point. It is this point exactly that makes clear that the so-called "colour problem" in the United States, as elsewhere in the world, is not a thing of race, but a thing of class. Those in power (the whites) have kept down the Negro and the coloured, and we have the seemingly racial anomaly of colour against itself. It cannot be left as an anomaly of race, however, for it is a very distinct *class antagonism*.

In other words, the Negro bourgeois leaders fit in very well under the heading of what is called "white man's niggers." They are on the side of the white ruling class against their own race. That Dr. DuBois has only a little Negro blood has nothing to do

---

1 A boundary line between Pennsylvania and Maryland and extending to West Virginia; regarded as the boundary between northern and southern US states or, prior to the Civil War, between slave states and free.

with it, he is known as and professes to be a Negro. What are we to call such "race men" (a sufficiently self-explanatory term for those who feel they should lead, counsel, and act for their people) who lay aside all honesty, responsibility, energy and common sense to tell the world merely that the Negro is really getting on, or just deplore, that he is not "getting a square deal," as see any Negro newspaper, with the exception of the *Harlem Liberator*—*The Crisis* leading the field? We see in this the hypocritical, placatory, pandering spirit addressing itself to the uneasy conscience of some small fraction of white America, and aiming at hoodwinking the coloured race into believing itself *free*, merely through the white philanthropy and culture that have resulted in a few thousands exchanging the maximum of bad conditions in the South, and on the land, and in factories for ... segregation and discrimination in the North. We call this spirit treachery.

Appendix A: Imperial Eyes

1. Mary Gaunt, from *Alone in West Africa* (1912)

[In 1911, Mary Eliza Bakewell Gaunt (1872–1942) made her second trip to West Africa, financed by her publisher T. Werner Laurie, who wanted her to produce a travel book. *Alone in West Africa* is the work that ensued. Gaunt had already published several novels set in Africa; the first two were even written before her initial visit in 1908. Their popularity, and the popularity of adventure travel by women in "exotic" climes, no doubt prompted the publishers to enlist Gaunt in this travel-writing project. For Gaunt, travel was a means to self-realisation and independence. The trope of the independent woman traveller is stressed even in the title of the book Gaunt wrote as a result of this trip.]

In the midst of great rejoicing, a good omen for me, I set my foot on African shore. I began my journeying, and I looked round to try and realise what manner of country was this I had come to—what manner of life I was to be part and parcel of.

These colonies on the West-African coast are as unlike as possible to the colony in which I first saw the light,[1] that my people have helped to build up. I fancy, perhaps, the Roman proconsul and the officials in his train, who came out to rule over Britain in the first century before Christ, must have led lives somewhat resembling those of the Britons who nowadays go out to West Africa. One thing is certain, those Italians must have grumbled perpetually about the inclemency and unhealthiness of the climate of these northern isles; they probably had a great deal to say about the fever and ague that was rife. They were accustomed to certain luxuries that civilizations had made into necessities, and they came to a land where all the people were traders and agriculturalists of a most primitive sort. They were exiles in a cold grey land, and they felt it bitterly. They came to replenish their purses, and when those purses were fairly full they returned to their own land gladly.

The position describes three-quarters of the Englishmen in West Africa today; but between the Roman and the savage Pict of Caledonia was never the gulf, the great gulf, which is fixed between even the educated African and the white man of whatever nationality. It is no good trying to hide the fact; between the white man and the black lies not

---

1 Australia.

only the culture and the knowledge of the west — that gulf might, and sometimes is bridged — but that other great bar, the barrier of sex. Tall, stalwart, handsome as is many a Negro, no white woman may take a black man for her husband and be respected by her own people; no white man may take a black girl, though her dark eyes be soft and tender, though her skin be as satin and her figure like that of the Venus of Milo,[1] and hope to introduce her among his friends as his wife. Even the missionaries who preach that the black man is a brother decline emphatically to receive him as a brother-in-law. And so we get, beginning here in the little colony of the Gambia, the handful of the ruling race set among a subject people; so the white man has always ruled the black; so, I think, he must always rule. It will be a bad day for the white when the black man rules. That there should be any mingling of the races is unthinkable; so I hope that the white man will always rule Africa with a strong hand.

2. Margery Perham, from *West African Passage* (1931-1932)

[*West African Passage* was published posthumously, in 1983, based on travel diaries from the early 1930s. The visit to Nigeria that it records enabled Dame Margery Freda Perham (1895-1982) to publish what would be her first academic monograph, *Native Administration in Nigeria* (1937) and thus to embark on her career as a historian of colonial administration and consultant to the colonial establishment. In a very different way than Mary Gaunt, travel was clearly also key to self-realisation for Perham. The terms of her identity construction emerge particularly clearly in this personal account of Nigeria. Perham's evident delight in being "the first white woman to …," her disdain for the "grovelling" of the native who is thereby pronounced unfit to wear an English uniform, and her approval for the effects on the natives of British colonial administration will be familiar tropes to students of colonial discourse.]

January 7

After half a morning with papers, Percival[2] took me to the native town. It sprawls sparsely within red mud walls, whose crumbling state is witness to the peace our presence has brought. Sentiment would repair them but this would need much labour and expense, so sentiment con-

---

1 Famous Greek sculpture discovered on island of Milos in 1820 and now housed in the Louvre in Paris.

2 D. A. Percival was an Assistant District Officer in Nigeria, and one of the administrative officers playing host to Margery Perham in Zaria, a town in northern Nigeria.

centrates upon the historic gateways and builds up their red arches. (The earth here is predominantly red.) Inside the city the universal huts of Central Africa and the flat mud buildings of the dry Muslim North stand among parcels of farmland. But buildings concentrate as we approach the seat of government. There is a wide space before the Emir's compound; to the right of this are the court and the treasury. We drove to the court, a delicate moment, as my conductors admitted, since my entry was not only that of a stranger but also of a woman. This raises a controversial point which will everywhere be left open for the decision of each political officer and of each lawcourt.

What followed rather confirmed all that critical southern officials had told me of their northern colleagues, that they are sometimes more Islamic in official matters than the Africans themselves. The Waziri (prime minister) and the Alkali (judge) came out to greet us with the slow and grave repetitions of the customary Hausa greetings. Then, through Percival, I offered to go and watch the court from outside through the women's grille. This, much to my surprise and relief, the Hausa officials refused. So I walked into the antechamber of the court. "Should my chair be put here?" I asked, indicating a modest position. "No." They had it brought right into the body of the court. So, with a sense that I had at once acted correctly and won the first round of the game, I entered, the first white woman to do so in any court in Nigeria, or so I was informed.

There was nothing in what I saw to add much to my sense of achievement. We were in a small building, almost in darkness since the light was able to peer only through holes knocked high in the lofty walls. The ceiling was curved with the natural arch made by the slow graceful shape of palm branches, placed close together and then covered over with clay. (I wonder if this is how arches were first invented.) On a slight dais was a sheepskin and upon it squatted the Alkali. To his right sat his three or four assistants; to his left his clerks, who bent themselves double over their books in which, writing in ink from right to left in the beautiful Arabic script, they entered the cases. The two litigants crouched before them, bent to the ground. In the grudging light the draped figures, speaking in low tones that lost themselves in the high roof, had some dignity. But I felt a sense of distaste. It was not only that, on closer view, they were one and all very dirty, even the heavily embroidered *riga* or gown of the Alkali carrying the stain of the dust and sweat of many days. More important, this secretive court offered no accommodation to the public and so clashed against my memories of the East African courts, wide open to the watching crowd.

The cases. A man accused his village-head of cutting down his tree;

the village-head had been twenty days in gaol awaiting the issue. As there were no witnesses, they were sent with the oath-giver to the mosque nearby to take the oath. The oath-giver returned to say that the complainant, faced with this grave test, had run away. So the village-head was cleared. The appeal to Allah seems effective. It also relieves the courts from taking such evidence. Next, a soldier came in to claim a divorce; his clean, trim, English-designed uniform did not seem suited to his grovelling in the dust before the judge.

From the court we went on to the treasury. Northern Nigeria leads the way in "colonial" Africa in the development of its Native Administrations, Lugard[1] having built upon the basis of what he found in the emirates, which appear to be much more advanced than anything in the rest of our African dependencies. And since his day they have been developed further, especially on the financial side. Fifty, and, in some emirates, seventy, percent of the taxation passes through the local [Native] treasury.

I spent an hour going through Zaria's treasury system. I am always impressed by seeing Africans handling local government finance partly because I know nothing of accountancy and have never kept the simplest accounts. At any rate, I was easily convinced by the quiet and courteous Treasurer and his staff that they are quite capable of receiving, banking and spending many thousands of pounds and this without loss or error that cannot immediately be detected. I must get used to the sight of these dignified Muslims in their turbans and flowing robes dealing with the complicated finance of a large emirate.

Lunch at three and a long evening up the town with a recuperated Mr Daniel,[2] examining the market, a rowdy, smelly affair, with a suffocating dust. Another dinner-party at night.

3. C.L.R. James, from *The Case for West Indian Self-Government* (1933)

[The essay from which this excerpt is drawn was originally published in a pamphlet series by Leonard Woolf, not long after C.L.R. James (1901-1989) arrived in England. James had drafted much of the argument for West Indian independence prior to his leaving Trinidad in 1931, and the

---

1   Frederick John Dealtry Lugard (1858-1945) British colonial administrator. He was the governor of Nigeria from 1912-1919, where he developed the doctrine of indirect rule that enabled the British to exercise control of the subject population through tradition-al native institutions. Great Britain subsequently adopted this practise in many of its African colonies.

2   F. Daniel was Acting Resident in Zaria.

essay combines socio-political description of Trinidad with witty, often satirical, observations about those occupying positions of power in colonial societies. Published prior to James's collaboration with George Padmore in the International African Service Bureau, and just on the cusp of his immersion in radical European political thought, *The Case for West Indian Self-Government* nonetheless resonates with that later political and intellectual work, and offers a powerful example of the cultural cargo borne on what Edward Said has termed "the voyage in."]

… When will British administrators learn the lesson and for the sake of future cordial relations give willingly and cheerfully what they know they will have to give at last? How do they serve their posterity by leaving them a heritage of bitterness and hate in every quarter of the globe? Solution of the problem there is but one — a constitution on democratic lines. This does not necessarily mean a form of government modelled plastically on the English or Dominion systems. Ceylon shows one way, Malta another. The West Indian legislators have their constitution ready. That is not a matter for debate here. But there will only be peace when in each colony the final decisions on policy and action rest with the elected representatives of the people. Hard things are being said today about parliamentary democracy, but the West Indian Colonies will not presume to reject it until England and the Dominions show them the way. The high qualification for membership of the Council must go. The high franchise for the power to vote must go. That tight-rope dancer, the nominated member, must vanish forever, and the representatives of the people thrown back upon the people.

No one expects that these Islands will, on assuming responsibility for themselves, immediately shed racial prejudice and economic depression. No one expects that by a change of constitutions the constitution of politicians will be changed. But though they will, when the occasions arise, disappoint the people, and deceive the people and even, in so-called crises, betray the people, yet there is one thing they will never be able to do — and that is, neglect the people. As long as society is constituted as it is at present that is the best that modern wage-slaves can ever hope to achieve.

For a community such as ours, where, although there is race prejudice, there is no race antagonism, where the people have reached their present level in wealth, education, and general culture, the Crown Colony system of government has no place. It was useful in its day, but that day is now over. It is a fraud, because it is based on assumptions of superiority which have no foundation in fact. Admirable as are their gifts in this direction, yet administrative capacity is not the monopoly of the English; and even if it were, charity begins at home, especially in these difficult times. The system is wicked, because to an extent far more than is immediately obvious it permits a privileged few to work their will on hundreds of thousands of defenceless people. But most of all is the system criminal because it uses England's overflow as a cork to choke down the natural expansion of the people. Always the West Indian of any ambition or sensibility has to see positions of honour and power in his own country filled by itinerant demi-gods who sit at their desks, ears cocked for the happy news of a retirement in Nigeria or a death in Hong-Kong; when they go and others of the same kind take their places, while men often better than they stand outside rejected and despised. And even were the Colonial Office officials ideally suited to their posts the situation would not be better, but worse than it is. For the more efficient they are, the more do they act as a blight upon those vigorous and able men whose home is their island, and who, in the natural course of events, would rise to power and influence. Governors and governed stand on either side of a gulf which no tinkering will bridge, and political energy is diverted into other channels or simply runs to waste. Britain will hold us down as long as she wishes. Her cruisers and aeroplanes ensure it. But a people like ours should be free to make its own failures and successes, free to gain that political wisdom and political experience which come only from the practice of political affairs. Otherwise, led as we are by a string, we remain without credit abroad and without self-respect at home, a bastard, feckless conglomeration of individuals, inspired by no common purpose, moving to no common end.

"Self-government when fit for it." That has always been the promise. Britain can well afford to keep it in this case, where evidence in favour is so overwhelming and she loses so little by keeping her word.

Appendix B: Miscegenation Blues

1. Albert Edward Wiggam, from "Woman's Place In Race Improvement," *The Fruit of the Family Tree* (1924)

[Albert Edward Wiggam (1875–1957) devoted his career as a writer and lecturer to the subject of eugenics, and was a member of the American Eugenics Society, among other organizations devoted to the promotion of eugenics. This excerpt from one of Wiggam's several books not only illustrates quite vividly the extent to which a particular conception of womanhood was implicated in race politics, but offers an example of so-called "positive" eugenics. One strategy among eugenicists was to discourage reproduction among those deemed degenerate; in contradistinction to this "negative" approach, a "positive" strategy entailed exhorting the "right sort" (white, middle-class Americans) to have more children.]

Woman's new Promised Land, the objective of her exodus from political bondage, science has at last discovered for her, and, through her, for the race. Its name is Eugenics. It is the land of the well-born. It is for woman to determine whether or not the race shall enter it. Walt Whitman was its poet, the poet of this next great era of the world, when he cried, "Give us great persons, the rest will follow ... / Give the world a saner, ... well-begotten brood."[1]

If America does not produce a great race what else matters? And eugenics means that *the production of a great race* shall become the sum and meaning of all politics, the one living purpose of the state.

It is peculiarly to woman that America looks for the realization of this ideal. She is the natural conservator of the race, the guardian of its blood. Eugenics means the improvement of *life*, and if we can improve *life*, produce better human beings, they will themselves improve everything else. Only a noble race will or can build noble institutions.

---

1   I have been unable to identify this specific poem, but similar sentiments are to be found throughout Whitman's poetry and prose. See, for instance "On Blue Ontario's Shore" from *Leaves of Grass* where Whitman proclaims "Produce great persons, the rest follows." Whitman was influenced by the eugenicist discourses of his day in his mythopoetic construction of the poet-hero's perfect body, as he was by other medical pseudo-sciences such as phrenology, pathognomy, magnetism and electrical biology. Harold Aspiz documents the relationship between these discourses and Whitman's poetics of the body in *Walt Whitman and the Body Beautiful* (Chicago: U of Illinois P, 1980). Wiggam undoubtedly quotes Whitman approvingly in ignorance of the poet's homosexuality.

And this improvement of life, the perfecting of the babe at her breast, is not only woman's supreme duty, but is her one deathless passion. At last her new freedom has given her the opportunity to make *her natural passion her political platform.*

What, then, is eugenics? What is it all about? What does it propose to do? How does it propose to do it? These questions must be answered and the answers made as dramatic and human as securing clean streets, jailing grafters, or removing garbage. Otherwise eugenics will never get outside of a few dreamers' heads.

Ninety-nine educated persons out of a hundred imagine eugenics has something to do with sex-hygiene, vice campaigns, or personal health certificates before marriage. These are matters of public health and morals and bear only indirectly upon eugenics.

On the other hand the Eighteenth Amendment,[1] if it really prohibits, is the most tremendous "eugenic law" ever passed in the world's history, because it will profoundly influence the health, sanity and stamina of the generations yet unborn.

Some biologists believe it will weaken the race, because they believe alcohol has for ages killed off the weaklings and those lacking self-control; and that if such persons are permitted to live and reproduce and spread their inborn weakness, in time the whole race will become potential drunkards. Other biologists believe that counteracting factors will prevent this disaster. I shall not enter the controversy here. But I cite it as a tremendous eugenical problem, which is also a political problem.

Likewise, the baby-saving campaign, with all its noble impulses, many biologists believe will weaken the race by saving so many weaklings. Indeed nearly everybody, except trained biologists, believes that our fresh air campaigns, universal education, pure food, medical and dental inspection, our hospitals, reformatories and public health measures are already rapidly improving the race. But biology, I think, has proved that *if we stop here and do nothing else* the race will deteriorate rapidly; in fact is probably already deteriorating through the saving of the weak and unfit—not unfit, perhaps, in the sight of Heaven, but unfit for reproduction on earth. Beyond question an "improved environment" will deteriorate a race much more rapidly than a hard environment which weeds out the incompetents, weaklings and fools.

Now, the American woman must become enlightened upon these startling new discoveries. She must take a sound course in biology if she

---

1   The eighteenth amendment to the US Constitution concerned the "prohibition of intoxicating liquors." The amendment was proposed by Congress in 1917, and it was ratified by 1919, having been adopted by the requisite number of states.

wishes to be the true politician of the new social order. Otherwise she may wreck the very race she is trying to save. She may be throwing a stone to a drowning swimmer instead of a life-preserver.

Eugenics wishes to save all these good things for everybody. It does not believe in letting a single baby die. It desires whole-heartedly to "rescue the perishing, care for the dying," but it also offers a much wider program; it calls for a golden rule which will do unto both the born *and the unborn* as you would have both the born and the unborn do unto you.

The vast educational, social, religious and economic measures necessary to do this constitute the science of eugenics, and lift it into first rank as the last great political program of the human race. Here, indeed, is a program to stir the heart and brain of every woman with a militant and conquering ideal.

2. W.E.B. DuBois, "The Marrying of Black Folk" (1910)

[Originally published in *The Independent* October 13, 1910, this essay offers both an intelligent riposte to eugenicists and an analysis of the politics of so-called race-science in the American context. Repudiation of the social Darwinist principles informing eugenics was a central tenet of the Niagara Movement, forerunner of the NAACP; W.E.B. DuBois (1868-1963) was a founding member of both organizations, and 1910 marks the inaugural year of the latter. DuBois's own mixed racial origins remain an unspoken but nonetheless significant subtext.]

A white man of the South writes me:

> The crux of the race problem is intermarriage, and on that you do not deliver yourself …. If some Southern white men seem to deny to the Negro those rights which are called civil and political, it is because they fear the exercise of them by the Negro will lead to race amalgamation.
>
> The Southern white man is not moved, I think, by hatred of the Negro; he is moved by the fear of amalgamation.

A Northern white man writes concerning me:

> Is he asking for social equality in the sense that the races shall freely intermarry?

A brown man of India follows with these words:

I am sending you the following questions on which I would like to have your opinion, which if you so desire may be kept confidential as long as you wish:

1. Whether the industrial and intellectual process of the Negro would minimize or on the contrary heighten the race conflict?

2. Whether the intermarriage of the whites and the Negroes would be beneficial to the two races?

I recognize the various difficulties in answering the two questions and so I assure you of the secrecy again, if you so desire. It is a known fact that the whites in the United States would hate to marry with the Negroes. They also claim that such intermarriage would produce a progeny inferior to both the races.

Wherefore as a black man of America who has thought much on these problems I offer the following:

Marriage Credo

I believe that a grown man of sound body and mind has a right to marry any sane, healthy woman of marriageable age who wishes to marry him.

I believe that a man has a right to choose his own wife, but not to choose wives for other men.

I believe that in general the best results follow when persons marry in their own social group; provided there is such freedom in the formation of social classes as will permit the grouping of persons on the whole, according to intellect, culture, physical and moral health and personal agreeableness.

I believe that there are human stocks with whom it is physically unwise to intermarry, but to think that these stocks are all colored or that there are no such white stocks is unscientific and false.

I believe that intermarriage between races is apt to unite incompatible personalities, irreconcilable ideals and different grades of culture. Insofar as they do this they should be discouraged. Where, however, this is not the case, such unions are not necessarily undesirable and race blending may lead, and often has led, to new, gifted, and desirable stocks and individuals, as witness the English nation, the Homo Europeus, the

Egyptians, and such men as Robert Browning, Aleksander Pushkin and Frederick Douglass.

I believe that the mingling of blood between white and black and yellow races is neither "unnatural" nor physically deleterious. Mulattoes, Eurasians, and the like have been insulted and hated and loaded with obloquy for obvious reasons, but there is no adequate scientific proof of their necessary physical degeneracy, nor has the will of God in the matter of race purity been revealed to persons whose credibility and scientific poise command general respect.

I believe that the bad social effects often seen in "colored" strains of blood are for the most part due to the character of the unions and the social taboo on the offspring. Within bounds of reason and decency such taboo is justified insofar as it seeks to preserve family morality, guard the transmission of culture, and foster group ideals. It is unjustifiable and monstrous when it seeks without rule or reason to preserve mankind in separate airtight apartments, despite the tremendous economic and intellectual trend toward human brotherhood; when it arbitrarily limits human friendships and courtesies, penalizes affections, undermines sexual morals, and bans, excommunicates, and exorcises millions of honest men and women of mixed blood for no fault of theirs; and when it cruelly punishes hundreds of others who refuse to submit to impudent dictation in the sacredly personal matter of the choice of their consorts.

I believe that the man who fears to train and civilize Negroes lest eventually they intermarry with whites fears a curious dilemma; either he assumes that whites object to Negroes on purely racial grounds, in which case education can have absolutely no effect, or he makes the antipathy mainly cultural and then opposes human culture. If further he thinks the racial objection valid but unrealized by the mass, and therefore seeks to emphasize it by the repression, injustice and deliberate lying of a caste system, then, as all history teaches, the proposed remedy is worse than the disease, and the true remedy lies not in further degradation of the degraded but in national training in ethics of marriage and the responsibilities of sexual selection.

I believe the world has so much to learn as to the physical results of marriage that it is not well to dogmatize; whether or not it eventually be proven true that the intermarriage of some races is physically or socially undesirable, the best and indeed the only way to secure on the part of the white men and black the world over the safest corresponding social conduct lies thru education and social justice to both races.

I believe that in this respect the South has sinned well nigh beyond redemption and that any people who seek to save their own daughters by making other men's daughters helpless prostitutes before their sons, and who load a race with lies and chains lest that race prove themselves their equals, will have and deserve to have a resultant physical and moral degeneration far worse than any possible honest and open racial amalgamation could bring.

I believe that all so-called "laws against intermarriage" are simply wicked devices to make the seduction of women easy and without penalty, and should be forthwith repealed. Instead of such legislation each group should be trained to self-respect and not forced, ridiculed or ostracized into loss of individuality and into a dead level of absolute uniformity, on penalty of economic slavery and spiritual death. Jim Crow legislation is an open bribe to amalgamation. For this reason arbitrary and humiliating segregation and subordination should be abandoned and it should be made possible and desirable to be at once an American and a Negro. In this way and in this way only will race integrity be maintained through race pride, as long as there is the slightest reason for or advantage in maintaining such integrity. After all, most people even of the same race and nation and neighbourhood do not marry each other; but despite this they may live together like national civilized beings in mutual help and progress.

I believe that practically there is little cause to regard the intermingling of the major groups of the earth's people as a serious present problem, and that insofar as it is a present or future problem it cannot be met by inhumanity, barbarism and the methods of the jungle. It is precisely this sort of treatment of black men in slavery and since that has produced two or three million mulattoes in the United States.

I believe that a wholesale intermarriage of races during the present generations would be a social calamity by reason of the wide cultural, ethical and traditional differences. Whether or not this will be true a hundred or a thousand years hence I do not know and I am not acquainted with any one who does know. I am willing in this matter to let the unborn future grapple with its own problems, for I believe that with regard to so personal a thing as marriage a desire to impose on future generations one's own judgment not by reason and argument, but by physical force, is *prima facie* evidence of the logical weakness of one's cause.

I believe, finally, that if we avoid hysteria, seek the uplift of all classes and races to their highest possibilities, promote international peace, and allow men to mingle naturally without artificial stimulus or attempted segregation, racial intermarriage, becoming thus a matter of intelligent individual judgment, will for many ages, if not forever, maintain in the world the integrity and individuality of the three great divisions of man; and this not simply for the good of and at the behest of any one race which recently arrogantly assumes the heritage of the earth, but for the highest upbuilding of all peoples in the great ideal of human brotherhood.

3. Ida B. Wells-Barnett, from *Southern Horrors: Lynch Law in All its Phases* (1892)

[In March of 1892, three black store owners, whose joint business competed with one belonging to a white merchant, were lynched in Memphis, Tennessee. These men were friends of Ida B. Wells (1862–1931), who promptly wrote about the lynching in the newspaper she edited and co-owned, the *Memphis Free Speech*. The publication endangered Wells's own life; the newspaper office was destroyed and her partner forced to leave town. Wells was in New York at the time and was advised not to return to Memphis. *Southern Horrors* opens by citing Wells's own editorial, and extends and develops the analysis she employed in the article that proved so incendiary to her white readers.]

The New Cry

The appeal of Southern whites to Northern sympathy and sanction, the adroit, insidious plea made by Bishop Fitzgerald for suspension of judgment because those "who condemn lynching express no sympathy for the *white* woman in the case," falls to the ground in the light of the foregoing.[1]

From this exposition of the race issue in lynch law, the whole matter is explained by the well-known opposition growing out of slavery to the progress of the race. This is crystallized in the oft-repeated slogan: "This is a white man's country and the white man must rule." The South resented giving the Afro-American his freedom, the ballot box and the

---

1 In the preceding chapter, Wells-Barnett outlined several cases where white women "confessed" to having initiated sexual relations with black men.

Civil Rights Law. The raids of the Ku Klux and White Liners[1] to subvert reconstruction government, the Hamburg and Ellenton, South Carolina, the Copiah County, Mississippi, and the Lafayette Parish, Louisiana, massacres[2] were excused as the natural resentment of intelligence against government by ignorance.

Honest white men practically conceded the necessity of intelligence murdering ignorance to correct the mistake of the general government, and the race was left to the tender mercies of the solid South. Thoughtful Afro-Americans with the strong arm of the government withdrawn and with the hope to stop such wholesale massacres urged the race to sacrifice its political rights for sake of peace. They honestly believed the race should fit itself for government, and when that should be done, the objection to race participation in politics would be removed.

But the sacrifice did not remove the trouble, nor move the South to justice. One by one the Southern States have legally (?) disfranchised the Afro-American, and since the repeal of the Civil Rights Bill nearly every Southern State has passed separate car laws with a penalty against their infringement. The race regardless of advancement is penned into filthy, stifling partitions cut off from smoking cars. All this while, although the political cause has been removed, the butcheries of black men at Barnwell, South Carolina, Carrolton, Mississippi, Waycross, Georgia, and Memphis, Tennessee, have gone on; also the flaying alive of a man in Kentucky, the burning of one in Arkansas, the hanging of a fifteen year old girl in Louisiana, a woman in Jackson, Tennessee, and one in Hollendale, Mississippi, until the dark and bloody record of the South shows 728 Afro-Americans lynched during the past eight years. Not fifty of these were for political causes; the rest were for all manner of accusations from that of rape of white women, to the case of the boy Will Lewis who was hanged at Tullahoma, Tennessee, last year for being drunk and "sassy" to white folks.

These statistics compiled by the Chicago Tribune were given the first of this year (1892). Since then, not less than one hundred and fifty have

---

1   A term used interchangeably with the Ku Klux Klan.

2   Massacres and race riots such as these were numerous and can be understood in terms of the racial tension that was pervasive in the South during Reconstruction (c1869–1876), which saw increased rights for blacks and the subversion of the antebellum order. Historians connect many of these events with southern Democrats' opposition to Reconstruction under a federal Republican government. For example, the Ellenton, South Carolina race riot, on September 20, 1876, two months before a federal election, involved the killing of up to 100 black persons by a trainload of Red Shirts, a white, pro-Democrat and Anti-Reconstructionist organization.

been known to have met violent death at the hands of cruel bloodthirsty mobs during the past nine months.

To palliate this record (which grows worse as the Afro-American becomes intelligent) and excuse some of the most heinous crimes that ever stained the history of a country, the South is shielding itself behind the plausible screen of defending the honour of its women. This, too, in the face of the fact that only *one-third* of the 728 victims to mobs have been *charged* with rape, to say nothing of those of that one-third who were innocent of the charge. A white correspondent of the Baltimore Sun declares that the Afro-American who was lynched in Chestertown, Maryland, in May for assault on a white girl was innocent; that the deed was done by a white man who had since disappeared. The girl herself maintained that her assailant was a white man. When that poor Afro-American was murdered, the whites excused their refusal of a trial on the ground that they wished to spare the white girl the mortification of having to testify in court.

This cry has had its effect. It has closed the heart, stifled the conscience, warped the judgment and hushed the voice of press and pulpit on the subject of lynch law throughout this "land of liberty." Men who stand high in the esteem of the public for Christian character, for moral and physical courage, for devotion to the principles of equal and exact justice to all, and for great sagacity, stand as cowards who fear to open their mouths before this great outrage. They do not see that by their tacit encouragement, their silent acquiescence, the black shadow of lawlessness in the form of lynch law is spreading its wings over the whole country.

Men who, like Governor Tillman, start the ball of lynch law rolling for a certain crime, are powerless to stop it when drunken or criminal white toughs feel like hanging an Afro-American on any pretext.

Even to the better class of Afro-Americans the crime of rape is so revolting they have too often taken the white man's word and given lynch law neither the investigation nor condemnation it deserved.

They forget that a concession of the right to lynch a man for a certain crime, not only concedes the right to lynch any person for any crime, but (so frequently is the cry of rape now raised) it is in a fair way to stamp us a race of rapists and desperadoes. They have gone on hoping and believing that general education and financial strength would solve the difficulty, and are devoting their energies to the accumulation of both.

The mob spirit has grown with the increasing intelligence of the Afro-American. It has left the out-of-the-way places where ignorance prevails, has thrown off the mask and with this new cry stalks in broad daylight in large cities, the centres of civilization, and is encouraged by the "leading citizens" and the press.

Appendix C: The Red and the Black

1. W. E. B. DuBois, "The Class Struggle" (1921)

[Originally published in *The Crisis*, the NAACP's official organ, this essay reveals W. E. B. DuBois's (1868-1963) liberal faith in the principles of reason in the struggle against racism. That DuBois felt called upon to defend the NAACP suggests that Cunard's attack on the organization and on DuBois expressed a more generally-held sentiment, particularly in the leftist circles she moved in. DuBois nonetheless identifies some of the tensions that emerged between race politics and class politics in Harlem in the early part of the century in a way that points up the limits of dogmatism. By the late 1930s DuBois himself came increasingly to be convinced of the value of Marxist principles for the struggle against imperialism.]

The NAACP has been accused of not being a "revolutionary" body. This is quite true. We do not believe in revolution. We expect revolutionary changes in many parts of this life and this world, but we expect these changes to come mainly through reason, human sympathy, and the education of children, and not by murder. We know that there have been times when organized murder seemed the only way out of wrong, but we believe those times have been very few, the cost of the remedy excessive, the results as terrible as beneficent, and we gravely doubt if, in the future, there will be any real recurrent necessity for such upheaval.

Whether this is true or not, the NAACP is organized to agitate, to investigate, to expose, to defend, to reason, to appeal. This is our program and this is the whole of our program. What human reform demands today is light — more light; clear thought, accurate knowledge, careful distinctions.

How far, for instance, does the dogma of the "class struggle" apply to black folk in the United States today? Theoretically we are a part of the world proletariat in the sense that we are mainly an exploited class of cheap labourers; but practically we are not a part of the white proletariat and are not recognized by that proletariat to any great extent. We are the victims of their physical oppression, social ostracism, economic exclusion and personal hatred; and when in self-defence we seek sheer subsistence we are howled down as "scabs."

Then consider another thing: The colored group is not yet divided into capitalists and labourers. There are only the beginnings of such a division. In one hundred years, if we develop along conventional lines, we would have such fully separated classes, but today to a very large extent our labourers are our capitalists and our capitalists are our labourers. Our small class of well-to-do men have come to affluence largely through manual toil and have never been physically or mentally separated from the toilers. Our professional classes are sons and daughters of porters, washerwomen, and labourers.

Under these circumstances, how silly it would be for us to try to apply the doctrine of the class struggle without modification or thought. Let us take a particular instance. Ten years ago the Negroes of New York City lived in hired tenement houses in Harlem, having gotten possession of them by paying higher rents than white tenants. If they had tried to escape these high rents and move into quarters where white labourers lived, the white labourers would have mobbed and murdered them. On the other hand, the white capitalists raised heaven and earth either to drive them out of Harlem or keep their rents high. Now between this devil and the deep sea, what ought the Negro socialist or the Negro radical or, for that matter, the Negro conservative do?

Manifestly, there was only one thing for him to do, and that was to buy Harlem; but the buying of real estate calls for capital and credit, and the institutions that deal in capital and credit are capitalistic institutions. If, now, the Negro had begun to fight capital in Harlem, what capital was he fighting? If he fought capital as represented by white big real estate interests, he was wise; but he was also just as wise when he fought labour, which insisted on segregating him in work and in residence.

If, on the other hand, he fought the accumulating capital in his own group, which was destined in the years 1915 to 1920 to pay down $5,000,000 for real estate in Harlem, then he was slapping himself in his own face. Because either he must furnish capital for the buying of his own home, or rest naked in the slums and swamps. It is for this reason that there is today a strong movement in Harlem for a Negro bank, and a movement which is going soon to be successful. This Negro bank eventually is going to bring into co-operation and concentration the resources of fifty or sixty other Negro banks in the United States, and this aggregation of capital is going to be used to break the power of white capital in enslaving and exploiting the darker world.

Whether this is a program of socialism or capitalism does not concern us. It is the only program that means salvation to the Negro race. The main danger and the central question of the capitalistic development through which the Negro-American group is forced to go is the question of the ultimate control of the capital which they must raise and use. If this capital is going to be controlled by a few men for their own benefit, then we are destined to suffer from our own capitalists exactly what we are suffering from white capitalists today. And while this is not a pleasant prospect, it is certainly no worse than the present actuality. If, on the other hand, because of our more democratic organization and our widespread interclass sympathy, we can introduce a more democratic control, taking advantage of what the white world is itself doing to introduce industrial democracy, then we may not only escape our present economic slavery but even guide and lead a distrait economic world.

2. Richard Wright, from *American Hunger* ([1944] 1977)

[The work that was posthumously published under the title *American Hunger* was originally conceived as part of Richard Wright's (1908-1960) autobiography, *Black Boy* (1945). The latter focused on Wright's experiences growing up in the South, while the section eventually published as *American Hunger* represented Wright's life in Chicago. In this excerpt about his early experiences as a writer and his efforts to align his politically-committed writing with Communist Party politics, Wright records the tensions he experienced as a consequence of the ways that race and writing were frequently contradictorily positioned in Communist Party practice.]

I had read widely in revolutionary literature, had observed many Communists, white and black, and had learned to know the daily hazards they faced and the sacrifices they made. I now wanted to give time to writing the book of biographical sketches I had planned. I did not know Negro Communists as well as I wanted to, and when, on many occasions, I had sought to question them about their feelings, their work, and their actions, they had been reticent. My zeal made me forget these rebuffs, for I was sure that an atmosphere of trust would be created as soon as I had explained my project to them.

The Communist Party fraction in the John Reed Club instructed me to ask my party cell—or "unit," as it was called—to assign me to full duty in the work of the club. I was instructed to give my unit a report of my activities; writing, organizing, speaking. I agreed to do this and wrote a report.

A unit, membership in which is obligatory for all Communists, is the party's basic form of organization. Unit meetings are held on certain nights which are kept secret for fear of police raids. Nothing treasonable transpires at these meetings; but, once one is a Communist, one does not have to be guilty of wrongdoings to attract the attention of the police.

At these meetings members pay their dues, are given party tasks, are instructed in the party's interpretation of world events.

I went to my first unit meeting—which was held in the Black Belt of the South Side[1]—and introduced myself to the Negro organizer.

"Welcome, comrade," he said, grinning. "We're glad to have a writer with us."

"I'm not much of a writer," I said.

The meeting started. About twenty Negroes were gathered. The time came for me to make my report and I took out my notes and told them how I had come to join the party, what few stray items I had published, what my duties were in the John Reed Club. I finished and waited for comment. There was silence. I looked about. Most of the comrades sat with bowed heads. Then I was surprised to catch a twitching smile on the lips of a Negro woman. Minutes passed. The Negro woman lifted her head and looked at the organizer. The organizer smothered a smile. Then the woman broke into unrestrained laughter, bending forward and burying her face in her hands. I stared. Had I said something funny?

"What's the matter?" I asked.

The giggling became general. The unit organizer, who had been dallying with his pencil, looked up.

"It's all right, comrade," he said. "We're glad to have a writer in the party."

There was more smothered laughter. Some of the more intelligent ones were striving to keep deadpan faces. What kind of people were these? I had made a serious report and now I heard giggles.

"I did the best I could," I said uneasily. "I realize that writing is not basic or important. But, given time, I think I can make a contribution."

"We know you can, comrade," the black organizer said.

His tone was more patronizing than that of a southern white man. I grew angry. I thought I knew these people, but evidently I did not. I wanted to take issue with their attitude, but caution urged me to talk it over with others first. I left the meeting baffled.

During the following days I learned through discreet questioning that I had seemed a fantastic element to the black Communists. I was shocked to hear that I, who had been only to grammar school, had been classified as an *intellectual*. What was an intellectual? I had never heard the word used in the sense in which it was applied to me. I had thought that they might refuse me on the grounds that I was not politically

---

1   Wright is referring to the south side of Chicago.

advanced; I had thought they might place me on probation; I had thought they might say I would have to be investigated. But they had simply laughed. And I began to realize why so few sensitive Negroes had had the gall to come as close to them as I had.

I learned, to my dismay, that the black Communists in my unit had commented upon my shined shoes, my clean shirt, and the tie I had worn. Above all, my manner of speech had seemed an alien thing to them.

"He talks like a book," one of the Negro comrades had said. And that was enough to condemn me forever as bourgeois.

The more I learned of the Negro Communists the more I found that they were not vicious, that they had no intention to hurt. They just did not know anything and did not want to learn anything. They felt that all questions had been answered, and anyone who asked new ones or tried to answer old ones was dangerous. The word "writer" was enough to make a black Chicago Communist feel that the man to whom the word applied had gone wrong.

I discovered that it was not wise to be seen reading books that were not endorsed by the Communist party. On one occasion I was asked to show a book that I carried under my arm. The comrade looked at it and shook his head.

"What're you reading this for?" he asked.

"It's interesting," I said.

"Reading bourgeois books can only confuse you, comrade," he said, returning the book.

"You seem convinced that I'm easily confused," I said.

"You know," he said, his voice dropping to a low, confidential tone, "Many comrades go wrong by reading the books of the bourgeoisie. The party in the Soviet Union had trouble with people like that."

"Didn't Lenin read bourgeois books?" I asked.

"But you're not Lenin," he shot at me.

"Are there some books reserved for some people to read, while others cannot read them?" I asked.

"Comrade, you do not understand," he said.

An invisible wall was building slowly between me and the people with whom I had cast my lot. Well, I would show them that all men who wrote books were not their enemies. I would communicate the meaning of their lives to people whom they could not reach; then, surely, my intentions would merit their confidence. I dismissed the warning about the Soviet Union's trouble with intellectuals. I felt that it simply did not apply to me. The problem I faced seemed a much simpler one. I had to win the confidence of people who had been misled so often that they were afraid of anybody who differed from themselves. Yet deep down I feared their militant ignorance.

Appendix D: Claude McKay, from A Long Way from Home: An Autobiography (1937)

[In this excerpt from his autobiography, Claude McKay (1889-1948) alludes to correspondence between himself and Nancy Cunard. McKay was living in Morocco when Cunard wrote to request that he contribute to her anthology. Their correspondence was initially quite friendly, and McKay expressed considerable enthusiasm about the *Negro* project. Cunard also served unofficially as a kind of literary agent for McKay, running errands to publishers on his behalf in Paris, and having Otto Theis do the same in London. Yet as this excerpt makes clear, their budding friendship came to an abrupt halt over Cunard's failure to remunerate McKay for his work. His analysis of the implications of this failure, and other facets of Cunard's work, are as insightful about the contradictions she embodied as they are sardonic.]

On Belonging to a Minority Group

It was in Africa that I was introduced to Nancy Cunard—an introduction by mail. Years before, when I saw her at a studio in Paris, she had been mentioned as a personage, but I had not been introduced. In Africa I received a pamphlet from Miss Cunard entitled *Black Man and White Ladyship*. The interesting pamphlet gave details about the Cunard daughter establishing a friendship with a Negro musician, of which the Cunard mother had disapproved.

Miss Cunard wrote that she was making a Negro anthology to dedicate to her Negro friend, and asked me to be a contributor. I promised that I would as soon as I found it possible to take time from the novel I was writing. That started an interesting correspondence between us.

Although I considered the contents of the Nancy Cunard pamphlet of absorbing interest and worthy of publication, I did not admire the style and tone of presentation.

After some months, Miss Cunard informed me that she was travelling to New York, and from there to the West Indies, including Jamaica. She asked me if I could introduce her to anybody in Jamaica who could put her in touch with the natives. I addressed her to my eldest brother, who is well-placed somewhere between the working masses and the controlling classes of Jamaica and has an excellent knowledge of both. From Jamaica Miss Cunard wrote again that she had landed in paradise after the purgatory of New York, where she was put in the spotlight by the newspapers, when it was discovered that she was residing in Harlem among the Negroes. My brother invited her to his home in the heartland of the banana, chocolate, and ginger region of Jamaica, and she stayed there two weeks with her Negro secretary. Both she and her secretary were extolling my brother's hospitality and the warmth and kindliness of the peasants. Miss Cunard said she particularly liked my brother's face, and she sent me a snapshot of him.

Meanwhile I had come to the point of a breakdown while working on my novel in Morocco; and besides I was in pecuniary difficulties. Nevertheless I wrote an article for Miss Cunard's anthology and forwarded it to her on her return to France. Miss Cunard extravagantly praised the article and said it was one of the best and also that I was one of the best, whatever that "best" meant. She said she would use it with a full-page photograph of myself which was done by a friend of ours, the photographer, Berenice Abbot.[1]

However, she did not accompany her praise by a cheque, and I requested payment. I was in need of money. Miss Cunard replied that she was not paying contributors and that my article was too long after all. She was doing the book for the benefit of the Negro race and she had thought that every Negro would be glad to contribute something for nothing. She had suffered and sacrificed a fortune for Negroes, she said.

I comprehended Miss Cunard's way of reasoning. Yet in spite of the penalty she had to pay for her interest in the Negro, I did not consider it my bounden duty to write for her without remuneration. Miss Cunard would have been shocked at the idea of asking the printers and binders to print and bind her charitable book without remuneration. But in spite of her ultra-modern attitude toward life, apparently she still clung to the antiquated and aristocratic and very British idea that artists should perform for noble and rich people for prestige instead of remuneration.

I might say that I too have suffered a lot for my knowledge of, and contact with, the white race. Yet if I were composing an anthology of the white hell, it never would have occurred to me that all sympathetic white writers and artists owed me a free contribution. I suppose it takes a modern white aristocrat to indulge in that kind of archaic traditional thinking.

As Miss Cunard would not pay for my article, I requested its return. She said she was going to take extracts from it. I forbade her to touch it.

---

1 Berenice Abbot (1898-1991) American photographer known for portraits and documentary work.

That made her mad, *comme une vache enragée.*[1] My brother also was supposed to do an article on the Jamaica banana industry for Miss Cunard. He decided not to. And suddenly Miss Cunard did not like his face any more. She wrote that he was big and fat.

In her pamphlet *Black Man and White Ladyship* the reader gets the impression that the Cunard daughter enjoys taking a Negro stick to beat the Cunard mother. Miss Cunard seemed to have been ultra-modern in ideas and contacts without alarming Lady Cunard, who was a little modern herself. Then Miss Cunard became aware of the Negro by way of jazz in Venice. And soon also she was made aware that her mother would not accept her friendship with a Negro. Other white women have come up against that problem. It is not merely a problem of people of different races; people of different religions and of different classes know the unreasonableness and the bitterness of it. The mother Cunard drastically reduced the income of the daughter Cunard. The daughter replied with the pamphlet *Black Man and White Ladyship*, which was not published for sale but probably for spite. In telling the story of her friendship, Miss Cunard among other things ridicules her mother's American accent. Yet the American Negroes she professes to like speak the same language as her mother, with slight variations.

Writing in her strange, heavy and ineffectual giant of a *Negro* anthology, Miss Cunard has this to say of me: "His people [the characters of my novels] and himself have the wrong kind of race-consciousness; they ring themselves in."[2]

The statement is interesting, not so much from the narrow personal as from the broader social angle of a minority group of people and its relationship to friends who belong to the majority group. It leaves me wondering whether it would be altogether such a bad thing if by ringing itself in closer together, a weak, disunited and suppressed group of people could thereby develop group pride and strength and self-respect!

It is hell to belong to a suppressed minority and outcast group. For to most members of the powerful majority, you are not a person; you are a problem. And every crusading crank imagines he knows how to solve your problem. I think I am a rebel mainly from psychological reasons, which have always been more important to me than economic. As a member of a weak minority, you are not supposed to criticize your friends of the strong majority. You will be damned mean and ungrateful. Therefore you and your group must be content with lower critical standards.

---

1   Like an enraged cow.
2   In "Harlem Reviewed."

Select Bibliography

Works by Nancy Cunard

These Were the Hours. Memories of my Hours Press, Reanville and Paris, 1928-1931. Carbondale: Southern Illinois University Press, 1969.

G.M.: Memories of George Moore. London: Hart-Davis, 1956.

Grand Man: Memories of Norman Douglas. London: Secker and Warburg, 1954.

Poèmes à la France, 1939-1944. (ed.) Paris: P. Seghers, 1946.

Relève into Maquis. Derby: The Grasshopper Press, 1944.

The White Man's Duty: An Analysis of the Colonial Question. (with George Padmore) London: W.H. Allen, 1942.

Authors Take Sides on the Spanish Civil War. (ed.) London: Left Review, 1937.

Negro. An Anthology. (ed.) London: Wishart & Co., 1934.

Black Man and White Ladyship. Toulon: Imp. A. Bordato, 1931.

Henry-Music. Paris: Hours Press, 1930.

Poems (two). London: Aquila Press, 1930.

Parallax. London: Hogarth Press, 1925.

Sublunary. London: Hodder and Stoughton, 1923.

Outlaws. London: Elkin, Mathews and Murrot, 1921.

Works about Nancy Cunard

Benstock, Shari. *Women of the Left Bank.* Austin: U of Texas P, 1986.

Bröck, Sabine. "Do White Ladies Get the Blues?" *IEAS Women's Studies Newsletter* 2 (April 1992).

Chisholm, Anne. *Nancy Cunard. A Biography.* New York: Knopf, 1979.

Crowder, Henry. *As Wonderful as All That? Henry Crowder's Memoir of his Affair with Nancy Cunard.* Ed. Robert Allen. Navarro, CA: Wild Trees P, 1987.

Douglas, Ann. *Terrible Honesty: Mongrel Manhattan in the 1920s.* New York: Farrar, Straus and Giroux, 1995.

Ford, Hugh. *Published in Paris: American and British Writers, Printers, and Publishers in Paris 1920-1939.* New York: Macmillan, 1975.

——, ed. *Nancy Cunard: Brave Poet, Indomitable Rebel, 1896-1965.* Philadelphia: Chilton, 1968.

Friedman, Susan Stanford. "Nancy Cunard." *The Gender of Modernism.* Ed. Bonnie Kime Scott. Bloomington: Indiana UP, 1990: 63-67.

Marcus, Jane. "Bonding and Bondage: Nancy Cunard and the Making of the Negro Anthology." *Borders, Boundaries, and Traces.* Ed. Mae Gwendolyn Henderson. New York: Routledge, 1995: 33-63.

McSpadden, Holly. "Crossing Racial Borders: Nancy Cunard's Political Modernisms." PhD Dissertation, University of Texas-Austin, 1996.

———. "Black Culture and White Women: Identity Politics and the Erasure of Nancy Cunard." MA Report, University of Texas-Austin, 1991.

Moynagh, Maureen. "Cunard's Lines: Political Tourism and its Texts." *New Formations* 34 (Summer 1998): 70-90.

North, Michael. *The Dialect of Modernism. Race, Language, and Twentieth-Century Literature.* New York and Oxford: Oxford UP, 1994.

Background

Alloula, Malek. *The Colonial Harem.* Minneapolis: U of Minnesota P, 1986.

Baker, Houston A. Jr. *Modernism and the Harlem Renaissance.* Chicago: U of Chicago P, 1987.

Baucom, Ian. *Out of Place: Englishness, Empire, and Locations of Identity.* Princeton: Princeton UP, 1999.

Blunt, Alison and Gillian Rose, eds. *Writing Women and Space: Colonial and Postcolonial Geographies.* New York: Guilford, 1994.

Burton, Antoinette. *Burdens of History: British Feminists, Indian Women, and Imperial Culture, 1865-1915.* Chapel Hill and London: University of North Carolina Press, 1994.

Carby, Hazel. *Reconstructing Womanhood: The Emergence of the Afro-American Woman Novelist.* Oxford: Oxford UP, 1987.

———. "Proletarian or Revolutionary Literature: C.L.R. James and the Politics of the Trinidadian Renaissance." *South Atlantic Quarterly* 87,1 (1988): 39-52.

Edwards, Brent Hayes. "The Ethnics of Surrealism." *Transition* 78 (1999): 84-135.

Felski, Rita. *The Gender of Modernity.* Cambridge, MA: Harvard UP, 1995.

Giles, Judy and Tim Middleton, eds. *Writing Englishness, 1900-1950.* London: Routledge, 1995.

Gilroy, Paul. *The Black Atlantic. Modernity and Double-Consciousness.* Cambridge: Harvard UP, 1994.

Grewal, Inderpal. *The Home and the Harem: Nation, Gender, Empire, and the Cultures of Travel.* Durham: Duke UP, 1996.

Hall, Catherine. *White, Male and Middle Class. Explorations in Feminism and History.* New York and London: Routledge, 1992.

Hooker, James. *Black Revolutionary: George Padmore's Path from Communism to Pan-Africanism.* New York, London: Praeger, 1967.

Kelley, Robin D. and Sidney J. Lemelle, eds. *Imagining Home: Class, Culture and Nationalism in the African Diaspora.* London: Verso, 1994.

Lewis, David Levering. *When Harlem Was in Vogue.* New York: Knopf, 1981.

Maxwell, William. *New Negro, Old Left: African-American Writing and Communism Between the Wars.* New York: Columbia UP, 1999.

McClintock, Anne. *Imperial Leather.* New York: Routledge, 1995.

Mills, Sara. *Discourses of Difference: An Analysis of Women's Travel Writing and Colonialism.* London and New York: Routledge, 1992.

Naison, Mark. *Communists in Harlem During the Depression.* Urbana: U of Illinois P, 1983.

Porter, Bernard. "The Edwardians and their Empire." *Edwardian England.* New Brunswick, NJ: Rutgers UP, 1982: 128-144.

Pratt, Mary Louise. *Imperial Eyes: Essays in Travel Writing and Transculturation.* New York: Routledge, 1992.

Robinson, Cedric. *Black Marxism.* London: Zed, 1983.

Said, Edward. *Culture and Imperialism.* New York: Vintage, 1994.

Smethurst, James Edward. *The New Red Negro: The Literary Left and African American Poetry, 1930-1946.* New York: Oxford UP, 1999.

Smith-Rosenberg, Carroll. *Disorderly Conduct: Visions of Gender in Victorian America.* Oxford: Oxford UP, 1985.

Solomon, Mark. *The Cry Was Unity: Communists and African Americans, 1917-1936.* Jackson, MS: UP of Mississippi, 1998.

Spivak, Gayatri. "Three Women's Texts and a Critique of Imperialism." *Critical Inquiry* 12, 3 (1985): 243-261.

Stallabrass, Julian. "The Idea of the Primitive: British Art and Anthropology 1918-1930." *New Left Review* 183 (1990): 95-115.

Stoler, Ann Laura. "Making Empire Respectable: The Politics of Race and Sexual Morality in Twentieth-Century Colonial Cultures." *Dangerous Liaisons: Gender, Nation and Postcolonial Perspectives.* Eds. Anne McClintock, Aamir Mufti, and Ella Shohat. Minneapolis: U of Minnesota P, 1997: 344-373.

Torgovnik, Marianna. *Gone Primitive. Savage Intellects, Modern Lives.* Chicago and London: U of Chicago P, 1990.

Williams, Raymond. *The Politics of Modernism.* London: Verso, 1989.